D. H. Lawrence
Interviews and Recollections

Volume I

Also by Norman Page

Dickens: *Bleak House* (*editor*)
Dickens: *Hard Times, Great Expectations* and
Our Mutual Friend – Casebook (*editor*)
E. M. Forster's Posthumous Fiction
Hardy: *Jude the Obscure* (*editor*)
Speech in the English Novel
Tennyson: Interviews and Recollections (*editor*)
The Language of Jane Austen
Thomas Hardy
Thomas Hardy: the Writer and his Background (*editor*)
Wilkie Collins: the Critical Heritage (*editor*)

D. H. LAWRENCE

Interviews and Recollections

Volume 1

Edited by

Norman Page
Professor of English
University of Alberta

First published 1981 by
THE MACMILLAN PRESS LTD
London and Basingstoke
Companies and representatives
throughout the world

First published in the USA 1981 by
BARNES & NOBLE BOOKS
81, Adams Drive
Totowa, New Jersey 07512

MACMILLAN ISBN 0 333 27081 9

BARNES & NOBLE ISBN 0 389 20031 x

Printed in Hong Kong

Contents

vi CONTENTS

Acknowledgements

The editor and publishers wish to thank the following who have kindly given permission for the use of copyright material:

George Allen & Unwin (Publishers) Ltd, for the extracts from Bertrand Russell's *Autobiography*, vol. II: *1914–1944*.
Associated Book Publishers Ltd, for the extract from *D. H. Lawrence* by Hugh Kingsmill, published by Methuen and Co. Ltd.
Cambridge University Press and the Estate of the late Helen Corke, for the extracts from her book *In Our Infancy: an Autobiography*.
Jonathan Cape Ltd, Sophie Partridge Trust and Holt, Rinehart and Winston Inc., for the extract from *Carrington: Letters and Extracts from her Diaries*, edited by David Garnett.
Frank Cass & Co. Ltd, for the extracts from *D. H. Lawrence: a Personal Record* by E. T. (Jessie Chambers).
Chatto & Windus Ltd and Harcourt, Brace, Jovanovich Inc., for the extracts from *The Golden Echo,* © 1953, and *The Flowers of the Forest,* © 1955, by David Garnett.
Chatto & Windus Ltd and Harper & Row, Publishers, Inc., for the extracts from *The Letters of Aldous Huxley,* edited by Grover Smith; copyright © 1969 by Laura Huxley and Grover Smith.
Chatto & Windus Ltd and Viking Penguin Inc., for the extracts from the introduction to *The Letters of D. H. Lawrence*, edited by Aldous Huxley; © 1932 by the Estate of D. H. Lawrence; © renewed 1960 by Angelo Ravagli and C. Montague Weekley.
A. W. Coates, on behalf of Dr J. D. Chambers, Mrs Olive Hopkin, and the University of Wisconsin Press, for the extracts from *D. H. Lawrence: a Composite Biography*, vol. 1, edited by Edward Nehls.
Rosica Colin Ltd, on behalf of the Estate of Richard Aldington, for the extract from *Life for Life's Sake*.
Curtis Brown Ltd, New York, for the extract from *Memoirs of a Polyglot* by William Gerhardi.
Faber & Faber Ltd and Alfred A. Knopf Inc., for the extracts from *Ottoline: the Early Memoirs of Lady Ottoline Morrell* and *Ottoline at Garsington: Memoirs of Lady Ottoline Morrell, 1915–1918*, both edited by R. Gathorne-Hardy.
Granada Publishing Ltd, for the extracts from *Two Memoirs* by J. M. Keynes, published by Rupert Hart-Davis Ltd in 1949.

Harper & Row, Publishers, Inc., for the extracts from *Journey with Genius* by Witter Bynner (The John Day Co. Inc.); © 1951 by Witter Bynner.

William Heinemann Ltd and Farrar, Straus & Giroux Inc., for the extract from *The Priest of Love* by Harry T. Moore; © 1954, 1962, 1974 by Harry T. Moore.

David Higham Associates Ltd, on behalf of Ford Madox Ford, and Liveright Publishing Corp., for the extracts from *Return to Yesterday*; © 1932 by Ford Madox Ford; © renewed 1959 by Janice Ford Biala.

David Higham Associates Ltd, on behalf of Malcolm Muggeridge, for 'An Interview with Helen Corke' from *The Listener*, 25 July 1968.

London Magazine, for 'Lawrence in Bandol' by Brewster Ghiselin, from *London Magazine*, no. 5, December 1958; and the extracts from 'Conversations with Lawrence' by Brigit Patmore, from *London Magazine*, no. 4, June 1957.

Macdonald and Jane's Publishers Ltd, for the extract from *Life Interests* by Douglas Goldring.

Maxwell Aley Associates, on behalf of the Estate of Ford Madox Ford, for the extracts from *Portraits from Life: Memories and Criticisms*.

Henry S. Monroe and the Modern Poetry Association, for the extract from *Poetry*, no. 34, May 1930.

A. D. Peters & Co. Ltd, on behalf of Rebecca West, for the extract from *Ending in Earnest: a Literary Log*.

Laurence Pollinger Ltd and the Estate of the late Mrs Frieda Lawrence Ravagli, for the extracts from *Not I, but the Wind* by Frieda Lawrence.

Anne Powys-Lybbe, on behalf of John Manchester, for the extracts from *Lawrence and Brett: a Friendship*.

The Society of Authors as the literary representative of the Estate of John Middleton Murry, for the extracts from *Reminiscences of D. H. Lawrence* and *Son of Woman*.

Times Newspapers Ltd, for the extract by John Middleton Murry from *The Times Literary Supplement*, 13 May 1930.

Viking Penguin Inc., for the extract from *Writers at Work: the 'Paris Review' Interviews*, second series (1963), edited by G. Plimpton.

A. P. Watt Ltd, on behalf of the Estate of Cecil Gray for the extracts from *Peter Warlock: a Memoir of Philip Heseltine*.

Weidenfeld & Nicolson Ltd, for the extracts from *D. H. Lawrence: Novelist, Poet, Prophet*, edited by Stephen Spender.

Introduction

' . . . this man has something different and superior in kind, not degree'
Aldous Huxley, diary entry for 27 December 1927[1]

'There are some writers a serious interest in whose work leads inevitably to a discussion of their personalities.'

F. R. Leavis[2]

The circumstances of Lawrence's short but restless life brought him into contact with a large number of men and women, both the famous and the obscure. Their recorded reactions—and a surprising number of them seem to have been impelled, sooner or later, to try to catch in words the experience of meeting or knowing Lawrence—cover the whole gamut from hostility to hero-worship; but repeatedly, in one way or another, designedly or otherwise, they bear witness to the extraordinary impact of his personality. For Aldous Huxley, writing soon after Lawrence's death, he was 'the most extraordinary and impressive human being I have ever known'; and Helen Corke recalled, some sixty years after the event, that she had 'felt from the earliest association with Lawrence that here was an experience which in some way was out beyond the bounds of ordinary human experience'. What is in question, it is clear, is a reaction to the man rather than to his writings. The intensity of his response to everyday experiences gave to many of those who knew him a deeper awareness of the human capacity for seeing and feeling, so that to go for a walk with Lawrence or even to share a household task was to live for the moment more fully: 'No task seemed dull or monotonous to him', wrote Jessie Chambers, for he 'brought such vitality to the doing that he transformed it into something creative'. A less emotionally committed friend of his youth, Jessie's brother David Chambers, has confirmed that 'he imparted some of his own intensity of living to the rest of us', and many years later Harriet Monroe (who met Lawrence for only a few hours on a single occasion) noted that 'one felt an urge for life in his company'. That Jessie Chambers, who had not seen him or heard from him for seventeen years, should have believed she heard his voice on the day he died, and that his ghost should have appeared to his stepdaughter Barbara Barr—such accounts may elicit different reactions from different readers, but there is a certain appropriateness in the claim that so powerful an individual presence was not quick to fade.

Lawrence was aware of his own gift for winning devotion, and was prepared at times to play quite consciously a heroic and even a Messianic role. The bizarre and sad Café Royal episode, of which several accounts survive, was the most dramatic instance of a lifelong search for disciples. Yet Lawrence's temperament, and temper, allied to his passionate conviction that candour was essential in human relationships, meant that he also enjoyed in generous measure the gift of making enemies. For these reasons, the multitudinous surviving accounts of him compose a portrait that is not only many-faceted but often self-contradictory. To correct the bias of one witness by examining the testimony of others is a prudent proceeding: if the reader is judge, the witnesses as well as the subject of the inquiry must be regarded as being on trial.

The documents in the present collection represent a selection from a very large and disparate body of existing materials, and constitute a more or less continuous narrative of Lawrence's life from childhood onwards. They form not so much a biography as the raw materials for a biography: lacking the single focus and unified interpretation of a finished biographical study, they nevertheless have the advantage of speaking from first-hand knowledge, sometimes brief, sometimes extending over many years, and from a great variety of viewpoints and kinds of involvement. Although the arrangement is broadly chronological, I have sometimes preferred to preserve the integrity of a single witness's recollections rather than to split them into a series of fragments; in this way, what is lost on the swings of chronology is gained on the roundabouts of a more sustained sense of the narrator's personal experience of Lawrence. I have not attempted to remove all repetitions—indeed, I have sometimes deliberately presented accounts of the same incident (for instance, the Café Royal episode) by different observers. Such juxtapositions are apt to offer striking testimony to the hazards of any biographical or quasi-biographical enterprise, where more or less allowance must always be made for the unreliability of witnesses (deliberate misrepresentation being usually less in question than the omissions and distortions of fallible human memory). Memoirists often find it convenient to share some of the conventions of autobiographical fiction, such as total recall of conversations anything up to forty years old. (It is salutary to remember that Vladimir Nabokov once spent an entire evening talking to James Joyce and later confessed that not a single scrap of their conversation had remained with him.[3]) Still, a witness may be demonstrably inaccurate over details and yet succeed in conveying the essence of an encounter. Where memory has plainly or probably been at fault on questions of fact, I have tried to indicate this in my notes.

The notes themselves do not attempt to explain every reference in the extracts: I have passed silently over the more obvious or trivial allusions and have concentrated on providing what is necessary to render the accounts intelligible, as well as furnishing bibliographical references which will lead the interested reader or conscientious student to other sources. The chronology of Lawrence's life and career which follows this introduction has obviated the need for much repetitive detail in the notes.

I owe a considerable debt to Edward Nehls's three-volume 'composite biography' of Lawrence. That book, however, is now more than twenty years old, and some useful material has become available since its publication; moreover, the sheer bulk and inclusiveness of Nehls's work makes it an unwieldy tool for the student and excessive in its demands on the general reader's time and patience. My own aim has been a greater selectiveness and concentration without the loss of what is indispensable, the continuous sense of the variety of Lawrence's experiences and contacts.

Throughout this collection the following shortened forms of reference are used:

Complete Poems—*The Complete Poems of D. H. Lawrence*, ed. Vivian de Sola Pinto and Warren Roberts (London: Heinemann, 1964).

Letters—*The Letters of D. H. Lawrence*, ed. Aldous Huxley (London: Heinemann, 1932).

Moore—Harry T. Moore, *The Intelligent Heart: the Story of D. H. Lawrence* (London: Heinemann, 1955).

Nehls—Edward Nehls, *D. H. Lawrence: a Composite Biography* (Madison: University of Wisconsin Press, 1957–9) 3 vols.

Phoenix—*Phoenix: the Posthumous Papers of D. H. Lawrence*, ed. Edward D. McDonald (London: Heinemann, 1936).

Phoenix II—*Phoenix II: Uncollected, Unpublished, and Other Prose Works by D. H. Lawrence*, ed. Warren Roberts and Harry T. Moore (London: Heinemann, 1968).

Warren Roberts's *A Bibliography of D. H. Lawrence* (London: Rupert Hart-Davis, 1963) has been invaluable to me.

In the extracts given, spelling errors in the originals have been silently corrected, American spellings have been anglicised, and the spelling of names has been rendered consistent throughout.

All biographical undertakings are open to the charges of triviality and irrelevance, and it seems that custom cannot stale the jokes about Keats's laundry-bills. But a charge is not a conviction, and though this is not the place to enter into a full-scale defence of the uses of literary biography, I believe a short answer can be given to the objection that it is, say, *Sons and Lovers* and *The Rainbow* that alone matter, and that Lawrence's poignant friendship with Jessie Chambers or his quarrels with Frieda are worthy of attention only to the addict of literary gossip or the sentimentalist. To an unusual extent Lawrence's life and his work were all of a piece: his life enacted the convictions and insights recorded in his writings, his books grew directly from his responses to the people he met and the places he visited. For Lawrence, writing was a daily activity, like cooking a meal, and derived from daily experience. Some of the recollections gathered in this book reveal that the awareness and judgement of human character and behaviour which is part of his strength as a novelist was also part of his natural response to the process of living: 'in assessing human relationships [he] had an uncanny gift', writes Barbara Barr, while Ivy Litvinoff comments that 'he just said what other people didn't even know they were thinking'. And everything he wrote bore the stamp of his complex personality, a sense of which—set down at the time, or recalled through recollected moments or passages of experience or through the generalising and summarising power of memory long after the event—is vividly conveyed through the diversity of testimonies assembled in these volumes.

NOTES

1. *Letters*, p. xxix.
2. 'D. H. Lawrence and Professor Irving Babbitt', *Scrutiny*, 1 (1932) p. 273.
3. Andrew Field, *Nabokov: His Life in Part* (Harmondsworth: Penguin, 1978) p. 209.

A Lawrence Chronology

1885 David Herbert Lawrence born at Eastwood, Nottinghamshire, on 11 September, the fourth child of Arthur and Lydia Lawrence.

1893–8 Attends Beauvale Board School.

1898–1901 Attends Nottingham High School, assisted by a county council scholarship.

1901 Meets Jessie Chambers; becomes a clerk in a Nottingham factory (autumn); his brother, William Ernest Lawrence, dies at the age of 23 of pneumonia with complications; Lawrence himself is seriously ill with pneumonia in the winter of 1901/2.

1902 Becomes a teacher at the British School, Eastwood.

1903 Becomes a pupil-teacher at Ilkeston, Derbyshire; meets Louie Burrows.

1904 Placed first in England and Wales in the King's Scholarship examination (December).

1905 Returns to the British School, Eastwood, in order to earn his college fees.

1906 Begins a two-year teachers' certificate course at University College, Nottingham; starts to write a novel (later published as *The White Peacock*).

1908 Becomes a teacher at Davidson Road School, Croydon; meets Helen Corke.

1909 Lawrence's first published work appears in *The English Review*—sent to the editor, F. M. Hueffer, by Jessie Chambers (November).

1910 Lawrence's mother dies (December).

1911 *The White Peacock* published (January). Lawrence becomes ill, and is eventually forced to give up teaching (December).

1912 Lawrence meets Frieda Weekley (April). They go to Germany together, and later to Italy (May); *The Trespasser* is published.

1913 *Love Poems and Others* (February) and *Sons and Lovers* (May) published. Returns to England (June). To Germany, then to Italy (August).

1914 Frieda receives a divorce from Ernest Weekley (May). Lawrence and Frieda married in London (13 July). They move to Chesham, Buckinghamshire (August). *The Prussian Officer and Other Stories* published (November).

1915 The Lawrences live at Greatham, Sussex (January–July); later in the year they move to Hampstead, then to Zennor, Cornwall. *The*

Rainbow published (September). *The Rainbow* declared obscene (November); an expurgated edition is published in New York.

1916 *Twilight in Italy* (June) and *Amores: Poems* (July) published.

1917 The Lawrences are ordered to leave Cornwall and to stay away from the coast (October); after a brief visit to London, they move to Derbyshire. *Look! We Have Come Through!* (poems) published (November) in an expurgated edition.

1918 *New Poems* published (October).

1919 The Lawrences go to Italy (November).

1920 The Lawrences move to Sicily (March). *Women in Love* published in New York (privately printed); *The Lost Girl* published in London (November).

1921 *Psychoanalysis and the Unconscious* (May), *Women in Love*, first London publication (June). and *Sea and Sardinia* (December) appear.

1922 The Lawrences travel to Ceylon (February). They arrive in Australia, visit Sydney, and settle briefly in Thirroul, New South Wales, where Lawrence writes *Kangaroo* (May). They arrive in Taos, New Mexico (September). During this year, *Aaron's Rod* (April), *Fantasia of the Unconscious* (October) and *England, My England and Other Stories* are published.

1923 The Lawrences visit Mexico City and later New York. Frieda travels alone to England and Germany (August); Lawrence goes to Los Angeles and Mexico, and travels to Europe in November. Publication of a volume containing 'The Ladybird', 'The Fox', and 'The Captain's Doll' (March); *Studies in Classic American Literature* (August); *Kangaroo* (September); *Birds, Beasts and Flowers* (poems) (October).

1924 Lawrence revisits the Midlands; Lawrence and Frieda visit Germany (February); they return to New Mexico, this time accompanied by Dorothy Brett (March); to Kiowa Ranch (May); to Mexico City (October). *The Boy in the Bush*, by Lawrence and M. L. Skinner, published (August); Maurice Magnus's *Memoirs of the Foreign Legion* appears (October), with a long introduction by Lawrence.

1925 Lawrence becomes seriously ill, and tuberculosis is diagnosed. At Kiowa Ranch again (April); the Lawrences leave the United States and travel to Italy via England and Germany (September). Translation of Verga's *Little Novels of Sicily* appears (March); *St Mawr* (May), *Reflections on the Death of a Porcupine and Other Essays* published (December).

1926 *The Plumed Serpent* published (January.). They move to the Villa Mirenda, Florence (May).

1927 Lawrence visits Etruscan sites (spring). *Mornings in Mexico* published (June)

1928 The Lawrences move to Switzerland and later to Bandol, France.

The Woman Who Rode Away and Other Stories published (May); *Lady Chatterley's Lover* privately printed in Florence (July); *Collected Poems* published (September).

1929   In Paris (March); in Spain (April); Lawrence goes to Italy, Frieda to London, where an exhibition of Lawrence's paintings opens on 14 June; thirteen pictures are removed from the gallery by the police (5 July); Lawrence goes to Baden-Baden, Germany, and later (September) returns to Bandol. *Lady Chatterley's Lover* privately printed in Paris (May); *The Paintings of D. H. Lawrence*, with an introduction by Lawrence, privately printed (June); *Pansies* (poems) published in an expurgated edition (July); *The Escaped Cock* (later retitled *The Man Who Died*) published (September); *Pornography and Obscenity* published (November).

1930   Lawrence dies in Vence, France (2 March). *Nettles* (March), *Assorted Articles* (April), *The Virgin and the Gipsy* (May), *A Propos of 'Lady Chatterley's Lover'* (June), and *Love Among the Haystacks and Other Pieces* (November) published.

1931   *Apocalypse* published (June).

1932   Expurgated edition of *Lady Chatterley's Lover* published in London (February) and New York (September). *Etruscan Places* and *The Letters of D. H. Lawrence* (September), *Last Poems* (October) published.

1933   *The Lovely Lady* (short stories) published (January).

1934   *A Modern Lover* (short stories) published (October).

1935   Lawrence's body cremated and the ashes taken to New Mexico.

1936   *Phoenix: the Posthumous Papers* published (October). A second collection, *Phoenix II*, followed in 1968.

1959   First unexpurgated edition of *Lady Chatterley's Lover* published in the United States and later (1960) in England.

Lawrence's Boyhood*

W. E. HOPKIN

My first meeting with D. H. Lawrence, or rather my first sight of him, was in 1885 when he was a few weeks old. One day as I was passing the opening into Victoria Street, Eastwood, Mrs Lawrence[1] came out on the main road with her newest baby in a three-wheeled pram with ironbound wheels. I stopped and asked how the baby was faring. She uncovered his face and I saw a puny, fragile little specimen. I could understand the doubts expressed by Mrs Lawrence about being able to 'rear' him. Years later Lawrence said to me: 'Before I went to school I was a snuffy-nosed little beggar, seldom without a cold.'

Eastwood, Nottinghamshire, where Lawrence was born, is a busy little town on the Derbyshire border. It depends on coal mines for its prosperity, but there are none in Eastwood itself. The nearest are Moorgreen and Brinsley just within a mile. It was at Brinsley Colliery that John Arthur Lawrence,[2] the writer's father, spent his working days. He was a good miner, had an independent spirit and resented interference from the Colliery officials. In appearance he was a handsome man with a black beard and fairly high coloured cheeks. He was a very accomplished dancer in his younger days.

Lydia, Lawrence's mother, was a small woman of considerable refinement and culture. In her teens she composed poetry, some of which appeared in magazines in the district in which she then lived. As the wife of a miner in a mining community she was out of her element. It was largely, I think, because of her difference from most of the wives about her that she soon became president of the newly founded Co-Operative Women's Guild.

Being a total stranger to mining life and habits she was shocked when Arthur came home from the pit the first day after the honeymoon looking more like a negro than the man she kissed as he left home for work in the morning. When he insisted on having his dinner after merely washing his hands she was very upset. Arthur told her that coal dust was *clean* dirt, and that it was the habit of all miners to do the same, but she still protested. Then when as the crowning point he insisted on having his bath in the

---

* From 'D. H. Lawrence: A Personal Memoir', broadcast by the BBC on 17 August 1949 and first published by Nehls, 1, pp. 21–5.

'dolly tub' in front of the kitchen fire and she must wash his back, her cup of anger overflowed, and that was the beginning of the rift. Husband and wife were both determined creatures and neither would give way. It is not for outsiders to judge, but I'm sure that if she had shown tact and patience things might have been very different. Arthur Lawrence was not of the material to mould into his wife's idea of a gentleman. He was one naturally.

The house where Lawrence was born is in a steeply descending street. It has been described by some writers as a sort of mean tenement in a maze of dreary streets. As a matter of fact it is quite a decent house, and from the front door one can see a really beautiful bit of countryside sloping to the north. Mrs Lawrence had a shop where she sold baby clothes, ribbons, etc. in order to try and augment her husband's earnings. It proved a failure and when Lawrence was two years old the family moved to a house in Breach Bottoms, two long blocks of houses better than those in Victoria Street and in open country. They stayed there for some years and then went to a privately owned house in Walker Street. This house had a bay window which looked out on the fields and woodlands known as High Park, and the young folk felt they had gone up a step in society.

David Herbert, or as he was known locally, 'Bert' Lawrence, was always a good scholar. He attended Beauvale School until he was 13, when he won a scholarship and went to the High School in Nottingham. Later he attended a training centre at Ilkeston and was first in England and Wales in the Uncertificated Teachers Examination.

Young Lawrence was very sensitive, or as his schoolfellows said, 'Mardy',[3] which is a term used to signify a sort of babyish disposition. Never in his life could he bear anything like severe criticism. He either got extremely angry or worried and upset. In his later school and college days he had a few male friends, but in his elementary school days he did not get on with other boys. They despised him because he couldn't take part in their games. I well remember the day when I was passing the school as the scholars were leaving for dinner. He was walking between two girls, and a number of Breach Boys walked behind him monotonously chanting 'Dicky Dicky Denches plays with the Wenches.' That charge branded any boy as effeminate—the local term is 'Mardarse'. Bert's chin was in the air as though he cared no jot but his eyes were full of anger and mortification.

In those days things at home were in a bad way. The everlasting quarrels between his father and mother played havoc with his mind, and he used to lie awake in terrible fear that his father would do his mother a mischief. There were periods when peace reigned, and his sister Ada once told me that then the home was a very happy one, for the father did all kinds of things for the youngsters. The greatest single influence in Lawrence's life was his devotion to his mother. As is the wont of mothers, the weakly one of the family received a double share of love and attention, to which Bert responded in full measure, and there grew between them a love stronger and deeper than is usual between parent and child. To see them together sometimes was to imagine them fond lovers. She lavished on him some of the love her husband would have had if all had been well between them, and his passionate love for her made up in some measure for what she lacked from Arthur.

There was no kinship of soul between the father and son. The father was of the earth earthy, and the son, even in early life, was quite often up in the clouds.

Mother and son had a very perfect understanding. Had she taken a tenth part of the trouble, or shall I say pleasure, in trying to understand her husband what a fine family the Lawrences might have been.

As a boy and through his adolescence Lawrence was very fond of indoor games, and especially charades (dances too when the room was suitable). Whatever games were played he must be the leader. If his side failed to win he was very cross. I remember one evening at a party at the house of a friend he pitched into me for what he called 'deliberate cheating'. We had agreed to act book titles and we entered the room studying a book each and aimlessly wandering about. Lawrence failed to get the title, and when I said it was *The Student's Rome* he went into a temper.

He liked a sing-song, so I bought the *Oxford Song Book*. His favourite was the 'Elephant Battery' which he rattled through at a great pace. A few years later he developed a habit I disliked. If any person he took a dislike to was in the room he would not speak but sat silent and sullen. When the person had gone he asked angrily what the devil we had asked him for.

From his early days Lawrence had a great love for nature and the countryside. It was a delight to go rambling with him. How he acquired his knowledge I never knew. He seemed to be one of those rare persons that receive direct revelation from some source. When out with him I occasionally noticed that he would make brief notes on any bit of paper from his pocket. Even as a youth he seemed to see things differently from other folk, and his descriptions were often unusual but illuminating. One sunny June afternoon we came across an old farmhouse with moss-grown tiles near a brook. It was a sleepy sort of day and no breeze stirred the leaves. No person was in sight and the whole place seemed asleep. Lawrence looked at it for a few seconds, and then said, 'That house is brooding over its past.' In the next field we sat down to rest and Lawrence, with half-closed eyes, told us what incidents the old house was recalling. One of the girls exclaimed, 'Why don't you write stories, Bert?' A year or two later I came across the same idea in one of his books. I have been looking it up and it is in *The White Peacock*.

His talents were varied and for a long time I could not make up my mind what he would eventually become. At one time he had a craze for drawing and painting, and I dare say there are still one or two fire-screens and oddments in some of the cottages. He told stories well, and would sometimes recite poetry. His likes and dislikes were decided, and sometimes violent, and especially so later in his career, but it was the same as a boy. He had no use for neuters—he was of the same opinion as the writer of the couplet,

> Neuters in their middle way of steering
> Are neither fish, flesh, fowl, nor good red herring.

From boyhood he always spoke correctly and he was remarkably good in his writing.

Along with that he had an intimate knowledge of the local dialect which is a mixture of border Nottinghamshire and Derbyshire. Sometimes when at my house he and I would speak it for a time, much to the bewilderment of any visitor from elsewhere. These words—'How are you getting on? I hear you have been ill. I do hope it was nothing serious' spoken in the dialect would be—'How are ter gerrin on surrey? I hear as thou's bin badly. I dow hope its nowt serious.'

When Lawrence left Beauvale Elementary School he was not distinguished for anything, unless it was his tidy habits and his love of study, and a marked difference from the rest. Two things were against him—the teasing and contempt of his schoolfellows, and, what bit deeply into his daily life, the constant and bitter quarrels at home. It was, I think, his weakness and unpopularity with boys that drove him into the arms of girls. He was more in the company of girls than boys, and I used to notice that he had not much use for the Plain Janes. His girl friends were all good-looking and vivacious. In this connection I recall an amusing incident. Later on whenever it was known that Lawrence was staying with us we were invaded by swarms of soulful females—usually schoolteachers. As they came in I gave up my seat. Lawrence said: 'For goodness' sake don't be polite. Let 'em find their own. When you get to Heaven you'll get up for every blessed woman who enters until the last seat is gone, and then you'll fall backwards into Hell and serve you jolly well right.'

NOTES

W. E. Hopkin (1862–1951) was an Eastwood resident and a friend of Lawrence. He became a magistrate and a county councillor.

1. Lydia Lawrence, née Beardsall (1852–1910).
2. Arthur Lawrence (1846–1924) married Lydia Beardsall on 27 December 1875.
3. Lawrence uses the dialect word 'mardarsed' in his poems (see, for example, 'The Collier's Wife').

Mother and Son*

MAY HOLBROOK

So now on my first visit to the Lawrence house, I was warmly welcomed and taken in to be shown with pride the parlour, the carpet, the suite, the vases and ornaments, the family group in a handsome frame on the wall facing the bay window. We peeped through the curtains at the wide view over the valley crowning its far side. They turned again to the family group, telling me when and where taken, and I stood admiring everything when the elder sister asked:

'Have you got a suite?'

'Mind your own business,' snapped the mother. 'If you ask me no questions, you get no lies, do you, child?'

She was a short, robust woman with a heavy, plodding step, her thick hair greying, shrewd grey eyes, and a kindly smile. She drooped slightly, and carried her head bent to one side a little, as if weary and discouraged. Her black dress and the apron tied around her waist bore signs of work about which she complained and was rebellious. Her expression changed swiftly from the sympathetic to the combative. In Chapel she sat at the entrance of their pew. She wore a small black bonnet with the ribbons tied very neatly, sitting with downcast eyes, her head slightly on one side. Her eldest son[1] was dark and quiet-looking, his brother[2] was brilliant with flashing eyes and teeth, and unruly, tawny hair. He was popular with the night-school boys to whom he taught shorthand and with the athletes. He had an irresistible smile and seemed to find difficulty in sitting still so long, so he took down the sermon in shorthand sometimes. There were the two sisters[3] between whom Bert was sandwiched. Only on very rare occasions did I see the father in Chapel. He looked handsome in a rugged way: black curly hair and beard streaked slightly with silver; blue eyes smiling kindly in a rugged face, glancing over the congregation with a friendly air; well-built and strong in figure; and a genial manner. By comparison the mother appeared bitter, disillusioned, and austere. Her attire was black, as I recall it.

On Sunday morning was Sunday School followed by Chapel. In the afternoon was school in the big schoolroom, boys on one side, girls on the other, in small groups, each class with its teacher. Some Sundays 'pieces'

* From a memoir first published by Nehls, III, pp. 554–5, 557–8.

were said, and the Sunday Bert was told to say his piece he stood on the raised dais speechless, till a titter ran through the room. Then he was allowed to look at a sheet of paper from his jacket pocket; just one glance, and unfalteringly he went to the end. But I don't remember seeing him on the platform ever again. I said 'pieces' to my mother's intense disapproval, but at the special request of our young Scots minister, whose wife provided my 'pieces'. Sunday evening found us again at Chapel. Sunday was the big day for both our families. We went to different day schools because we lived in different parishes, but the brook drew children to play at the sheep-bridge where we also used to watch the shearing of a few sheep in the spring.

Bert was ten when first I went to his home, and Saturday mornings found him cheerfully helping in the work, cleaning boots or knives and forks, with an apron tied under his armpits, a smudge on his face, and his thick, fine hair rumpled. Whatever he was doing, he was merry with lots to say. One morning he was waiting for me. 'I must show you Mother's flowers,' he said, skipping about while the milk was put away, and then led me through the scullery into the yard where a bit of space made a drying ground for the wash, its line-post between the house and the ash pit. A tiny spot like a tablecloth was protected by a few bits of board for palings, and here bloomed a handful of flowers. Bert hopped on one foot as he excitedly explained:

'Mother calls it her "wilderness". They're all mixed together, they're best that way. It's a wilderness because they're all mixed together. They're lovely, aren't they?'

'It's a "wilderness" right enough, isn't it, child?' said the mother. 'I just took the seeds and scattered them all together. He thinks they're pretty, but they're nothing, are they, child?'

'Oh, I think they're ever so nice, don't you?' insisted her son, hopping from one foot to the other, and said when I was dubious: 'Well, anyway, they're better than none, and I think Mother's wilderness is lovely.'

He always spoke rapidly and in a high voice tingling with excitement or perhaps enthusiasm.

*   *   *

One dull, heavy morning I came upon mother and son at the end of the entry. I thought Mrs Lawrence must have a headache. Her elbow was on the coping stone on the low wall, her head resting on her hand. In her black dress and soiled apron she impressed me as one in deep misery.

Bert came a few steps to meet me, and said in a tense voice:

'I've won that scholarship.'[4]

My eyes and mouth opened in speechless admiration, and his face suddenly shone with joy, then clouded with anxiety.

'She's wondering if she'll let me go. I hope she does. I want to go.'

The mother didn't change her position, but stared out over the wide valley as she said:

'I don't know what to do, child. He's told you they both won the scholarship.'

The other boy had been forgotten. I hardly knew him. I said I was glad, and asked when would High School start? She had not altered her position, and stared over our heads to far tree-clad hills.

'I don't know that I shall let him go.'

Bert stood digging the toes of one foot in the dust, hanging his head, and said tensely, 'You will let me go. I know you will.'

'Oh, shall I?' she queried tartly.

'Yes, you will,' he repeated very low and vibrant. 'I know you will.'

She stepped away from the wall and shook and tossed her head.

'Aye, if I can pinch it out of the pennies, he knows I'll let him go. He knows, oh, he knows right enough.' Bert glanced with a face puckered with varying emotions, and she continued, appealing to me, 'It takes money, doesn't it, child?'

But Bert broke in, 'There is some money found, Mother.'

'Aye, my lad, there's a little found, but there's a lot wants finding. Why, look at his clothes and boots and dinners and train fare and books.'

'There's enough for books and train fare and a little more, I think, and I can wear my Sunday suit and boots,' he arranged eagerly.

'And they won't wear out? And what will you wear for Sunday? Tell me that. Oh, I don't know!'

And she turned up to the entry with her weary step and her shoulders a little more bowed.

'Skimp, skimp, I'm tired of skimping.'

The next time I went, it was all settled that somehow means should be found for Bert to attend the High School at Nottingham.

NOTES

May Holbrook, née Chambers (1883–1955), a sister of Jessie Chambers (see p. 31). She became a schoolteacher and later emigrated to Canada.

1. George Lawrence, born 1876.
2. William Ernest Lawrence (usually known as Ernest), born 1878. He died suddenly in London in 1901, and is the prototype of William in *Sons and Lovers*.
3. Emily (born 1882) and Lettice Ada (born 1887).
4. A county council scholarship to Nottingham High School, won by Lawrence in 1898 on the basis of a competitive examination.

Family Life*

ADA LAWRENCE

In spite of the fact that luxuries of any kind were unknown to us, much of our early life was very happy, and many days are fixed in my memory, days of such care-free joy with Bert that I know I can never experience again. It seemed inevitable that Bert should spend his life creating things. He was never content to copy others, and perhaps found more pleasure in inventing games than in playing them.

We had to create our happiness. There was little ready-made about us. We were always conscious of poverty and the endless struggle for bread. Perhaps many other children of mining folk knew frequently enough that they had not enough to eat. We were conscious of more. The anxieties of our mother were shared by us. She never concealed the fact that she had not enough money to clothe and feed us as adequately as she wished. The sight of father coming up the field at midday took all the pleasure from our games. It meant that on Friday night he would be short of half a day's pay. I don't remember him giving mother more than thirty-five shillings a week. So much was rare. The usual amount was twenty-five. The rent was five shillings and rates were extra. She baked the bread, made what clothes she could for us and schemed day and night so that we should have enough to eat. It was the terrible indignity of such poverty that embittered my brother so much.

My brother was a delicate and sensitive child and became morbid frequently, so that it was difficult to approach him. Sometimes, for no apparent reason, he would burst into tears and irritate mother, who would say 'Bless the child—whatever is he crying for now?' Bert invariably sobbed, 'I don't know', and continued to cry.

Excepting him we all went to school when we were five years old. He stayed at home until he was seven and during his first few years of school life displayed no remarkable ability. He worked under the shadow of Ernest, who was set up by the headmaster as a model for the other children. He told Bert that he would never be fit to tie his brother's bootlaces—a meaningless prophecy which did not help Ernest and merely depressed

* From Ada Lawrence and G. Stuart Gelder, *Young Lorenzo: Early Life of D. H. Lawrence* (London: Martin Secker, 1932) pp. 34–6, 40–3.

and discouraged Bert, who in spite of it won a scholarship which entitled him to attend Nottingham High School for three years.

* * *

I wonder if many children of wealthier homes got as much real joy as we did out of Christmas preparations. The most exciting days were when we searched for holly and the kissing bunch. (We never had a Christmas tree.) Sometimes we tramped miles to find berried branches, but often had to be content with small pieces tied into a large bunch, which we hung from a hook in the ceiling. Then out came the wooden box containing the treasures we had saved for years. I remember the chief decoration was an angel with feathery wings, keeping guard over the glistening balls, apples and other shining things. Each picture was decorated with a sprig of holly, and a bunch of mistletoe was hung by Bert in some secret spot. We plucked the duck or goose, while mother made mince-pies. Whatever the circumstances our stockings were always well filled, with a sugar pig and mince-pie at the top. Usually we each had a book or some small toy. Once my chief present was a suite of doll's furniture, while Bert had a delightful farmyard with fowls possessing real feathers and red flannel combs. The *Chatterbox* and the *Prize* had never given us such happiness, and the games we played were weird and wonderful.

For breakfast on Christmas morning there was a pork pie with a piece of holly stuck in the top. The table would not have been complete without it. At night we had our party, and crowds of young folk came. Until the death of Ernest, mother always took part in our games and joined in our songs. He had been the life and soul of them. After he died she would stay in the kitchen in her rocking chair, pretending to read. We knew where her thoughts were, and it always cast a shadow over the fun.

A few years after the death of Ernest we went to live in Lynn Croft, to a house owned by friends. The street was not so pleasant as the one we had left, but there was a lovely garden with a field at the end of it. Mother was happy here amongst the flowers. She knew every one.

At this house there was a large garret, and here on Christmas Eve we arranged a dance. Bert said we must wax the floor, and persuaded mother to give us two candles, which we shredded and rubbed into the wood by sliding about for half an hour or so. We decorated the beams with Chinese lanterns, hung a fancy curtain here and there, and put bits of mistletoe wherever there was room.

There were about eight couples. For music we depended on George, a school friend, and Eddie (who is now my husband). George's repertoire was quite varied, and we managed the polka, waltz, minuet and even lancers with great enthusiasm. But as poor Eddie could only play from memory the waltz *Love's Golden Dream Is O'er*, we had *Love's Golden Dream* for waltz, polka, and valeta, until perspiration dropped from the end of the violinist's nose.

All the girls loved to dance with Bert. His movements were so light. It was a thrilling moment when a lantern caught fire, and we nearly blew our heads off and stamped through the floor in putting it out.

Someone suggested ghost stories, and we trooped downstairs into the parlour, put out the light and gathered round the fire.

Bert, of course, told the tale, plunging into a ghastly adventure until our hair nearly stood on end. When he reached the most thrilling point he hesitated. Suddenly there was a most horrible banging and clattering just outside the door. We shrieked with terror and sat with palpitating hearts, and in marched George, who had been instructed by Bert to create the pandemonium at the critical moment, and who, strange to say, had not been missed. Mother sat in the kitchen alone, but content because we were happy.

NOTE

Lettice Ada Clarke, née Lawrence (1887–1948), was Lawrence's younger sister; she married in 1913.

'I am Going to be an Author'*

W. E. HOPKIN

By the time he had left Beauvale School [Lawrence] had formed the friendship with Jessie Chambers, the Miriam of his book.[1] They did their lessons together in a little alcove in the kitchen of the Haggs Farm. He usually finished first and would write odds and ends of verses and whole poems on odd bits of paper which he usually left lying about.

One Sunday evening when my wife and daughter were preparing supper and we were sitting on either side of the fire chatting, he startled me by suddenly leaning across and exclaiming, 'Willie, I am going to be an author.' I said, 'Are you, Bert? Well, if you think you have a gift for writing, go ahead. You must be prepared to have your manuscripts returned a few times, but if you have talent some publisher will discover it.' His face flushed slightly as he replied, 'I have genius! I know I have.' I treated it as

* From 'D. H. Lawrence: A Personal Memoir', in Nehls, I, pp. 70–1.

the pardonable conceit of a clever youth who *knew he was clever*, and told him I wished him the success he hoped for.

At that time he had three very good and helpful friends to whom he owed much, and to one in particular. Those who have read *The Lost Girl* will remember the local draper Lawrence describes so meticulously. This man's two daughters had a private governess, a very highly educated woman, and she spared no pains in helping Bert in his education—many times in after life he expressed his gratitude for what she had done. Undoubtedly he had the root of the matter in him, and it was only waiting a favourable environment to bring it to life and growth. I am quite sure that the unhappy events of his home life, terrible as he found them, had a profound effect and, perhaps, a helpful one on his life and writing. His mental makeup made something to fight an absolute necessity if the best was to emerge—at its best. Two happenings a few years later bear out my belief. He and Frieda were very much in love, but they quarrelled at times like the very devil. One day he said to me: 'Some of my acquaintances seem to think Frieda and I are wrongly mated. She is the one possible woman for me, for I must have opposition—something to fight or I shall go under.'

One day as we walked along the street I was incautious enough to ask him why he did not marry Jessie. He very angrily told me to mind my own damned business. A few minutes later he apologised and said: 'It would have been a fatal step. I should have had too easy a life, nearly everything my own way, and my genius would have been destroyed.' That belief was persistent in him. Even in his teens he allowed nothing to come between him and what he wanted for his writing.

NOTE

1. *Sons and Lovers*. On Jessie Chambers, see below, p. 31.

At Haggs Farm*

ADA LAWRENCE

When Bert was about sixteen we met the Chambers family at Haggs Farm, the Willey Farm of *Sons and Lovers*, the home of Miriam.[1]

We three were pupil teachers at different schools and attended the pupil teachers' centre at Ilkeston two or three times a week. Miriam's mother, a

* From *Young Lorenzo: Early Life of D. H. Lawrence*, pp. 44–50.

small, brown-eyed woman, with a gentle disposition, encouraged the friendship between her daughter and my brother; Miriam inherited her mother's large brown eyes. Her figure was a little ungainly as she walked with her head and shoulders bent forward, but her black silky hair had a natural wave and from her shoulders upward she was beautiful.

I think she first attracted Bert because she was so different from the gay, thoughtless girls we knew in the district. She was always very much in earnest about something or other, either her school work or a book, or her failing to understand her younger brothers or be understood by them. They delighted to offend her with little vulgarities.

Unlike us, she was not interested in new clothes or sweethearts, and until her meeting with my brother she had made no friend.

To know someone ready to listen to his ideas and views and accept his theories and beliefs, was a new experience for him. She shared his enthusiasm for the beauties of nature and poetry, and he loved the life at the farm—the companionship of the lads and her father. She claimed him before all others and their friendship continued for several years. Although mother accused him of being in love he would not admit it. Sometimes he said he was tired of the farm and Miriam and then mother would be glad, thinking he was all hers again. But after a restless weekend the desire to see Miriam again would become too strong, and when mother saw him wheeling his bicycle down the garden path she would say bitterly, 'So—he couldn't keep away after all his talk about not caring.' He was twenty-five when he and Miriam parted.

We spent many days in the country, and to Bert everything in the fields and woods was familiar. An Easter ramble I shall never forget was to Wingfield Manor, a lovely ruin near Matlock in the Derbyshire hills. It was a beautiful sunny Monday. We were up early, and packed lunches of veal sandwiches and hot cross buns. At nine o'clock the Haggs farm party arrived and we set off—four boys and three girls. We took the train to Alfreton, and Bert, who liked old buildings, said we must look round the church. He took a great deal of interest in architecture. But when we saw the Easter decorations, masses of daffodils, narcissus and Lent Lillies, he said we must sing a hymn or two, and threatened awful punishments if anyone laughed or treated the occasion lightly. I played the organ and we sang. After the boys had explored the belfry we set off for Wingfield.

Nothing escaped my brother's notice on the way, however deep in conversation he might be. He was the first to see the baby rabbit or cock-pheasant, the first primrose, or the fascinating male and female flowers of the larch.

At last we saw the ruins high up on a grassy slope. Bert loved the old place with its turrets and lonely crypt. Wallflowers grew among the stonework of the tower, and we climbed to the top to look over the deep lined face of Derbyshire. We reviled Cromwell and his men, who had destroyed the Manor, and spent a great deal of sympathy on Mary Queen of Scots who was imprisoned there.

We went on to Crich Stand, where a tower stands on an immense cliff near a small village. It is said that on a fine day one can see Lincoln Cathedral from the top of the tower. The beautiful valley of the Derwent lies below.

After passing through Holloway and Lea (the home of Florence Nightingale), we came to Whatstandswell, where we discovered we were terribly hungry. Lunch had been eaten long ago. When we had set aside our train fare from Ambergate to Langley Mill we pooled the remainder of the money. It amounted to sevenpence. 'Now,' said Bert, who was always the leader and was never ruffled by emergency, 'we must get some bread and butter from a cottage.' It was astonishing how much he got for so little. We drank from a spring. My brother's descriptions of the country in his novels and articles show how deeply he felt about it, and how much he knew of it.

Haggs farm was about three miles from Eastwood—a lovely walk past Moorgreen Reservoir, over fields, and through a little wood carpeted in spring with forget-me-nots. The farm house was low and long and the outbuildings adjoined it. There was a little strip of garden at the front, a gate separating it from the wood. At the back was a stack yard. Beyond it the fields stretched to Felley Mill (the Strelley Mill of *The White Peacock*). The three sons helped their father. The two daughters were schoolteachers. We climbed the apple trees, see-sawed, played hide and seek in the grain, and Bert tried his hand at milking cows.

In winter when work was finished we gathered round the piano in the parlour, and sang songs from a book, which Bert had given to me, and played charades.

Mr Chambers rented two fine mowing fields opposite Greasley church, and each year Bert helped with the haymaking, going early in the morning and working until after sundown. He could drive the cutting machines and load as well as the others, and had a wonderful amount of energy. While they worked we prepared huge quantities of bread and meat and currant-pies by the shady hedge side. One night, Bert and George, one of the sons, decided to sleep by a haystack, but were joined in the early hours by a tramp, whose company wasn't exactly peaceful. They kept to their beds after that. This part of the country is described by my brother in 'Love among the Haystacks'.

Some of our happiest hours were spent at our old piano with its faded green silk front. It had to be touched gently to bring out the tinkling notes. Bert bought me Chopin waltzes, music by Tschaikowsky and Brahms, Boosey's song books, and opera selections. He could not play but sat by my side for hours at a time encouraging me to practise difficult pieces. Sometimes they seemed beyond me and I was often on the verge of tears, begging to be left alone, but he insisted that I should persevere and hummed the air while I struggled with its complications. We sang duets— Mendelssohn's *Maybells and Flowers*, *The Passage Bird's Farewell*, and Rubinstein's *Song of the Birds*, but no one else heard them. There were sing-songs at Haggs Farm but our duets were never given there. He only sang them for his and my amusement.

Then he decided he would learn to play the piano. He could read music easily and thought he could master the rest as effortlessly as he painted and wrote. I remember how he shut himself in the front room and for half an hour or so we heard him labouring with simple scales and exercises. Then came a loud crash of keys and an exasperated young man stalked into the kitchen. His patience was exhausted and he refused to strum his fingers off over 'beastly scales' any longer. He never tried again and was content to sit with me and hum and sing.

NOTE

For a note on Ada Lawrence, see p. 10.
   1. In other words, Jessie Chambers (see below, p. 31).

The Friendship with 'Miriam'*

JESSIE CHAMBERS

My first clear recollection of D. H. Lawrence goes back to the Congregational Sunday School at Eastwood which we both attended. On a Sunday afternoon in each month the superintendent used to organise recitations instead of the usual lessons. We were sitting in groups, each with a teacher, the boys on one side of the long room, the girls on the other. The little dais at the end where the superintendent stood seemed far away, and the poems were seldom worth listening to, so that when a slight, fair boy of about eleven mounted the platform, my attention was only attracted when it became evident that he could not remember the beginning of his poem. He stood nervous and alert, the perfect pattern of a scholarship boy, and whispers went round that it was 'Bert Lawrence'. His elder sister was sitting near the platform, giggling at his distress. He opened his lips several times, only to find that the words would not come. The room grew ominously still. The white-haired, rosy-cheeked superintendent smiled

* From E. T. (Jessie Chambers), *D. H. Lawrence: A Personal Record*, 2nd edn, ed. J. D. Chambers (London: Frank Cass, 1965) pp. 15–16, 21–32, 38–42, 92–105, 108–9, 115–16, 182–4; the book was originally published in 1935.

encouragement, and Lawrence's sister giggled hysterically. At last the boy turned a tortured face to the superintendent and made a request, which was granted by a cordial nod. Lawrence thereupon drew a sheet of note paper from the inside pocket of his coat, glanced at it, then recited the poem correctly, and got down from the platform with a white face.

*   *   *

There was talk of Mrs Lawrence paying us a visit when first we went to live at the farm, but we had been there three years before she came. Eventually father told Lawrence how to find the field path and the way through the Warren, and so bring his mother by the short cut. It was on a day in early summer when the small, vigorous woman, and the slender boy she called Bertie, came into the farmyard, so still in the afternoon sunshine. Mother went out to greet them, and as she took them into the parlour, Mrs Lawrence, complaining of the heat, said in her crisp way:
'I'm thankful you haven't got a fire in here.'
We sat down to an early tea before the rest of the family came in. I had to go into the kitchen to boil eggs, and was surprised when the tall, fair boy followed me, and stood silently looking about him in a curious, intent way. The new staircase that had been put in for us made a big bulge on one wall, with deep recesses at either end. The recess beside the fireplace had a little window looking into the back garden. Lawrence seemed to be taking everything in with his eyes. It made me feel uncomfortable to see the peculiarities of our kitchen subjected to such keen scrutiny.
When tea was over we went out of doors. Mrs Lawrence and mother moved away together, talking the incomprehensible talk of adults. Already I felt that Mrs Lawrence pitied mother on account of her big family, and for living in such a queer, out-of-the-way spot. There was a tinge of patronage in her voice.
Lawrence and I went into the field beyond the stackyard. He stood quite still there, as if fascinated with the view of the Annesley Hills and High Park wood, with the reservoir gleaming below.
The single point of interest he had for me lay in the fact that he was still a schoolboy, as his Eton coat and collar reminded me. My own schooling, which had been of the crudest, had finished six months before, and my lack of education was a bitter humiliation to me. I was aware that this rather aloof youth had been for some years at the High School, and that he had studied French and German. I fancied that his superior education enabled him to appreciate things which were inaccessible to me. It was with a sense of getting even with him that I asked him abruptly how old he was.
'Fifteen,' he replied with a quick glance.
'I thought so. I'm fourteen,' I responded, aware that my question had been uncivil.
'You go to school?' I continued.

'Yes, to the High,' he answered, and gave me no further information. 'I don't care for the name of Bertie,' I went on, with a vague feeling of hostility. 'It's a girlish name. Do they call you Bertie at school?' 'No, of course not. They call me Lawrence.' 'That's nicer, I think. I'd rather call you Lawrence.' 'Do call me Lawrence,' he replied quickly, 'I'd like it better.'

He was shy and withdrawn, as if taking in many impressions at once. I felt that I was lacking in courtesy towards him, but I was terribly afraid this High School boy might look down on me.

Merely to prove my independence I set out a little later to visit a friend who lived on the opposite side of the wood. At the door I ran into Lawrence. His penetrating glance went over my hat, my face, my cloak. 'Are you going out?' he asked, disapproval in his voice. He had been exploring the farm with my brothers and his face glowed with excitement. He was naturally pale, but the keenness of his glance and his swiftly changing expression made him seem vivid. I told him where I was going, and he asked excitedly:

'How do you get there? Which way do you go?'

'Through the wood,' I replied.

'You go through there?' he said eagerly, nodding towards the wood.

When I returned everybody was crowded in the kitchen and the conversation had turned upon books. My parents adored Barrie, *The Little Minister* and *A Window in Thrums*. The talk was lively and Mrs Lawrence seemed to be the pivot upon which the liveliness centred. She struck me as a bright, vivacious little woman, full of vitality, and amusingly emphatic in her way of speaking. Her face changed rapidly as she talked and she had a habit of driving home her views with vigorous shakes of the head. She took a keen interest in things around her. As she said of herself, she entered into her children's pursuits and kept young through them. The conversation was mainly between Mrs Lawrence, father, and my elder sister, with Lawrence joining in occasionally. I listened for awhile in silence, then ventured to mention my favourite author.

'Who likes Scott?'[1] I asked.

'*I* do,' Mrs Lawrence replied, beaming encouragement upon me.

After this visit Lawrence came to the farm nearly always on his mid-week half-holiday. He would step quietly into the kitchen, often bringing some magazine or other to our book-loving household. He seemed gentle and reserved, and talked chiefly to my father, who liked him. He was rather slow at making friends with my brothers, and we on our side were shy of him, and afraid lest he should give himself airs. I have no particular recollection of Lawrence during that first summer except as a quiet presence coming suddenly out of the sunshine into the kitchen, warm with the fragrance of baking bread. Father and he seemed to find a good deal in common, and I noticed from the first that father talked to him almost as if he were grown up. I remember hearing them discuss whether it was possible to store electricity, and father spoke as if he expected Lawrence to know all about it. Occasionally he would bring a copy of *Black and White*[2] and they would talk about the illustrations, and I heard Lawrence describe the method of reproduction. These discussions introduced an interesting variety into our somewhat uneventful days.

Lawrence's schooldays finished that summer and he became a clerk in a Nottingham warehouse. We saw rather less of him then, but I heard him tell mother, in a voice that was clearly an unconscious imitation of his mother's, how Ernest and his fiancée had spent a fortnight's holiday with them, and that it had proved something of a strain. In October Ernest paid a flying visit to Goose Fair, and the next week we heard that he was dangerously ill in London and his parents had been summoned to his bedside. Almost immediately afterwards came news of his death, and we felt stunned by the tragedy. His mother had him brought home and buried in the cemetery at New Eastwood. She told my mother later, that when she reached her son's bedside she could scarcely recognise him, his head and face were so swollen and inflamed. He had returned to London in the raw morning hours after an exhausting week-end, and she could only think that he had caught a chill which brought on the fatal erysipelas. Telling me about this tragic journey years later she said:

'Yes, and I had to do everything myself, find out about the trains and how to get to Ernest's lodgings. His father was with me but he was no help; he stood just as if he was dazed.'

Only a few weeks after Ernest's death father came home from the milk-round with more bad news. It was Bertie this time, down with pneumonia. Mother looked stricken.

'I don't know whatever Mrs Lawrence will do if that son's taken from her,' she said. 'She told me when she was here with him that however much she loved Ernest it was nothing to what she felt for the one she brought with her. He had always meant more to her than any of the others.'

The trouble in the Lawrence family cast a gloom over our household, and mother inquired anxiously every day for news. It seemed a long time before father brought word that the patient was out of danger. His mother's nursing had saved his life, was the general verdict. When he was convalescent he began to send messages by father, begging one of us to go and see him. My sister took him a bunch of snowdrops that grew beneath the parlour window. She told us how gay he was, and how keenly he was looking forward to coming to the Haggs again, as soon as he was strong enough. His mother said he had grown so much in bed, she was sure his suits would all be too short for him.

On a day in early spring father brought him along in the milk-float. Mother and I watched from the kitchen window as the tall, thin youth in a dark overcoat stepped down from the float and walked slowly up the garden path.

'How white he is, how thin, poor lad,' mother was saying. He came into the kitchen, frail but eager, delighted to be with us again. Father seemed equally delighted. I do not know why my parents loved Lawrence as they did, but they were as glad at his recovery as if he had been their own son. They told him he was to come up just when he liked.

'Come up through the Warren, Bert,' father said. 'You want to get the smell o'them pine trees into your lungs. They're reckoned to be good for weak chests, aren't they? Take deep breaths and get your lungs full of the scent.'

From then his visits were a matter of course, and he became almost one of the family. He told us rather shamefacedly that his mother said he might as well pack his things and come and live with us. In later years he said that in those days he was only happy when he was either at The Haggs or on the way there. He vastly enjoyed the freedom of his long convalescence, and spent a month at Skegness with an aunt who kept a 'select' boarding-house on the front. He sent long descriptive letters to the family in general, in one of which he said that he could stand in his aunt's drawing-room and watch the tide rolling in through the window. My sister wrote back at once and said what an uncomfortable drawing-room his aunt's must be, with the tide rolling in through the window! He came home quite strong, and I heard father say what a rare good lad Bert was to his mother. He would blacklead the grate and scrub the floor. Lawrence told me himself that he never minded father seeing him with a coarse apron tied round his waist, but if he heard my brother's step in the entry he whipped it off on the instant, fearing he would despise him for doing housework.

At that period I was in a state of furious discontent and rebellion. I was the family drudge and hated it. My lack of education was a constant humiliation. The desire for knowledge and a longing for beauty tortured me. I came to the conclusion that unless I could achieve some degree of education I had better never have been born. I quarrelled continually with my brothers, who tried to order me about. I felt an Ishmael, with my hand against everybody, and everybody's hand against me. I did not know that Lawrence was aware of my state of mind, but one day he suddenly took an end of chalk from his pocket and wrote on the stable door:

Nil desperandum.

'What does it mean?' I asked, although I knew.

'Never despair,' he replied, with an enigmatic smile, and ran away.

Eventually I succeeded in making myself so disagreeable that mother in desperation sent me back to school and I became a pupil-teacher. Then began an arduous life of studying, teaching, and helping with the housework, which still somehow left time for the most exciting games.

It was by now an established rule that Lawrence should come to tea on a Saturday, and when he entered the house he brought a holiday atmosphere with him. It was not merely that we were all nice with him, he knew how to make us nicer to one another. Even my eldest brother thawed when Lawrence was there. He brought a pack of cards, and taught us

THE FRIENDSHIP WITH 'MIRIAM'   19

whist, and we played fast and furious, with the younger children crowding round to watch, and Lawrence excitedly scolding and correcting us. When he was in the mood he could be very funny, particularly when mimicking the members of the Christian Endeavour class repeating in turn 'The servant of the Lord is like a well-filled house. . .'. He used to say that our laughter was Homeric. He would have us dance in our little kitchen, and once while we paused for breath he said:

'Father says one ought to be able to dance on a threepenny bit.'

He seldom spoke of his father and we at once exclaimed:

'Why, does your father dance?'

'He used to, when he was a young man. He ran a dancing class at one time,' he replied briefly.

It seemed unbelievable; we had never thought of his father in that light.

Lawrence was extraordinarily kind and willing to help with whatever task was afoot. He was most considerate towards mother, with her big, unruly family, so hard to manage, each of us at a different stage of development, each making a different demand upon her. Several times when he came in and found her with more to do than she could get through he fetched water for the boiler, tidied up the hearth, and made a fire in the parlour where my sister (who was also a pupil-teacher) and I did our lessons. And I well remember a basket of tiny pickling onions that stood on the stone slab outside the back door for weeks, waiting to be peeled. They suddenly disappeared, and mother said that Bert had peeled them; he just sat down and did them without saying a word to anyone. No task seemed dull or monotonous to him. He brought such vitality to the doing that he transformed it into something creative.

It was the same at harvest time. Lawrence would spend whole days working with my father and brothers in the fields at Greasley. These fields lay four miles away, and we used to pack a big basket of provisions to last all day, so that hay harvest had a picnic flavour. Father enjoyed Lawrence's company quite as much as the rest of us. There was for years a fine understanding between them, a sympathy and recognition of what was best in each other. I heard father say to mother:

'Work goes like fun when Bert's there, it's no trouble at all to keep them going.'

It was true; in those early days Lawrence seemed so happy that merely to be alive and walking about was an adventure, and his gift for creating an atmosphere of good fellowship made work a joy. One could not help being affected by his vitality and charm. Mother made a remark that set me speculating. She said:

'I should like to be next to Bert in heaven.'

I did hope heaven wouldn't turn out to be a sort of eternal Sunday school. Our ideas of heaven must have been remarkably concrete, for Mrs Lawrence told mother that she looked forward more to meeting her son Ernest in heaven than Jesus Christ Himself.

Lawrence's speech abounded in vivid and oddly characteristic turns. I remember hearing him say in his blithe way:

'Ah, there's a custard for dinner, it rejoiceth my heart to see.' If he wanted a small piece of cake he would say in his rather high-pitched voice, 'Only give me a smeggin.' Anything he didn't like was 'a measly thing' and an inferior thing 'wasn't a patch' on something else. He amused us mightily by showing us how a girl acquaintance laughed. He would open his mouth wide and emit a sudden explosive giggle that was so comically like the original we laughed to exhaustion. He told us the story of his father bringing home a whole ham and then stopping payment for it each week out of the housekeeping money.

'Mother carried on about it week after week,' said Lawrence, with a touch of pained recollection in his voice. 'At last father could stand it no longer, and when mother began again he turned and looked at her, "Woman, how'd tha feeace"[3] he said, and I nearly felt sorry for him.'

We laughed uproariously, and Lawrence laughed too, a little ruefully.

'And did she stop then?' we asked.

'Oh, yes,' he said, 'even mother had to laugh.'

*   *   *

When Lawrence discovered that we had never seen the sea, he persuaded mother to let us go on a day trip to Skegness. His own intense enjoyment gave a keener edge to our pleasure. He knew all the landmarks on the way, and would not let us miss a single point of interest. We had to rush to the carriage window to observe the graceful lines of Gedling Church spire rising sheer out of the valley. Further on there was Bottesford Church with its handsome dog-toothed ornament, and we tried to descry the outline of Belvoir Castle standing high on its ridge. At Boston we craned our necks to catch a glimpse of the famous Stump dominating the fens with its sombre dignity. But it was more than merely *seeing* these landmarks; it was a kind of immediate possession, as though to have missed seeing them would have been to lose an essential moment of life. An outing with Lawrence was a memorable experience. There was a sense of immediacy; each moment as it came seemed to be a culminating point of existence. His face, and particularly his eyes, were alight with eagerness that we should miss nothing of what stirred his own delight so deeply.

At the seaside we found a greyish day, and I saw that what mattered was not the colour of the sea, about which I had wondered so much, but the expanse, and the wide horizon, and the quite different quality of light. We paddled, and dried our feet in the sand, and [Lawrence's younger sister] called in her tone of conscious ownership to her brother to dry her feet for her. He made a gesture of protest, but obeyed all the same, kneeling and dusting the sand from her feet with his handkerchief. We ate our lunch on the beach, and after tea, which we had in a café, went to buy presents to take home. As Lawrence was the only one of us who had tasted melon he bought one and we retired into an arbour in the public gardens to eat it. He assured us it would be delicious, and cut it into half a dozen strips. Mine tasted like turnip, and was quite as hard. But that was a secondary consideration; we had eaten melon; it was an experience the more. Lawrence had a knack of describing where he had been and what he had done in such a way as to make one feel that the thing he had seen was one of the few things in the world really worth seeing, and what he had done was just what any vitally alive person would want to do. But he was apologetic about the melon; the one he had tasted previously really had been delicious—this wasn't a patch on it, he assured us.

When Goose Fair came round Lawrence wanted me to join a party for a jaunt round the Fair, but mother gave a blank refusal. He sent me a postcard from the café where they had tea at a table in a window overlooking the whole panorama of the Fair, and he managed to convey the full flavour of his palpitating excitement. When he got home he wrote a long account of what they had done, and headed the letter 'The Diary of a Butterfly to a Moth'. I maliciously showed it to mother.

'A butterfly to a moth?' she said. 'What does he mean? Who is the moth? Are you the moth?' Her anger helped to mollify my disappointment.

But we had some wonderful outings. Mrs Lawrence was an active member of the Women's Co-Operative Guild, and sometimes she and a friend would make up a party and hire a brake to take us to Matlock, and it was Lawrence who prevailed upon my parents to let my sister and me accompany them. Best of all, though, were the tramps we had in parties of a dozen or so, all young people. These were genuine explorations of the countryside, and Lawrence was always the originator and the leader. He would walk briskly along with his lithe, light step, tirelessly observant, his eager eyes taking everything in, his pale skin whipped into colour. We had an exhilarating walk to Condnor Castle one bitterly cold day in a Christmas holiday, along the frozen black mud of the towing path by the canal, the icy wind whipping a finer ecstasy into our blood, and imparting a flavour that was more than mortal to the sandwiches and biscuits we munched as we went along. The little, crumbling, ivy-covered ruin that Cromwell had demolished was full of the romance of bygone days. We peopled it in imagination with its former inhabitants—ourselves more splendidly situated.

There was a memorable outing when we took train to Alfreton and walked from there to Wingfield Manor, then on to Crich Stand, and through the woods to Whatstandwell where we hoped to get a train home, but found the station locked up. We were tired and hungry and beyond our train fare could muster only a few pence amongst us to buy bread and butter at a cottage. But we were supremely happy. Lawrence seemed to have a knowledge of the countryside as he had of flowers; he could tell us something about every place we passed through, as if he had already shared in its life.

It was on one of these walks—we had been to the Hemlock Stone, the curious outcrop of ancient rock that stands alone like a sentinel on the very edge of a big industrial region—that I had a sudden flash of insight which made me see Lawrence in a totally new light. We were walking along anyhow, singly, or in twos and threes. I happened to be alone, admiring the bronze tips of the maple in the hedge. Suddenly I turned and saw Lawrence in the middle of the road, bending over an umbrella. There was something in his attitude that arrested me. His stooping figure had a look of intensity, almost of anguish. For a moment I saw him as a symbolic figure. I was deeply moved and walked back to him.

'What is the matter?' I asked.

'It was Ern's umbrella, and mother will be wild if I take it home broken,' he replied.

We walked on together, but I did not tell him what I had seen. This was perhaps the beginning of our awareness of sympathy for one another.

Christmas was a wonderful time. There were parties at one house or another during the holidays, and always thrilling charades at our house, with Lawrence directing things, and father joining in the play like one of us. Then towards midnight, to escort our friends through the Warren and over the dim field path, singing, with the stars flashing above the silent woods, and the pale light over the water, was perhaps the most wonderful bit of all. We seemed to be living in a world within a world, created out of the energy of the imagination. Life in those days was full to the brim, pressed down, and running over.

*   *   *

One of the most treasured possessions of the Lawrence household was a set of large volumes bound in green cloth containing long extracts from famous authors. The books had belonged to Ernest, and were regarded with a reverence amounting to awe. Lawrence must have made many literary acquaintances through the medium of these volumes. As a mark of rare favour I was once allowed to borrow one of them, but the favour was never repeated.

The first book I recollect Lawrence bringing to me was Louisa Alcott's *Little Women*. We thought the story delightful, and set about finding correspondences. I was Jo, there was no doubt about that, and Lawrence was Laurie. 'Only not quite so nice, do you think?' he said with a glance that asked to be contradicted. Not long afterwards he brought Watts-Dunton's *Aylwin*, and then was very contrite because he thought the ghost scene might have frightened me.

'I ought not to have given it to you,' he said repeatedly, and asked anxiously if mother was angry with him.

Both his family and mine were members of the library which was part of the Mechanics' Institute at Eastwood and was open only for two hours on Thursday evenings. How it came about that Lawrence and I usually went to the library together to choose the books for our respective families, I don't remember, but the visit to the library was at that time the outstanding event of the week. As a rule I should put the books to be returned in the milk-cart, and father would leave them at his home. Lawrence would change the books for us, if it happened to be wet and I was unable to go, and send up the new ones next morning. But I always went if possible, though Lawrence inevitably did most of the choosing. He would take possession of my list and pounce on the book he was looking for; he always seemed to know just where to look for it. We were both excited by this hunting among books. Even then he seemed to be acquainted with nearly everything in the little library. We had also to bear in mind the varying tastes of the two families, and the matter of selection was sometimes a lengthy business. On more than one occasion when I placed the books we proposed to take for our family upon the counter, the old librarian, who gave his time and services to the Institution, would regard me gravely over his glasses, and say:

'Young lady, you are entitled to one bound volume and one magazine,' but he rarely insisted on the letter of the law. Then Lawrence and I would set off for my home literally burdened with books. During the walk we discussed what we had read last, but our discussion was not exactly criticism, indeed it was not criticism at all, but a vivid re-creation of the substance of our reading. Lawrence would ask me in his abrupt way what I thought of such and such a character, and we would compare notes and talk out our differences. The characters interested us most, and there was usually a more or less unconscious identification of them with ourselves, so that our reading became a kind of personal experience. Scott's novels in particular we talked over in this way, and the scenes and events of his stories were more real to us than our actual surroundings. We read Rider Haggard at about the same time, but somehow he never provided the same rich basis for discussion. I remember how Lawrence pressed me to read Anthony Hope's *Rupert of Hentzau* and *The Prisoner of Zenda*.[4] 'You will like them, I'm certain you'll like them,' he assured me, and I did like them, but all the same I felt they were trivial. A quite different book that he recommended me to read and that impressed me profoundly was Dean Farrar's *Darkness and Dawn*.[5] This period, when Lawrence would be 16–17, was a kind of orgy of reading. I think we were hardly aware of the outside world.

When I called for Lawrence to accompany me to the library, if no one else was in the house, he would take a volume of poetry from the bookcase (Longfellow in the early days) and read to me, always, as it seemed, with one ear cocked for an alien footstep. In this way he read to me most of *Hiawatha*, which I thought long-winded and rather thin, and *Evangeline*, which again Lawrence liked far better than I did. He seemed disappointed when I did not care for the poems he read, so I kept my opinion to myself, for I could never bear to hurt his feelings. He used to look so delicately excited, sitting there on the sofa, his head resting on one of his small, vigorous hands, and the other with fingers ready to turn the page, ready to close the book and swiftly put it away if a step should sound outside in the entry. In time he read Tennyson's *Morte d'Arthur*, which I really did like, and *Lancelot and Elaine*, that struck me as a revolting story. But when he came to *Maud*, dwelling especially on the lyrical passages, and read:

> Birds in the high Hall garden
> When twilight was falling,
> Maud, Maud, Maud, Maud,
> They were crying and calling,

which evoked memories of our own wood, then I thought that was what poetry should be like. Later on he would read 'Ulysses' and would often quote: 'Though much is taken, much abides'. Other poems he read to me time after time were 'The Lotus Eaters' and 'The Lady of Shalott', which he somehow hinted applied to me, and 'Locksley Hall', where again he conveyed the impression that he was telling me something about himself.

Scott was succeeded in our affections by Dickens, with *David Copperfield* pre-eminent. I was aware even then that Lawrence felt an affinity with the hero of that story—'the nicest young man in the world', he would quote mischievously. *Bleak House* and *Dombey and Son* were great favourites. And to say that we *read* the books gives no adequate idea of what really happened. It was the entering into possession of a new world, a widening and enlargement of life. There was *The Cloister and the Hearth* that we all tried to read together, Lawrence and those of our family who were old enough to read, almost snatching the book out of one another's hands in our eagerness to follow Gerard's thrilling adventures. And how we each described the particular bit of the story that had given us the greatest thrill! Then we read Fennimore Cooper's *Last of the Mohicans* and *The Pathfinder*, with its impression of the expanse of level lake and silence, and R. L. Stevenson's *Treasure Island* and *Kidnapped*. But when Lawrence spoke of *The Master of Ballantrae* there was quite another tone. 'Do read it,' he begged. 'I want to know what you think of it. It's not a bit like Stevenson's other books.'

Lorna Doone was a story after our own hearts, which we all re-enacted in fancy on our own Annesley Hills. One of the patches of woodland we named Bagworthy Forest, and we scoured down the hillside with imaginary Doones at our heels.

It was on a wintry Sunday afternoon that we explored Felley Mill Farm for the first time—a little crowd of us, my elder brother and sister, my younger brothers, Lawrence and I. Like Annesley Lodge Farm it was unoccupied, the poisoned ground lying fallow, recovering from intensive rabbit farming. We went cautiously through the little side gate into the garden, down which the windows of the two parlours looked blankly. There were snowdrops under the windows, and we gathered some, putting them with ivy leaves which we pulled from the stone wall beside the millrace, where the wheel used to be, and where now the water slid down with a ceaseless rush into the pond below. The mill-pond was on our left, higher than our heads. We watched the water rushing down and smelt the acrid odour from the mould under the ivy leaves. Then we went through the little gate at the end of the garden and up the steep slope of the sluice, and crossed to the far side of the pond. As there was no one to forbid us we went to the extreme end and walked over the ice to the islet covered with low alders and brushwood. It was pure adventure. The snowdrops and the ivy leaves and the smell of the earth mould, the ceaseless rushing of the water and our own excitement created an impression of something more real and permanent than our actual presence there. We seemed momentarily to have penetrated to the abiding spirit of the place.

With *Adam Bede* and *The Mill on the Floss* we found ourselves in deeper waters. Lawrence adored *The Mill on the Floss*, but always declared that George Eliot had 'gone and spoilt it half way through'. He could not forgive the marriage of the vital Maggie Tulliver to the cripple Philip. He used to say: 'It was wrong, wrong. She should never have made her do it.' When, later on, we came to Schopenhauer's essay on *The Metaphysics of Love*, against the passage: 'The third consideration is the *skeleton*, since it is the foundation of the type of the species. Next to old age and disease, nothing disgusts us so much as a deformed shape; even the most beautiful face cannot make amends for it.' Lawrence wrote in the margin: 'Maggie Tulliver and Philip'. Maggie Tulliver was his favourite heroine. He used to say that the smooth branches of the beech trees (which he especially admired) reminded him of Maggie Tulliver's arms. Over *Romola* he shook his head: 'Poor George Eliot, she said the writing of *Romola* made an old woman of her.'

A book that exercised a real fascination over him was *Jane Eyre*. He seemed to brood over the relationship between Jane and Rochester, whose attitude in particular interested him. 'He calls her a *thing*,' he said to me. 'You know, where he finds Jane in the rosegarden, and he says, "You curious thing." How could one say that in French? It would have to be *chose*. It wouldn't go at all.'

Thackeray's *Vanity Fair* took the household by storm, my father being as eager as any of us. We found a big illustrated volume of *The Four Georges and English Humorists*, and the rollicking Dick Steele and the prim Addison stood out as real figures, the first of the journalists. It was at the house of Lawrence's headmaster that we came across a volume of Hogarth's drawings and delighted in their bold portrayal of life. There also we found a big volume of Swift's writings, and read a short account of his life. Swift, towering menacingly above his age, impressed us deeply. Lawrence told me about Stella and the *Little Journal*, and we pondered their strange love story.

This might be called the second period of our reading. The first was a sheer revelling in books, the second was almost purely receptive, then we reached the stage which in my mind coincides roughly with my introduction to Palgrave's *Golden Treasury of Songs and Lyrics*, when I was eighteen. This became a kind of Bible to us. Lawrence carried the little red volume in his pocket and read to me on every opportunity, usually out in the fields. He must have read almost every poem to me at one time or another, but those that stand out most clearly in my memory are Shelley's 'The Invitation', 'The Recollection', 'Rarely, rarely comest thou', 'Ode to the West Wind', and 'Swiftly walk over the western wave'. Of Wordsworth there was 'The Solitary Reaper', 'I wandered lonely as a cloud', and the 'Ode on Intimations of Immortality', while Keats' 'La Belle Dame Sans Merci' seemed to have the tang of our own dank meadows. These, with others, he would read to me over and over again, and he pointed out that Book IV comprised nearly half the volume. 'Getting nearer to our own day,' he said significantly.

In Book III he was very fond of Cowper's two poems to Mary Unwin. Underneath the second of the two he wrote: 'Poor Cowper, when he felt he was going mad again.' He liked Burns, and when he had read 'Mary Morison', he said, smiling: 'No one was quite so deft as Burns at turning a compliment.' We had many favourites in Book II. Lawrence adored Herbert's 'The Gifts of God' and talked to me about the mystical quality of the poets of that age. Against Shirley's 'Death the Leveller' he wrote in my copy: 'This poem De Quincey says he heard sung in a chamber of a tiny Welsh inn where he was staying awhile during his rambles. The unseen singer was a young Methodist girl, and although used to operatic performances De Quincey was more pleased and delighted with her song than he had even been before or since.' Lawrence underlined:

> Only the actions of the just
> Smell sweet and blossom in their dust.

He liked 'Fair Helen'[6] very much, and later he taught it to his boys in the Croydon school. He used to say that boys ought to learn love poems at school, as a preparation for love in real life. 'The Great Adventurer' was another favourite: 'Cromwell—in love?' he wrote beneath the poem. Book I was for us mainly Shakespeare's Sonnets, and we marvelled at their perfection and their nearness. All this was spread over a number of years, and meant more to our development than one knows how to put into words. At Christmas we exchanged tiny gift books. Lawrence gave me once a selection of Shelley and at other times *The Blessed Damozel* and the *Rubáiyát of Omar Khayyám*, and I gave him Blake's *Songs of Innocence* and *Songs of Experience*.

We read essays, too, at this time. Bacon's *Essays* was one of our set books. Lawrence detested Bacon's calculated moralising, but he adored Lamb, and dwelt affectionately on 'Dream Children' and 'The South Sea House', and we chuckled over 'A Dissertation on Roast Pig'. He read and liked Emerson's *Essays* and became wildly enthusiastic over Thoreau's *Walden*, especially the essay on 'The Ponds'. I remember Lawrence waiting one morning of a holiday to accompany my brother who was going to work in the Greasley fields, and telling us meanwhile how Thoreau built himself a hut in the woods and lived beside the pond. It was a still, sunless morning, with a brooding light over the landscape, and the atmosphere he conveyed in his description seemed to tally perfectly with that particular morning.

Then we came to Carlyle. Lawrence said that he was reading the *French Revolution* with Carlyle on one knee and the dictionary on the other. He was loud in his denunciation of Carlyle's affectation of a German style, but he insisted on my reading the book. The stabbing of Marat by Charlotte Corday excited him—just like a bit out of *A Tale of Two Cities*, he said. We read also *Heroes and Hero Worship* and *Sartor Resartus*. This was in the spring of 1906 just before Lawrence went to College, and his early flamboyant delight in reading was changing into a seriousness that was at times almost frightening in its intensity. He said to me weightily, 'I feel I have something to say', and again, 'I think it will be didactic.'

Other books that belong to this period were Mrs Gaskell's *Cranford*, and I remember the glow of his tender delight in that simple tale. And there was *Alice in Wonderland* that we bought for the little ones and revelled in ourselves. A book that Lawrence absolutely forbade me to read was *Wuthering Heights*.

'*You* mustn't read it,' he said in his excited way. And when I asked why not, he said:

'You mustn't, that's all. It might upset you.' I said I meant to read it anyhow, and then he became serious and made me promise I wouldn't. His mother had read it, and I remember hearing her say with comic exaggeration what she would like to do to 'that Heathcliffe', only she pronounced it 'Hethcliffe'.

Once when we had just left his home Lawrence said to me, 'I don't believe they were like us when they were young, do you? Our parents, I mean. I don't imagine mother ever read Carlyle. It was Annie Swan,[7] I think.'

And another time he said:

'I'm sure they don't feel things as we do, I don't care what they say. They talk about them too much. If you really feel a thing deeply you can't talk about it, can you?'

Lawrence now began to talk definitely of writing. He said he thought he should try a novel, and wanted me to try to write one too, so that we could compare notes.

'The usual plan is to take two couples and develop their relationships,' he said. 'Most of George Eliot's are on that plan. Anyhow, I don't want a plot, I should be bored with it. I shall try two couples for a start.'

It was in the Whitsuntide holiday that he brought the first pages to me. I had been away from home, and returned to find Lawrence waiting uneasily. Out in the fields he gave me the manuscript and asked me if I had any to show him. I shook my head.

'We've broken the ice,' he said in a tense voice. He told me to put the writing away and read it when he had gone. I was to tell him what I thought of it the next time he came. I was interested to find that his story was laid around Felley Mill Farm. These first pages described himself standing on the banks of the mill-pond, watching the fish glide in and out. The farm had a tenant now, and Lawrence had accompanied me there several times on some errand or other. From now on he brought some pages almost every time he came up. He would pass them to me in secret and wait restlessly until we were out in the fields and he could begin to talk about his writing. One evening we were looking for the little purple orchids that were to be found only in the Long Close, and Lawrence was saying:

'I'm afraid it will be a mosaic. My time's so broken up. In the morning when I should love to sit down to it I have to go to school. And when you've done the day's teaching all your brightness has gone. By the time I get back to the writing I'm another man. I don't see how there can be any continuity about it. It will have to be a mosaic, a mosaic of moods.'

What fascinated me about his writing was the way he would weave incidents from our daily life into it. Mother was looking in the wood for the nest of a hen that was laying away, and came across an old kettle containing a nest and a bright-eyed robin sitting on her eggs. We showed it to Lawrence, who seemed moved at the sight. Soon after it appeared in his writing, described with amazing exactness and intensity of observation. Then there was the lark's nest, a mere hole where a cow's hoof had sunk into the soft ground, and the four speckled eggs lying there, so unprotected. Lawrence knelt beside it, almost trembling with excitement. We went to look at it each time he came until at last the quivering bubs[8] lay on the ground, with feathers fine like hairs.

A fragment of conversation about writing and writers comes back to me. We were in the wood where the stiff clay soil was waterlogged in all except the driest seasons, and we were picking our way carefully over the muddy patches.

'You see, it was really George Eliot who started it all,' Lawrence was saying in the deliberate way he had of speaking when he was trying to work something out in his own mind. 'And how wild they all were with her for

doing it. It was she who started putting all the action inside. Before, you
know, with Fielding and the others, it had been outside. Now I wonder
which is right?'

I always found myself most interested in what people thought and
experienced within themselves, so I ventured the opinion that George Eliot
had been right.

'I wonder if she was,' Lawrence replied thoughtfully. 'You know I can't
help thinking there ought to be a bit of both.'

* * *

Sometimes we had a play-reading at home. We read *Macbeth* with father
taking the part of Macduff, and horrified at the speech he had to make
when he came face to face with Macbeth. He stopped to exclaim, 'Oh dear,
oh dear! How awful!' Lawrence stood knitting his brows, half-amused,
half-vexed at the interruption. He was excited and inclined to be
domineering over the play-readings, but we knew him too well to take
offence. He admired Ibsen tremendously, and recommended my brother
to give me a volume of his plays on my birthday, so we read *Rosmersholm*,
which was Lawrence's favourite, and *The Lady from the Sea*, of which he
gave us a full description in advance, saying it was the most poetical of
Ibsen's plays that he had read. Finally we read *Hedda Gabler* which he
thoroughly disliked. I remember how severely he took me to task for
omitting a phrase about someone who used to 'keep mistresses'. I simply
couldn't read it aloud. Lawrence said nothing at the time, but he taxed me
with it later. 'Why did you miss that passage—about mistresses? You
should have read it as it stood. What do you want to make such evasions
for....'

We went to the theatre occasionally. I saw *Hamlet* for the first time with
Lawrence and my brother. Lawrence was intensely excited. He went
through Hamlet's soliloquy afterwards in our kitchen—'To be, or not to
be . . .' And it was the same when we had seen *Macbeth*—'Is this a dagger I
see before me, the handle towards my hand . . . ?' grasping at an
imaginary dagger. It was his characteristic blending of the serious with the
comic. Of course we laughed at him, but the two aspects were plainly
visible. Going to the theatre was the same as reading, Lawrence identified
himself with the play, and for the time being lived in its atmosphere. Now
and again we saw a D'Oyly Carte opera—Lawrence was often humming a
tune from *Il Trovatore*—and we heard *Tannhäuser*. Once on a Saturday
afternoon we went to a Gilbert and Sullivan opera, and on another
occasion we saw Galsworthy's *Strife*.[9]

While Lawrence was at college Sarah Bernhardt came to our theatre at
Nottingham, and he went to see her in *La Dame aux Camélias*. The next day
he wrote to me that the play had so upset him that at the end he rushed
from his place and found himself battering at the doors until an attendant

came and let him out. He ran to the station to find the last train gone, and had to walk home. He added, 'I feel frightened. I realise that I, too, might become enslaved to a woman.' On the Saturday afternoon he came up and told us all about the play, and showed us how Sarah Bernhardt died in the last scene. He looked quite worn out with emotion.

*   *   *

Lawrence was constantly bringing his writing to me, and I always had to tell him what I thought of it. He would ask whether the characters had developed, and whether the conversation was natural, if it was what people really would say. He found conversation easy and wondered if it was too easy. He feared he had a tendency towards verbosity; perhaps he ought to condense his writing more . . . Saturday evening was the best time for talking over his work, but in a busy household like ours I naturally had to help. Sometimes when he very much wanted to talk, Lawrence would follow me from the kitchen into the parlour and back again from parlour to kitchen until I was free to sit down and talk to him. He always declared that he did the writing for me.

'Every bit I do is for you,' he said. 'Whenever I've done a fresh bit I think to myself: "What will she say to this?"' And of his poetry he said, 'All my poetry belongs to you.'

I had not a high opinion of the first version of *The White Peacock*, in which George married Letty. Lawrence persuaded me on a Saturday morning when I happened to be going into Nottingham, to take a tram ride out to Basford and bring him word what the registry office looked like. It was a solid, square building, the most unromantic place imaginable. I can see now his bright, subtle smile when I told him my impressions. The next pages of writing he brought to me described George and Letty being married there.

*   *   *

The autumn of his mother's dying imposed a terrible strain upon Lawrence. He was never the same man again. He came home on alternate weekends to be with her. I saw him several times, and although he was superficially interested in things one could not help feeling how terribly alone he was in his grief. Love was unavailing, no matter how sincere or how selfless. In his presence one felt only the horror of sheer hopelessness. His mother's death completed the break-up of the old life, that had proved so rich in experience and achievement.

A fortnight or so before his mother's death I had occasion to call at the village post office and a letter from Lawrence was handed to me. In the dim light I read: 'I was in the train with X on Saturday and I suddenly asked her to marry me. I never meant to. But she accepted me and I shall stick to it. I've written to her father . . . I'll go over the old ground again, if you like, and explain. Do you want me to say little, or nothing, or much? I'll say anything you like, only I can't help it, I'm made this way.'

Lawrence was with his mother when she died. He sent word to me, and on a Sunday morning, the day before her funeral, we met and walked once more on the familiar lanes. As we passed the reservoir a beggar whined for alms. Lawrence brutally tossed a coin to him, and the man grovelled for it in the dust. I looked at Lawrence in anger, and he answered:

'Yes, a man has sunk pretty low when he can take a copper in that fashion.'

I told him he had done wrong to involve X in the impasse of our relationship: 'You should not have drawn X into things,' I said. 'She has no idea of the real state of affairs.'

'With *should* and *ought* I have nothing to do,' Lawrence replied coldly. We walked on in anguish of spirit. At the railway track leading down to the pits we remained standing a long time. We seemed to be completely shut in by the grey December day, quite removed from the world of human contact. Suddenly out of the gloom a collier appeared on his way to work. He had a red scarf round his neck and a tea-can was sticking out of his pocket. He looked at us with startled eyes. Lawrence glanced at him as he passed.

'There you are,' he said, 'A story by Chekhov—"The Man in the Red Muffler".'

We waited some time longer, then Lawrence looked at me with intensity. 'You know—I've always loved mother,' he said in a strangled voice.

'I know you have,' I replied.

'I don't mean that,' he returned quickly. 'I've *loved* her, like a lover. That's why I could never love you.'

With that he silently gave me a draft of the poems he had just written: 'The End', 'The Bride', 'The Virgin Mother'.

After his mother's death Lawrence was like a rudderless ship—'a leaf blown in the wind' was his favourite simile for himself.

NOTES

Jessie Chambers (1886–1944), later Jessie Wood, lived at Haggs Farm and was the most important friend of Lawrence's youth. She is portrayed as Miriam in *Sons and Lovers* and by Lawrence and others was variously nicknamed 'Miriam', 'Muriel', 'The Princess', and 'E.T.' (these initials, under which her memoir was originally published, are those of Eunice Temple, the heroine of an unpublished novel by Jessie Chambers). She married in 1915. She is the subject of Helen Corke's *D. H. Lawrence's 'Princess': A Memory of Jessie Chambers* (Thames Ditton: Merle Press, 1951), which includes many letters; for the last of them, see p. 300 below.

1. Compare the introductory description of Miriam in Chapter VII of *Sons and Lovers* (for example, 'The girl was romantic in her soul. Everywhere was a Walter Scott heroine being loved by men with helmets or with plumes in their caps. . . .').

2. An illustrated weekly which ran from 1891 to 1912.

3. 'Hold your face' ('Be quiet').

4. Pseudonym of Anthony Hope Hawkins, whose adventure stories were widely popular. The two titles mentioned were published in 1898 and 1894, respectively.

5. The full title of this novel by Frederic William Farrar is *Darkness and Dawn, or Scenes in the Days of Nero: an Historic Tale* (1891).

6. The title given by the anthologist Francis Palgrave to the anonymous ballad beginning 'I wish I were where Helen lies'.

7. A popular sentimental novelist with a wide female readership.

8. Dialect word for young birds.

9. This must be an error of recollection, since *Strife* was first produced only on 9 March 1909, by which time Lawrence had settled in Croydon.

Adolescence*

J. D. CHAMBERS

My memory of D. H. Lawrence goes back to when he was a young man of eighteen—tall, pale, with the liveliest eyes I have ever seen and a high-pitched voice that would trail off into a squeak of excitement or of exasperation. He had originally come to help in the hayfield as part of his convalescence from an attack of pneumonia and had by the time I remember him become almost a member of the family—certainly the most exciting person I had ever met.

I adored him for what he was: high-spirited, infectiously gay, galvanising every company, whether at work or at play, into new and more intense activity, making them bigger, better, cleverer than they were by nature, and imparting to them some of his own inexhaustible zest for life. When he came into the hayfield, as he often did in those endlessly sunny summers of one's boyhood, work went with an unaccustomed swing; he worked along with my father and brothers, staggering under massive forkfuls of hay and keeping up his side of the haycart by sheer nervous energy, for in physique he was not their equal though he was taller. And at tea time, hampers

* J. D. Chambers's memoir was originally broadcast by the BBC and subsequently appeared in condensed form in *The Listener*, XL (7 Oct 1948) p. 515, under the title 'Memories of D. H. Lawrence as a Boy'. The full version is printed by Nehls, I, pp. 47–51.

would be mysteriously unearthed and tea time in the hayfield was turned into a picnic; how it happened I never quite knew, but I suspect the news got around that Bert was helping in Chambers' fields at Greasley and his sister or his friends, mainly girls studying at the pupil-teacher centre at Ilkeston, would take the opportunity of bringing a contribution to a picnic that might well become an impromptu dance, a game at duck or hide and seek and would certainly be memorable for high spirits and reckless fun. At any rate, I remember them after forty years.

But to me, as a mere child, he was at his greatest in charades. There have never been such charades since. My favourite role was to play the part of corpse so that I could be brought in with one eye and both ears very wide open. By this happy arrangement I had nothing to do but I missed nothing. On one unforgettable occasion, I played the same role on both sides, the most complete success I have ever known. I remember him playing the part of coachman, sitting on our parlour table and suddenly jumping up to whip up the horses, with the effect of bringing my father's tall hat, which he had borrowed for the part, into violent contact with the ceiling and ramming it over his ears and face, to my quite inexpressible delight; and another, when he played the part of Pharaoh, with the milksile[1] on his head for crown, and hardened his heart ineluctably against the pleas of Moses and the children of Israel. Besides charades, he introduced whist, chess, dancing, singing and, above all, reinforced the flow of books until it became a flood in our family circle. In regard to singing, he contrived to make my brothers and sisters learn their parts from tonic sol-fa, and even went into the cowshed to teach them while they were milking. We sang *Friars of Orders Grey, Two Grenadiers, Caro Mio Ben, Larboard Watch* and a host of others which I can never hear even now without an echo of those family sing-songs with Bert conducting and singing all parts as required although he had by far the poorest singing voice of us all. And when he left us to start out on his two and a half mile walk through fields and woods, heavy with sticky mud or bathed in translucent moonlight, we gathered outside and sang in full-throated family chorus what would now be called our signature tune—*A Tavern in the Town*—or shattered the midnight stillness by a final crashing rendering of *Larboard Watch*. There was no need to worry about neighbours, we had only one, and they would be fast asleep by then, and there was no other house for a mile, only deep woods and silent meadows and pastures.

A word must be said about these woods: they formed an essential part of the setting which made Lawrence what he was. A miner's son, living in a row of miners' cottages at Eastwood, with the noise and smoke of collieries, smouldering pit banks and a clanking headstock on his very doorstep, he came to the fields and woods at the Haggs as into a new world, a species of fairy land, where the contact with nature was direct and free; where a robin building in an old kettle, a lark in a beast's hoofmark left in the stiff clay, and above all the white embroidery of lady smocks and the foam of bluebells over the wood in spring were a matter for perpetual wonder and genuine excitement. I have seen these things since, but never with the same thrill as when Bert was there to see them. He imparted some of his own intensity of living to the rest of us; later, when life became difficult for him, he imparted something of his own sense of the enigma of life. So great was the weight of gloom he cast over us of his own insoluble conflicts and in which he involved us that he contributed to an abiding apprehension of tragedy behind the gayest, brightest exterior which has stayed with me ever since.

There was, from the beginning, a hint of something incalculable and uncontrollable about him. I remember very early in his association with us, when he was only a lad, eighteen or so, and I a youngster of five, seeing him fly into a rage at something one of my brothers had done, and chase him with his long legs and lay him out flat on his face with a blow on the back of his neck. In such moods he was beside himself. There was another occasion when he terrified me by jumping backwards and forwards across a millrace at Felley Mill farm. The water poured in a swift green avalanche down a shute about a yard and a half wide: too wide to step across but by no means easy to jump because of the sloping sides; but Lawrence jumped repeatedly backwards and forwards across it like an antelope, as though defying death itself, while I stood holding my breath with fear. I have seen the shute since and I still cannot see how it was done.

There was the streak of the incalculable, almost the uncanny, about him that drew him apart even when he was most intimate to make him feared as something out of the ordinary as well as loved as one of ourselves. But it was the feeling of love for him which predominated in the early years. He was irresistible because of his impetuous acts of kindness and generosity, his willingness to help my mother with household tasks, with cookery, washing, peeling onions, fetching in coal from the coal heap outside. I remember him helping me with this one day when I stood petrified in the pouring rain and the hurly-burly of a summer thunderstorm. He darted out to help me, picked up the coal and hurried me in along with it while my brothers watched shamefaced at the window where they had sat jeering at me as brothers do. Such incalculable acts of kindness endeared him to us; he was Bert, as much one of the household as any of us, and vested with a peculiar authority. What he said went with our rather unruly and outspoken family. I remember it was his especial duty to see that the rare delicacies, such as a tin of fruit or salmon, were fairly distributed at Sunday tea-time, a not easy task with a household of nine plus Lawrence himself and a friend or two he may have brought along with him. And needless to say, his opinions were vested with similar authority. They were expressed with such vehemence, opposition was borne down with such irresistible raillery, or a storm of invective that was too fantastic to wound but too devastating to answer.

He was also a master of mimicry, and brought teachers, preachers, neighbours and his parents to life by his mastery of the local trick of speech or expression. His story about his father and the ham he bought has remained a family classic! His father bought the ham and presented it to his wife but deducted a proportion of the cost from the housekeeping every week until it was paid off. Lawrence's mother protested volubly on each occasion until the father, at the end of his patience, said 'Woman, owd theee feeace.' Even his mother had to laugh. Our tea table rocked, the reverberations are still not quite dead; they are heard sometimes in Canada to this day, where all but one of those who witnessed the scene now are.

There were the liveliest discussions about books I have ever known. Lawrence invested books with the attributes of something alive; we lived in their world rather than in our own. Rebecca looking down from the battlements of Torquilstone, Carver Doone carrying Lorna across his saddle bows, the footsteps of Lucy Gray ending at the broken bridge:[2] it is difficult to think that these things never actually happened. And there were rampageous arguments on politics, especially votes for women, with Lawrence leading the younger generation against their parents. But deeper divisions began to develop. Lawrence, like ourselves, had been brought up in the evangelical circle of a Congregational Chapel,[3] Buttys' Lump, as it was called locally, but he soon began to doubt, and from doubt he turned to mockery and disdain. I remember walking through the Warren one summer evening after Chapel with Lawrence and the family. Lawrence was in one of his destructive moods, and he broke into a stream of raillery at the expense of the Congregational ministers whom we had recently been listening to. I was a mere boy at the time, but I remember the shocked silence in which my elders received this outburst and the sense of impotence they felt before this torrent of strange talk. He declared in favour of a sceptical materialism and carried my eldest brother with him. It was from him that I received the echo of Lawrence's ideas in later years. My mother—and I believe his—was deeply disturbed. She began to see Lawrence in a new light.

It was about this time that another episode occurred which is worth recalling. My eldest sister, May, was engaged to a young stonemason whom Lawrence hated. He was lively and full of tall stories that kept us children in shrieks of laughter and I think Lawrence was jealous of him, and he generally took care to keep out of his way. But he took symbolic vengeance on him by smashing a stone carving which he had made and presented to my sister, claiming that it was intended as a likeness. Lawrence made fun of it unmercifully and finally—I can see him now— lifted our heavy coal pick above his head and brought it down on the symbol of his rival with all his might and smashed it to pieces. If asked he would perhaps have justified this whim of hate and jealousy by repeating a saying of his which my eldest brother—one of the few men friends he had at this time—was fond of quoting: 'With *should* and *ought* I have nothing to do'; and there can be no doubt that Lawrence felt he could not be bound by the conventional standards which were recognised if not respected by others.

Yet, in spite of this assumption of moral sovereignty he was the least free of men. He was entangled in conflicting loyalties from which he was unable to break loose, his abnormally strong affection for his mother and his feeling of dependence upon Miriam of *Sons and Lovers*. His love for his mother did not admit of any relationship other than that of plaything for another woman; but Miriam was an integral part of his emotional life. He left us to take a post in London, but day after day parcels of manuscript came for Miriam to read that later materialised into *The White Peacock* and *Sons and Lovers*. He insisted on submitting his work to her unerring judgement of what was best in him, even though for her it was a process of laceration.

A time came when it could be borne no longer; the stream of manuscripts stopped and Lawrence gradually dropped out of our lives. He came to see us once more, but he was strained and ill at ease. He went away, leaving a sense of desolation yet relief, and we never saw him again.

NOTES

J. D. (David) Chambers, a younger brother of Jessie Chambers, became a teacher at the University of Nottingham.

  1. Strainer for milk.

  2. The allusions are, respectively, to Scott's *Ivanhoe*, Blackmore's *Lorna Doone*, and Wordsworth's poem 'Lucy Gray'.

  3. In a late essay, 'Hymns in a Man's Life' (first published in the *Evening News*, 13 Oct 1928; repr. in *Phoenix* II), Lawrence records his sense of the lasting effect upon him of 'the rather banal Nonconformist hymns that penetrated through and through my childhood'.

Recollections of a 'Pagan'*

GEORGE H. NEVILLE

It is an amazing thing that so little should generally be known, and so much mystery be made, of the early life and circumstances of David Herbert Lawrence, in view of the fact that there are so many persons living

* 'The Early Days of D. H. Lawrence': this account appeared in the form of a letter to the editor of the *London Mercury*, XXIII (Mar 1931) pp. 477–80.

to-day who could each contribute quite an interesting 'something' to the story of those early days. The majority of us who formed that little band of comrades—we have been called 'Pagans'—of whom you have read in *The White Peacock* and *Sons and Lovers*, are still living, and each of us could tell a story of Lawrence; and what a different story from what might be expected in many quarters!

I am acutely conscious of the fact that it is really wrong to attempt to deal with the early life of Lawrence in a letter which will permit only of a bare recital of the simple facts. Each of the outstanding incidents of those early years should be considered carefully because of the impression it, individually, made upon this hyper-sensitive character. I have no hesitation in saying that one of the deepest impressions made upon Lawrence's young nature, affording an explanation of an attitude towards his father that must have appeared inexplicable to many people, was made when he discovered the true circumstances in which his mother and father were married; and I have still less hesitation in expressing the opinion that the 'Little Woman' [Lawrence's mother] never made a greater mistake than when she related those circumstances to us. His cynical attitude towards some women dates from an incident that occurred shortly after the death of his brother 'Ern', whom the whole family idolised. This attitude was further 'burnt' into him by the 'blistering' his young soul received during the time he was working as foreign correspondent to a firm of manufacturers in Nottingham. The girls at the factory appear to have taken a sheer delight in searing his youthful innocence. You may be of the opinion that such a remark is a queer one to be made in respect of D. H. Lawrence. It is; but believe me, it is a true one.

Briefly, the story of those early years is as follows: Arthur Lawrence, a young collier, a member of a family of miners from Brinsley, one of the numerous mining villages lying in the Eastwood district in Nottinghamshire, a dashing and good-looking youth, fond of dress and the gayest possible time, used to follow the custom of many youths of the district and run down to Nottingham most week-ends by one of the cheap market trains which always ran on Wednesdays and Saturdays.

I have never known quite definitely how the meeting came about, but I believe that it was at one of the numerous 'dances' or 'dancing classes' held in the city on Saturday nights, that he first met 'Lydia', the daughter of a tradesman carrying on business in the Peashill Rise district of the city, and a member of a family in quite good circumstances. Lydia promptly fell in love with the handsome, dark and curly-haired young collier. It is certain that there was considerable opposition from her people, but Lydia had that strain of stubbornness which she transmitted, in a marked degree, to each of her sons, and to David Herbert in particular, and her little toss of the head and irritating 'sniff' that I remember so well, were answers to all objections. She married Arthur Lawrence. There were five children, the names and order of birth being George, Emily, Ernest, David Herbert and Lettice Ada.

When I was seven years of age, my family moved into a house that Father had built in the Lynn Croft district of the Parish of Greasley, and all the children of our family began to attend the Beauvale Board Schools. Here it was that I first made the acquaintance of Lawrence, who was one year my senior and one standard higher in the school. He was a thin, pale, weakly lad, always scrupulously clean, neat and tidy, with no energy for our oft-times over-robust games and no apparent inclination to attempt to join us. A book and a quiet corner were always his delight and he would much more often be found with girl companions than with boys. He had a high-pitched, girlish voice which always rose in pitch with the least excitement, a feature which he retained to early manhood, as he retained also that impatient toss of the head he got from his mother and that unruly lock of hair that always would persist in drooping to one side of his high forehead.

Throughout the whole of his schoolboy years, he was known as 'Bert', and this was the name used by the whole of the members of the family. Occasionally, I have known a misguided woman, thinking to address him in a way which might be construed as showing liking or sympathy, call him 'Bertie', and this he positively hated, though I do not recall an instance when he allowed his resentment to be seen.

At this time, the Lawrences were living in 'The Breach', a typical agglomeration of colliery houses, spoilt by its abominable 'middle lane', a feature which D. H. Lawrence never forgot and always held as a sin committed by the colliery company responsible for the erection of such an unsavoury, unhealthy and unnecessary blot on the earth.

Ernest Lawrence, who received his early training in an office at Langley Mill, a neighbouring town just over the Derbyshire border, had made splendid progress and succeeded in obtaining a position, with plenty of prospects of advancement, in a very large London office. He was an exceptionally good son whose main thought appeared to be to do his best to help his mother and the other members of the family, and he was particularly anxious that his younger brother Bert, should have, if possible, a better educational start in life than he, himself, was able to get. Our old schoolmaster, Mr W. W. Whitehead, suggested that Lawrence ought to try to obtain one of the scholarships which the Notts County Council had recently commenced to offer, and he specially coached Lawrence for the examination. I remember the news coming through that Lawrence had been successful and was the first boy from that school to win such a scholarship. Dear old Whitehead positively beamed with joy at the success of his first entry in the County Competitions.

Just before he was twelve years of age, then, we find young Lawrence attending Nottingham High School, where Doctor James Gow was Head, and by this time, the Lawrences had moved to the Walker Street house, a move which they regarded as quite a distinct social advance. The following year, I had the honour of following in the footsteps of Lawrence, and the

'Beauvale Yell' celebrated the fact that Whitehead's candidate had again been successful.

Then followed our High School days together, starting from home shortly after seven o'clock in the morning and returning just before seven at night, with always a pile of lessons to do later, though we younger ones could always depend on a little real help from Lawrence with any knotty points during the tiresome train journey. Even in these days, Lawrence had that little, troublesome, hacking cough that used to bring his left hand so sharply to his mouth—a cough and an action that he never lost.

During holidays we always tramped; tramped, many times, the live-long day, and at least one day in every holiday we contrived to spend tramping the Derbyshire dales. It was chiefly during these tramps that we gathered our knowledge of the life of the fields and woods, and I think we gathered, pressed and mounted specimens of every plant, shrub and tree to be found for miles around. Lawrence was never very keen on the collection of insects, though he had a very profound knowledge of the insects of the locality, and the mounting and dressing of the specimens in this case fell entirely to my lot.

High School days over; and neither of us could follow our own inclination and become pupil teachers because we had not sufficient 'backing influence' to gain us admission. Lawrence started to work at the factory office in Nottingham, where he stayed for about twelve months, when he contracted pneumonia and for a considerable time his recovery appeared to be very improbable. As he slowly improved, it became very obvious that he ought not to attempt to continue his arduous duties in Nottingham. He still longed for the teaching profession, and so, after considerable 'effort', he was able to begin duties as a student at the Albert Street Schools, Eastwood, where Mr George Holderness was in charge.

The Education Act of 1904[1] made entry to the teaching profession quite a different matter from what it had been previously, and, in the following year, I had passed the entrance examination and was a student teacher at the Greasley Gilt Hill Schools, and, on certain days, joined Lawrence on our journeys to Ilkeston to attend the local centre for preparation for further examinations.

These were the days that saw the real gathering together of the 'Pagans'. The group was almost entirely composed of student teachers, of whom Lawrence and I were the only male members, with the occasional addition of Alan, the elder brother of 'Jess', to whom Lawrence, many years later, applied the name 'Princess'.

It was this period, too, that Lawrence began seriously to apply his mind to sketching, in which branch of the arts he had, as yet, been but a somewhat dilettante dabbler, and I think it was at this time also that he made up his mind that, some day, he would make his name as a writer. Let there be no misunderstanding about that; Lawrence, even in those early days, knew that he had the capacity for literary greatness and had thoroughly made up his mind to achieve it.

The 'Little Woman' had never appeared to be quite comfortable in the Walker Street house after the death of 'Ern', and a move was next made to the Lynn Croft house, chiefly owing to the influence of 'Franky' and 'Grit' of the 'Pagans', whose father owned the property. They remained at this house until the 'Little Woman' laid down the wearisome burden of her life, to the torture of the soul of Lawrence.

Student days over and his intermediate exam passed with flying colours, Lawrence was given a position as assistant master at the Albert Street Schools, but he realised that, to be in the profession without attendance at a training college, was a very serious handicap. The 'Little Woman' shared his opinion and, though it was obvious that it would mean a very great struggle to bear the expense, they decided that the sacrifice must be made, and they commenced saving every possible penny towards sending Lawrence to college. Thus the following year saw Lawrence beginning his studies at the Nottingham University College Day Training Section. As we all expected, he came through remarkably well and had an extraordinary success in the college finals.

It was during this University training period that the friendship between Lawrence and the 'Princess' reached its highest point, and Lawrence and I had a standing arrangement that, on the Saturday evenings, when I was playing cricket or football as the case might be, I would look round at his home. If he was not there, he would be at the farm—the home of the 'Princess'. The reason for this was that he was very seldom certain as to whether he would be going to the farm or not. If he settled down to write or sketch and the work progressed to his satisfaction, he would stick to it, very often until it was completed. But when the story did not develop to his liking, the 'Little Woman' would say, 'He's gone up there again, George. He lost his patience, crammed his papers into his pocket, snatched up his cap and went.' Usually, I would sit down for a chat or perhaps, if Ada chanced to be there or any of the 'Pagans' had called, we would indulge in a little singing—usually folk-songs or glees—until I thought Lawrence would be almost ready to start from the farm, and then I would be off to meet him on the way back.

I have seen it stated that the 'Princess' lived in the same village as Lawrence. This statement is entirely wrong. To go by the road from the Lawrences' home to the farm was a good three miles, but there was an unwritten permission for the family from the farm, and their friends, to take a short cut over the fields beyond the reservoir and through the woods, which reduced the journey to about two miles. If I reached the fields before meeting him, our old High School whistle call, sent out into the darkness at intervals, prevented us from missing each other in the darkness and, at the same time, told the keepers, who were always on the alert, that the trespassers were not the poachers against whom they had continually to guard.

Sometimes I got as far as the farm, where I would usually find Lawrence and the 'Princess' with their heads close together and the crumpled papers spread out in front of them; but the papers soon disappeared with my arrival.

The explanation of that is to be found in the fact that the 'Princess' was the only one of all the 'Pagans' who did anything at all to encourage Lawrence in his writings. We were enthusiastic on the subject of his sketches and paintings, but we all realised the danger of a literary career for him. The 'Princess', however, helped him by her encouragement and assistance and received some nasty remarks from some of the other 'Pagans' for her pains, but she was proof against all such pettiness, and her dark eyes would continue to gleam brightly and her lips to smile that everlastingly inscrutable smile of hers, as though she were saying to herself, 'Wait! You will see who laughs in the long run.'

College days over, Lawrence obtained a post as Assistant Master at the Addison[2] Road Council Schools, Croydon. I was at Stourbridge at this time, and the correspondence between Lawrence and me consisted chiefly of personal items, family news and always arrangements for the next holidays, when we should again be at home together. He was still writing short stories and discussing them with the 'Princess' in correspondence, and even part of the *White Peacock* was written at this time.

The 'Princess' has the credit for 'launching' Lawrence. I am quite certain that she would be the first to admit that he required no 'launching'. What did she do? She merely made surreptitious copies of manuscripts Lawrence had lent or sent to her to read and correct where necessary, and, without consulting Lawrence on the matter, she sent these copies on to the *English Review*. Hueffer[3] recognised that here was something for which he had been seeking—genius—as he, himself, expressed it when he and Lawrence met personally a short time later. And since then, so far as I am aware, the genius of Lawrence has never been questioned.

Success made his double task too heavy and again his over-taxed body cracked under the strain he was putting on it, and his ever-constant enemy—pneumonia—again almost claimed him. The 'Little Woman' had the dreadful experience of once more being called to the bedside of a son in the London area, and of making the journey full of doubts as to whether she would be able to reach him in time. In the case of 'Ern' she had been too late, but David Herbert had retained the vital spark of life and the unremitting care of the 'Little Woman' and the others forced back the grasping hands for the time being. After a period of recuperation, Lawrence made up his mind that it was impossible to continue as a teacher and continue a literary career at the same time. He gave up his profession to follow his star.

Shortly before the publication of *The Trespasser*, Lawrence was staying with me in a little village in the hills dividing Derbyshire from Staffordshire, and we spent much of the time on our walks over the hills, attempting to find a more suitable name for the story but without coming to any definite decision. Ultimately, I believe, Messrs Heinemann settled the matter for themselves.

While I was away in the daytime, Lawrence was busy with the final bringing into shape of *The Rainbow* and, at the time, I predicted trouble over the bedroom scene; but Lawrence was adamant. Later, when the trouble actually developed, and there appeared to be a chance of avoiding the trouble if Lawrence would consent to re-write that chapter, he not only maintained that attitude but declared that he would much rather destroy the whole manuscript than alter one jot or tittle of it 'for the sake of such a set of fools'. That was a flash of the real Lawrence.

Now, though I was just as well aware, as was Lawrence, that the incident therein portrayed was absolutely true to life, and had indeed occurred, I advised the line of least resistance and suggested a certain method of re-writing the chapter, by which it appeared to me that the main feature could be kept, while the trouble would be avoided. Lawrence, however, would have none of it. The book must stand or fall as it was. It fell; and to-day, book-lovers the world over are seeking copies of the American edition and paying extravagant prices to obtain them. Is there anyone who dares to assert that they are doing this because the book is indecent?

'Teufel,' he said to me when I tried to insist—the name was given to me by his idolised brother, 'Ern'—'Teufel, the real knowledge of the world consists of the related experiences of the men and women who have lived in it. To each human being separate experiences, thoughts and emotions come, and it is a duty which each one of us owes to the world, to add our own contributions just as we know them, whether they be the result of our own experiences or as related to us by others.'

I objected that living persons might be affected, hurt in the feelings, damaged in their reputations, upset in their homes, disgruntled in a thousand and one different ways.

And now the old, impatient Lawrence flashed to the surface again as he replied,

Just the same old Teufel! You always were such a sentimental devil— more's the pity. Think of the stories you could write if only you would let yourself go. Don't you see that we must each of us be prepared to take the responsibility for our own actions? How can anyone complain so long as the narrator tells the truth? And suppose their puny feelings are hurt, or, what is probably nearer the mark, they get a pain in their pride, what does it matter so their lesson is given to the world and they shall have taught others to avoid the mistakes they made?

You will note that Lawrence referred to one type of experience only. There you have the line he marked out for himself. There you have the line he followed; and in following that line, he had to show that truth, as we know it, must reveal much more of ugliness than of beauty. In the upshot, *The Rainbow* fell; and in falling, placed Lawrence in the very forefront of the novelists of his day in the considered judgement of those who read him rightly and are qualified to judge. From that time, Lawrence lived his life before the world and in a letter of this description, there is neither space nor need to dwell on what is already quite well known.

'Have you heard anything of poor old Bert lately?' That was always the question my sister asked me during the later years of his life, and her method of allusion to Lawrence well illustrates the general attitude towards him, of those who had any knowledge of him at all, who knew his lovable nature, who appreciated his real genius, who understood the splendid fight he made, both through circumstances and against a physique never at all robust; and all this, even though some of them may have considered that the line he had marked out for himself was a wrong line, or, at least, a misguided one.

Strong in his own strength, Lawrence forged on to his destiny—mental and bodily distress, exile and death; and in his death, he must have made the great discovery that death had brought to him more love and lovers than ever he had known in life and that their numbers were ever-increasing throughout the world. May this be balm to his spirit and cause him to rest in peace!

NOTES

George H. Neville was a year younger than Lawrence and knew him during his Eastwood and Croydon periods. He became a teacher.

1. An error for 1902.
2. An error for 'Davidson'.
3. See below, p. 63.

'Jehovah Junior' *

W. E. HOPKIN

One evening [in 1909] he came to me in a state of wild excitement and told me he had some poems accepted by the *English Review* and to crown everything he was invited to go to London to meet the Editor. He could

* From 'D. H. Lawrence: A Personal Memoir', Nehls, 1, pp. 71–4.

neither stand nor sit still for a moment and rushed off to begin making arrangements for the visit. A few days later when he had calmed down, I asked him how it all came about. He said, 'You know I always finished my homework first, and I sometimes wrote odds and ends of poetry on bits of paper which I left lying about. I did not know Jessie collected them and copied some of them out, nor did I know she had sent some to the *English Review* until this letter came.' I said, 'Bert, fancy owing your entry into the world of literature to your sweetheart! It's real romance!' He did not reply.

As I remarked, when Lawrence left the Elementary School he had not shown much sign of what was to follow. He was studious, careful, well-spoken and particular about his clothes. Perhaps he was held back by the fact that he was not happy there.

Some time ago I was talking to one of his old schoolfellows. He said, 'We were a bit hard on him for, after all, he couldn't help his constitution. But, thou knows, William, lads is allus cruel to one another. He wor a bit to blame for he wor rayther stuck up, and when Gaffer gin him a bit o' praise we didn't like it. When he got nigh fourteen he began hittin' back wi' his tongue an' he could get at us wheer it hurt.'

It was after leaving school that Lawrence began visiting us regularly. My wife one day said she very much objected to him putting a woman on his operating table for dissection and then saying in a sneering tone: 'There you are! That is a woman, body and soul.' He turned round and said: 'If I need any woman for my purpose—you included—I shall use you. Why the devil should you or any other woman come between me and the flowering of my genius?' He almost made me believe in the theory of reincarnation, for he had a most uncanny knowledge of women. I said to him more than once, 'Bert, you were a woman last time you were on earth'.

I have mentioned the profound influence his mother had on his whole life. She dominated every side of it, and her one desire was to see him become a great writer. When she passed away, he was so terribly affected I thought he would commit suicide. During the latter part of her illness he wrote some most poignant verse. His sister Ada had it and refused to allow it to be published, for she said it was too personal and full of agony.

When he was writing *The White Peacock*,[1] he and his mother criticised it together, and he rewrote parts of it until it satisfied them. When it was in the hands of the publisher his mother was nearing the end of her final illness, and she was feverishly anxious to see 'our Bert's first book'. He wrote and telegraphed daily and, at last, a special volume arrived. It was put into her hand, but no sign was given that she knew what it was and that added to Lawrence's grief. His grief at his mother's death was profound.

It was about this time I noticed a growing change in him. It did not seem to be introspection, but a delving deep into his mind and bringing up a strange mixture of ideas and beliefs. He always had a vivid and fertile imagination, but now he began to talk about not trusting to reason. He used to say, 'If you can't see these things with your very soul, and feel them here' (touching his middle) 'you will remain blind until you die.' In those earlier days, whether from design or because he was unsure, he would vehemently deny tomorrow what he had said today. It was difficult to know how to take him, and I was never sure whether he was 'having me on' or just posing the question to find where he himself stood. He could be very upsetting, and quite often after a long talk some of my cherished values had somehow become valueless. A few of them crept back after he had left the house, but I was never quite as sure as I had been. He often reminded me of a young child looking at the world with new eyes and questioning the beliefs and experiences of his elders.

One evening when he was holding forth to us he said: 'There are only two states, life and death. You, my boy, are dead.' I was going to interrupt but he held up his hand like a schoolmaster for silence and went on: 'You are dead. You move and think mechanically, and repeat the tricks you have been taught—at best you are an automaton. You, Sallie, have some glimmerings of life.' I was neither flattered nor pleased. When he was assured within himself, nothing would move him. 'I know I am right,' he would say.

When he talked about his dark Gods I was lost entirely—perhaps in those days I was too materially minded. They were very real to Lawrence. At first I was shocked when he exclaimed: 'Why do you put your trust in reason? If I do not feel it deep down inside it is not true, no matter what reason says.'

Despite his assertions, in practical life his reason stood him in good stead. He was always as careful over spending money as when he went shopping for his mother. For instance, when my daughter was staying with the Lawrences in Italy he sent her with Frieda shopping to Florence one day. Every item was put down on paper and the price they should pay. 'You will have enough to pay for a cup of coffee, too,' he said.

When he was well his conversation was brilliant. To me it sounded like someone reciting free verse. Indeed the poet was uppermost right through his life.

At that time, in his early teens, he toyed with the idea of joining the Socialists, but never took any part in politics. He pitched into me angrily for spending time over politics, and called me a damned fool. He also threatened to take me off in a book—he did thoroughly in his play *Touch and Go*.[2] He could be very charming and also abominably rude—tender and savage.

When he had used the money he received for his first book, and before his second was finished, he was nearly penniless, but a grant from a society saw him through.[3]

In his college and Croydon days, when he came to see or stay with us, he was restless mentally and spiritually. My wife accused him of spending his life between dreams and frenzy, but it seemed to me that his varying states arose from his continually delving deeply into himself, and the consequent changes were the result of his discoveries. One day I asked if he intended us to read his books as novels or as treatises on the experiences of spiritual and bodily awareness, and if he did which did he lay the most stress upon. He replied rather casually that if we read them simply as stories we should not get much satisfaction from them. Said he, 'When will you discover that what you call the intelligence is a something that cheats you and juggles you all the time. It can make you believe you are right when you are hopelessly wrong—you must have physical vision.'

'Is that another way of talking about instinct?' I asked.

'You can take it that way if you like,' he said.

In those days he seemed to be trying to find a philosophy for himself—something he could state in plain language, but I do not think he ever succeeded. 'When you realise that the primal consciousness in man' (a phrase he sometimes used in argument) 'is pre-mental, you will get some glimmerings of what I mean when I talk about and write about blood consciousness.' Even as a boy of 14 he questioned the accepted values. His schoolmaster at Beauvale once told me after Lawrence had left the school that young Bert was a note of interrogation—he was always wanting to know why. We often were startled by statements he made even when young, and he always sounded as though he was the final authority. I remember one lass saying as he came into the circle, 'Here comes Jehovah Junior!' It was a really apt description—he was always so very cocksure.

As small boy and during his elementary schooldays he was greatly attached to the Sunday School, and especially to the singing. And even when he had discarded those early beliefs he was always ready to talk about those times. Somebody remarked that his deeper insight into life and the nature of life was a sort of reward for doing justice to its depth and seriousness.

After his first attack of pneumonia his voice grew high-pitched and light, almost like a girl's.

I would readily admit that even in his early life he had a deeper insight than was given to most of us.

NOTES

1. 1906 to 1910.

2. A three-act play written in 1918 and published in 1920.

3. The reference to a grant awarded at this time is probably an error. Lawrence received £50 from the Royal Literary Fund a little later, in 1914.

Lawrence as a Teacher*

PHILIP SMITH

When Lawrence reported at the school I recall him to be tall, very thin though of large build. He had a shock of dark hair, small ginger moustache and vivid blue eyes. Later I noticed that his hands contrasted palpably with his general appearance. They were fragile, long-fingered, expressive, well controlled. Lawrence was not a robust being. He made no pretensions in the matter of dress. His expression always showed a kind of confident amusement. It was rarely serious. He did not appear to be perturbed with his new surroundings nor doubtful of his powers to succeed in his new duties. Circumstances permitted no gradual introduction to his work. A large class of boys, the regulation 60, awaited him, and he commenced at once.

The staff at Davidson at this time was composed of young men all of about Lawrence's age, and one woman, Miss Agnes Mason, who was considerably older. He was therefore not influenced by the normal professional practice of older men usually present in a school personnel, and was at liberty to work out his own salvation.

His well-known powers of concentration and untiring industry soon became apparent. He shirked none of the drudgery of the details which hamper the routine of a teacher's life. He was interested in Art, English and Biology. I kept for some years his note book recording a year's work in biology. The water-colour drawings and details of experimental exercises were models of correctness and clarity. His caustic humour often aroused suspicions as to the value of his most genial expressions. 'Let them play now,' he says. 'The world will teach them how to work.' To a youth called Cass, whose English was 'wanting' in every sense of the word, he remarks 'Write it down with an A, Cass, write it down with an A.' A perfectly harmless remark as it affected the particular individual [in other words, A for Ass].

Lawrence hated the slightest interference with his class work. On one occasion I followed a Ministerial Inspector into his room. The intrusion was unexpected and resented. A curious wailing of distressed voices issued from a far corner. The sounds were muffled by a large covering black-board. The words of a familiar song arose from the depths:

* Moore, pp. 77–9.

> Full fathom five thy father lies;
> Of his bones are coral made.

The class was reading *The Tempest*. The presentation expressed the usual thoroughness of Lawrence's attitude to the exercise in progress. It must not be spoiled by even official comment. Lawrence rushed with outstretched hands to the astounded visitor: 'Hush! Hush! Don't you hear? The sea chorus from *The Tempest*.' Those were the days of conventional methods of instruction, and Lawrence's excursions into dramatic expression were not likely to meet with full approval.

The same gentleman, some months later inquired, 'Where's this bookwriting fellow of yours?' Lawrence's classroom was indicated. 'I shall not go into his room,' he said. 'I have no intention of being pilloried in some book.'

Lawrence's ideas on the teaching of Art were also somewhat suspect. While I was conferring with another Board of Education inspector, a boy brought a large pastel drawing, still life, for inspection. After a glance, I made an ineffectual attempt to suppress the sketch. The official eye had, however, anticipated my effort. 'Is this sent for any particular reason?' I inquired. 'Mr Lawrence thought it was rather good,' the boy replied. The artist returned to his class leaving his masterpiece with us.

'Are you by any chance an artist?' inquired the wary dictator. 'No,' I replied. 'Neither am I,' he commented. 'We had better be careful about this man. After the session, without his knowledge, collect a sample of these drawings. I will send them to the Art Department at Kensington for an expert opinion.' Later they were returned by the inspector in person. 'Good thing we took the course we did,' he reported. 'The Department highly approves. You'll have a crowd of students down to worry you about them, I expect.'

At that period, there were in circulation a number of small periodicals designed to make some appeal to boys. Lawrence hit upon the idea of setting some of his pupils to contribute short articles to several of these publications. These he amplified and edited. Several were accepted, and to the vast surprise of the authors were actually paid for by postal orders for small sums. From henceforth the despised 'composition essay exercise' assumed an unexpected value in their eyes. Lawrence assumed quite voluntarily the responsibility for many of the least desired for school routine duties. This included the constant attention bestowed on the details connected with the school library. He used to affirm 'Let them read any rubbish they like as long as they read it at all. They will very soon discard the bad.'

Later, some of the boys discovered in a London evening news sheet one of his earlier 'School Poems'.[1] They devised a method of registering their disapproval of some lines by writing replies in verse which were affixed to his desk lid to meet his eye at morning school. They were, however, somewhat disappointed with the reactions aroused. Instead of disapproval or perhaps reproof, Lawrence was delighted and even indicated how the lines might have been improved.

Lawrence was greatly interested in a section of boys who attended the school from the English Actors' Home. Some of these pupils bore well-known names connected in the past with the English stage. For a school dramatic performance, Lawrence painted all the scenery, revised and added to the text of the drama and, after the initial rehearsals, remarked, 'These actor boys know more than we do about this kind of thing. We can't teach them the beginnings of play acting. Let them run this show as they think fit.' We agreed, with beneficial results.

NOTES

Philip F. T. Smith was the headmaster of Davidson Road School, Croydon, during the period when Lawrence was teaching there. His short memoir (from which only an extract is given) was written in 1951, some forty years after the time in question.

1. Lawrence wrote a number of poems based on the period he spent as a teacher. Among others, 'Last Lesson of the Afternoon' depicts the teacher's life in gloomy terms; 'The Best of School' offers a more contented picture of his lot; 'School on the Outskirts' portrays Davidson Road School (opened in 1907, and so still very new when Lawrence arrived there). Some of them were published as a sequence titled 'The Schoolmaster' in the *Westminster Gazette* (four issues, May–June 1912), and it was presumably one of these—possibly 'Afternoon: the Last Lesson' (as the first mentioned above was originally titled)—that the boys saw. The sequence was revised before its appearance in *Last Poems* (1932).

In Lodgings in Croydon*

HUGH KINGSMILL

Throughout his time at Croydon Lawrence lived with Mr Jones, a Lancashire man, who was the School Attendance Officer. Mr Jones, who has now retired, has given me a very interesting account of Lawrence during this period. Though Lawrence disliked teaching, Mr Jones said, he was conscientious about it, and got on well with the boys. He was good with children of any age, and when Hilda, Mr Jones's daughter, was six months old, Lawrence used to walk her up and down, exclaiming, 'You *shall* walk! You *shall* walk!' Mr Robertson, an elderly Scotsman, and

* From *D. H. Lawrence* (London: Methuen, 1938) pp. 36–9.

somewhat pompous, did not like Lawrence. When he came into the classroom, and the boys stood up, saying 'Good morning, sir,' Lawrence used to scowl, and would not 'sir' him.

I asked Mr Jones, who had been a professional footballer, what he thought of Lawrence's physique, and he said he was strong enough, and did his daily dozen in the bathroom, but already had trouble with his chest. Most men, Mr Jones added, thought Lawrence rather effeminate, but there was something about him which appealed to women. Some of them, his particular friends, used to call him Bert, but he was always Lawrence to men. Mr Jones knew the auburn-haired schoolmistress Miriam mentions [in *Sons and Lovers*]—he spoke of her as red-haired—and said that Lawrence was very bitter against her because she would not fall in with his wishes.

Lawrence generally stayed in in the evenings, sitting with a pad on his knee in front of the fire, writing his novels, but occasionally he went out with Mr Jones, and Mr Jones particularly remembered an evening when they went to the *Greyhound* after a visit, cut short by Lawrence, to a billiard saloon. At the *Greyhound* Lawrence asked for absinthe, and got into conversation with the French barmaid there, airing his French. On Sunday mornings he and Mr Jones used to paint together, copying from reproductions. Lawrence fancied classical subjects—one which Mr Jones remembered was of the Greek god Hermes with a young girl in a wood, some poppies lying about on the ground. There was a landscape by Lawrence in Mr Jones's drawing-room. Trying to get the clouds right, he had grown impatient and dabbed white paint on with his thumb. The thumb-marks showed clearly.

He smoked very seldom, perhaps five cigarettes a week, and hardly drank at all, and if he did take a glass of Mr Jones's beer, he insisted on providing a bottle in return. They used to argue a lot, especially about religion, against which Lawrence was very bitter, getting so worked up sometimes that he used to sit with his mouth open, so excited he couldn't say a word.

Lawrence was devoted to his mother, Mr Jones said, and became very morose after her death, but he had nothing good to say about his father, and it was really horrible the way he spoke about him. His brother came on a visit once, and Lawrence was patronising with him. Some London writers had recently taken Lawrence up, and when he came back from a week-end with them he used to speak with a different accent. On one of these occasions Mr Jones interrupted him with 'That's not your usual form of talk,' to which Lawrence haughtily replied, 'I don't understand what you mean.'

It was one of these week-ends which led to his leaving the Davidson Road School. He arrived back on the Sunday evening looking as if he was suffering from a frightful hang-over. The next morning he tried to get up for school, but was unable to, developed double pneumonia and nearly died. He went to Bournemouth to convalesce and sent in his resignation a bit later. Mr Jones, I gathered, had had as much of Lawrence at the end of three and a half years as he could stand, and had decided not to have him back if he returned to Croydon. The Joneses heard from him only once again, some months later, when he wrote mysteriously that something had happened which he was not at liberty to divulge, but which would become known in due course. 'It was the German lady,' Mr Jones said.

NOTE

'Hugh Kingsmill' was the pseudonym of Hugh Kingsmill Lunn (1889–1949).

An Editor's Impressions*

FORD MADOX FORD

[One day in 1909] I received a letter from a young schoolteacher[1] in Nottingham. I can still see the handwriting—as if drawn with sepia rather than written in ink, on grey-blue notepaper. It said that the writer knew a young man who wrote, as she thought, admirably but was too shy to send his work to editors. Would I care to see some of his writing?

In that way I came to read the first words of a new author:

The small locomotive engine, Number 4, came clanking, stumbling down from Selston with seven full waggons. It appeared round the corner with loud threats of speed, but the colt that it startled from among the gorse, which still flickered indistinctly in the raw afternoon, outdistanced it in a canter. A woman, walking up the railway line to Underwood, held her basket aside and watched the footplate of the engine advancing.

I was reading in the twilight in the long eighteenth-century room that was at once the office of the *English Review* and my drawing-room. My eyes were tired; I had been reading all day so I did not go any further with the story. It was called 'Odour of Chrysanthemums'. I laid it in the basket for accepted manuscripts. My secretary looked up and said:

* From *Portraits from Life: Memories and Criticisms* (Boston, Mass.: Houghton Mifflin, 1937) pp. 70–2, 75–89. The book was published in England under the title *Mightier than the Sword* (London: Allen & Unwin, 1938).

'You've got another genius?'

I answered: 'It's a big one this time', and went upstairs to dress...

It was a Trench dinner at the Pall Mall Restaurant—a Dutch Treat presided over by Herbert Trench,[2] the Poet, and Dutch Treats being then new in London, Trench dinners were real social events. You sat in groups of five at little tables and the big hall of the restaurant was quite full.

I was with Mr H. G. Wells, Mr Hilaire Belloc, Mr Maurice Baring, and Mr G. K. Chesterton. At other tables were other celebrities. In the middle of an astounding story about the Russian court, told by Mr Baring, who had lately returned from being first secretary or something at our embassy in St Petersburg, Mr Belloc's magnificent organ remarked to an innocent novelist called Kinross, who at the next table was discussing the New Testament with Ladies Londonderry and Randolph Churchill, the reigning beauties of that end of a reign:

'Our Lord?' Mr. Belloc's voice pealed among the marble columns and palms. 'What do _you_ know about Our Lord? Our Lord was a Gentleman.'

To turn the discussion I remarked to Mr Wells that I had discovered another genius, D. H. Lawrence by name; and, to carry on the good work, Mr Wells exclaimed—to some one at Lady Londonderry's table:

'Hurray, Fordie's discovered another genius! Called D. H. Lawrence!'

Before the evening was finished I had had two publishers asking me for the first refusal of D. H. Lawrence's first novel and, by that accident, Lawrence's name was already known in London before he even knew that any of his work had been submitted to an editor... The lady who had sent the story to me chooses to be known as 'E. T.' and she had not even told Lawrence that she was sending the MSS.

So next morning I sent Miss E. T. a letter, a little cautious in tenor, saying that I certainly liked the work she had sent me and asking her to ask her friend to call on me when he had the opportunity. I appear to have said that I thought Lawrence had great gifts, but that a literary career depended enormously on chance, and that if Lawrence had a good job in a school he had better stick to it for the present. It was probably a stupid thing to do and I have regretted it since for I was certain that that writer had great gifts and the sooner a writer who has great gifts takes his chance at writing, the better.

Miss E. T. in her lately published little book[3] on the youth of Lawrence—and a very charming and serviceable little book it is —seems to be under the impression that she sent me as a first instalment only poems by Lawrence. Actually she first asked me if I would care to see anything— and then should it be poetry or prose. And I had replied asking her to send both, so that she had sent me three poems about a schoolmaster's life . . . and 'Odour of Chrysanthemums'. I only mention this because I found the poems, afterwards, to be nice enough but not immensely striking. If I had read them first I should certainly have printed them—as indeed I did; but I think the impact of Lawrence's personality would have been much less vivid. . . .

It was therefore with a certain trepidation that I awaited the visit of Lawrence. If he was really the son of a working coal-miner, how exactly was I to approach him in conversation? Might he not, for instance, call me 'Sir'—and wouldn't it cause pain and confusion to stop him doing so? For myself I have always automatically regarded every human being as my equal—and myself, by corollary, as the equal of every other human being—except of course the King and my colonel on—not off—parade. But a working man was so unfamiliar as a proposition that I really did not know how to bring it off.

Indeed, E. T. in her account of the first lunch that I ever gave Lawrence and herself, relates that Ezra Pound—who has a genius for inappropriate interpolations—asked me how I should talk to a 'working man'. And she relates how she held her breath until, after a moment's hesitation, I answered that I should speak to him exactly as I spoke to anybody else.

Before that I had had some little time to wait for Lawrence's visit. I found him disturbing enough. It happened in this way:

It would appear that he was on his holidays and, as one can well believe, holidays on the seashore from a Croydon board-school were moments too precious to be interrupted even for a visit to a first editor. Indeed, as I heard afterwards, he had talked himself into such a conviction of immediate literary success that he could not believe in the existence of a literary career at all. He had, I mean, said so often that he was going to make immediately two thousand—pounds, not dollars—a year and had so often in schemes expended that two thousand a year in palaces with footmen that, when he came to himself and found that he had not so far printed a word, a literary career seemed part of a fairy tale such as no man had ever enjoyed. And there were no doubt shynesses. Obviously you cannot approach the utterly unknown without them. Yes, certainly there were shynesses.

It must have been on a Saturday because otherwise Lawrence would not have been free to leave his school and come up from Croydon, which was a suburb but not part—as poor Lawrence was to find to his cost—of London, and it cannot have been a Sunday because we were working. And I certainly must have been in the relaxed frame of mind that comes just before the end of the week. I was, I suppose, reading a manuscript or some proofs in a chair that looked towards the room door. My secretary, Miss Thomas, who afterwards won renown as the war secretary of Mr Lloyd George, presumably heard someone knocking at the outer door, for I was dimly aware that she got up from her desk, went out, and returned, passing me and saying, Mr Someone or other.

I was engrossed in my manuscript or proofs. Miss Thomas, imagining that she had been followed by the individual she had found at the outer

door, sat down at her desk and became engrossed in her work. And deep
peace reigned. The room was L-shaped, the upright of the L being long
and low, the rest forming an alcove in which was the door...And
suddenly, leaning against the wall beside the doorway, there was,
bewilderingly...a fox. A fox going to make a raid on the hen-roost before
him...

The impression that I had at my first sight of Lawrence is so strong with
me at this minute that the mere remembrance fills me with a queer
embarrassment. And indeed, only yesterday, reading again—or possibly
reading for the first time, for I did not remember it—Lawrence's story
called 'The Fox',[4] I really jumped when I came to his description of the fox
looking over its shoulder at the farm girl. Because it was evident that
Lawrence identified himself with the russet-haired human fox who was to
carry off the as-it-were hen-girl of the story.

And that emotion of my slightly tired, relaxed eyes and senses was not so
bad as a piece of sensitised imagination. The house itself was old and
reputed full of ghosts, lending itself to confusions of tired eyes...My
partner Marwood, sitting one evening near the front windows of the room
whilst I was looking for something in the drawer of the desk, said suddenly:

'There's a woman in lavender-coloured eighteenth-century dress
looking over your shoulder into that drawer.' And Marwood was the most
matter-of-fact, as it were himself eighteenth-century, Yorkshire Squire
that England of those days could have produced.

And I experienced then exactly the feeling of embarrassment that I was
afterwards to feel when I looked up from my deep thoughts and saw
Lawrence, leaning, as if panting, beside the doorpost...It was not so bad
an impression, founded as it was on the peculiar, as if sunshot tawny hair
and moustache of the fellow and his deep-set and luminous eyes. He had
not, in those days, the beard that afterwards obscured his chin—or I think
he had not. I think that on his holiday he had let his beard grow and, it
having been lately shaved off, the lower part of his face was rather pallid
and as if invisible, whereas his forehead and cheeks were rather high-
coloured. So that I had had only the impression of the fox-coloured hair
and moustache and the deep, wary, sardonic glance...as if he might be
going to devour me—or something that I possessed.

And that was really his attitude of mind. He had come, like the fox, with
his overflood of energy—his abounding vitality of passionate determination that seemed always too big for his frail body—to get something—
the hypnotic two thousand a year; from somewhere. And he stood looking
down on the 'fairish, fat, about forty' man—so he described me in his letter
home to E. T. —sprawling at his mercy, reading a manuscript before him.
And he remarked in a curiously deep, rather musical chest-voice:

'This isn't my idea, Sir, of an editor's office.'

That only added to my confusion. I had not the least idea of who this fellow was—and at the same time I had the idea from his relatively familiar address that it was someone I ought to recognise. But I was at least spared—since I did not know it was Lawrence—the real pain that his 'Sir' would have caused me had I known. For I should have hated to be given what I will call a caste Sir by anybody who could write as Lawrence could. But I was able to take it as the sort of 'Sir' that one addresses to one's hierarchically superior social equals...as the junior master addresses the Head, or the Major the Colonel. And that was it, for when a little later I reproached him for using that form of address, he said:

'But you are, aren't you, everybody's blessed Uncle and Headmaster?'

For the moment, not knowing how to keep up the conversation with an unknown, I launched out into a defence of my room. I pointed out the beauty of its long, low, harmonious proportions; the agreeable light that fell from windows at both ends with trees beyond one half of them; the pleasant nature of the Chippendale chairs and bureaus that had been in my family for several generations; the portrait of myself as a child by my grandfather, and his long drawings for stained glass. And I ended up by saying:

'Young man, I never enter this room, coming from out of doors, without a feeling of thankfulness and satisfaction such as I don't feel over many things in this world... All the while asking myself when I was going to pluck up my courage to say to this supervitalised creature from a world outside my own that I could not for the life of me remember who he was.

He continued to stand there, leaning still slightly against the doorpost with his head hanging a little as if he were looking for his exact thoughts. Then he raised his sardonic eyes to mine and said:

'That's all very well. But it doesn't look like a place in which one would make money.'

I said with the sort of pained gladness that one had to put on for that sort of speech:

'Oh, we don't make money here. We spend it.'

And he answered with deep seriousness:

'That's just it. The room may be all right for your private tastes...which aren't mine, though that does not matter. But it isn't one to inspire confidence in creditors. Or contributors.'

That fellow was really disturbing. It wasn't that his words were either jaunty or offensive. He uttered them as if they had been not so much assertions as gropings for truth. And a little, too, as if upon reflection I might agree with his idea and perhaps change my room or neighbourhood. And he added:

'So that, as a contributor, the first impression...

And he answered my immediate question with:

'You are proposing to publish a story of mine. Called 'Odour of Chrysanthemums'. So I might look at the matter from the point of view of a contributor.'

That cleared the matter up, but I don't know that it made Lawrence himself seem any less disturbing...

I have had indeed the same experience lately whilst I have been re-reading him for the purpose of this article. Each time that I have opened one of his books, or merely resumed reading one of his novels, I have had a feeling of disturbance—not so much as if something odd was going to happen to me but as if I myself might be going to do something eccentric. Then when I have read for a couple of minutes I go on reading with interest—in a little the spirit of a boy beginning a new adventure story...I will return to that side of the matter later.

Enthusiastic supporters of the more esoteric Lawrence will say that my perturbation is caused by my coming in contact with his as-it-were dryad nature. As if it were the sort of disturbing emotion caused in manufacturers or bankers by seeing, in a deep woodland, the God Pan—or Priapus—peeping round beside the trunk of an ancient oak. I daresay that may be something like it. At any rate if the God Pan did look at one round a trunk one might well feel as one felt when the something that was not merely eyesight peeped out at you from behind Lawrence's eyes.

For that was really what the sensation was like—as if something that was inside—inhabiting—Lawrence had the job of looking after him. It popped up, took a look at you through his pupils and, if it was satisfied, sank down and let you go on talking...Yes, it was really like that: as if, perhaps, a mother beast was looking after its young. For all I know it may have been that. Lawrence was extraordinarily—even to his detriment, I imagine—subservient to his mother, who would seem to have been a commonplace woman except for a jealousy that almost agonisedly transcended ordinary jealousies. I did not meet her but gathered as much from Lawrence's conversation about her. He talked about her and her opinions in a way that is unusual in young men out to make their fortunes.

On the other hand I did meet his father, from whom Lawrence seemed rather to shrink. He shrank from him, that is to say, in an official sort of way as if he had for so long been told to consider his father a disreputable person that he took it for granted that I or anyone else who came in contact with him might consider that Lawrence himself lost caste by having originated from any one of the sort. I think he was wrong. His father seemed by no means commonplace. He certainly drank...or no, he got drunk at times. But he exercised a good deal of influence over his mates in the mine and he was very ingenious with tools in his hands...and happy with them. That is in itself evidence of a creative gift such as in the next generation may become anything. It was probably not for nothing that the father of Jesus was a carpenter.

The darkest passage of his career and one that was as much as possible concealed was the fact that early in life he had conducted a dancing floor or saloon—or possibly a dancing floor in a saloon. Lawrence in mentioning the matter glanced at it so sideways that I had not the heart to try to find out from him what sort of an establishment it was. For what sort of dancing would there be in a modern, rather mushroom mining suburb of an old agricultural city of the Midlands in England?...I imagined it must have been something rather reckless and abandoned, resembling what took place in Poker Flat, Nevada.

In any case that early occupation of the father would seem to have been unknown to the mother at the time of the marriage and to have caused her infinite pain when at last the dark secret leaked out...pain that caused Lawrence, looking as it were from beside his mother's apron, to conceive almost a horror of his father...as if his father had struck her. For in the household the mother was regarded as a 'lady'. She had been the daughter of some sort of, I think impoverished, shopkeeper...It astonished me at the time that it should be considered—and still more that it should be considered by Lawrence himself—that a shopkeeper was the superior of a miner, for it seemed to me that anyone who could do things with his hands was a producer and so akin to the artist, whereas the shopkeeper was relatively effeminate and parasitic. But at any rate in those days Lawrence considered himself rather shudderingly as the product of a martyred lady-saint and a savage lower-class father. As far as it was given to him to do so, he oriented his thoughts and his character along the lines that would be approved by his mother and those in similar circumstances. And he seemed to have, in consequence, an interest and an appetite in 'things' such as few young artists can have had. I remember his expressing a satisfaction that seemed to me to be incomprehensible over the fact that his mother's house—which seemed to me to be like any other miner's cottage—had something— a double passage or an alcove on the stairs, I could not quite understand what, that none of the other miners' cottages had. But it ceased to seem incomprehensible when I understood that that satisfaction was not merely because that special appendage raised him above the other miners' sons; it was that it was, as it were, a proper homage that destiny paid to his suffering, exiled-patrician mother. At any rate it had given his mother infinite satisfaction as marking her off from the other miners' wives. The house was at the end of a row of cottage, giving on fields and, what was an almost greater cause for satisfaction to the children, its patch of garden was larger and more private than that of any of the other cottages. And they paid sixpence a week more rent for it. There were always pansies and Michaelmas daisies and wallflowers in the garden, according to the season.

The importance of these things in the childhood of a man who afterwards became himself so important and so tortured, should not be underestimated.

The perturbation that his sudden appearance caused me on that particular day lasted only a moment or two—and a similar perturbation and dying down of the emotion attended my every meeting with Lawrence, even if I met him twice on the same day at fairly short intervals. For the young man that succeeded to the fox appeared to be a rather keen, North Country or Midland, normal, puritanish businessman. Of that type!...I mean that always, at first, for a second or two, he seemed like the reckless robber of henroosts with gleaming eyes and a mouth watering for adventure and then, with the suddenness of a switched-off light, he became the investigator into the bases of the normal that he essentially was.

He told me later that what had passed through his mind as he had stood looking down on me was that there was nothing in particular to be shy about in the placid-looking elderly gentleman with his efficient-looking secretary. He had naturally been shy enough coming up in the Croydon train. Yet they sat there in a very unexciting, old-fashioned sort of a room...He had not yet come to regard Chippendale as 'antique'...And there really had run through his mind the idea that he might be able to make something out of them.

For it must be remembered that, all his life through, he considered that he had a 'mission'. As to its exact nature in those early days he was more than a little vague and I do not know that, in later years, he had any settled programme for his missionings. But missionaries of a Non-conformist revival type had been normal if notable figures of the landscape of his boyhood, and the idea of a man moving among and affecting the mentalities of crowds was a part of his mental paraphernalia. Moreover, it was in the tradition of the English standard writer. And he was tremendously up in the traditions of the standard writers. I have never known any young man of his age who was so well read in all the dullnesses that spread between Milton and George Eliot. In himself alone he was the justification of the Education Act, the passing of which, a decade or so before,[5] had split all England. He was, that is to say, the miner's son with nothing but pennies to spend on his education...and he moved amongst the high things of culture with a tranquil assurance that no one trained like myself in the famous middle-class schools of the country ever either exhibited or desired.

Well, I told him what he had done in writing 'Odour of Chrysanthemums' and he listened without much emotion to what would have sounded like extravagant praise to almost anyone else. And I more or less predicted to him what he would do. Over that he was a little more restive. I suppose that, intent on exploring the lives of artisans, I was inclined to prescribe to him a course of working-man novels, the idea of which he found oppressive. He wanted to try his hand at something more romantic and with more polished marble and gold and titled people among its furnishings.

I obviously could not blame him for that. A young man brought up in his circumstances would be less than human if he was not determined to have for himself two thousand a year and footmen and the intimacy of lords and, particularly, ladies. And you cannot make good novelists out of young men who are less than human. They will not understand the mainsprings of humanity.

On the other hand, Lawrence had inherited or imbibed from his mother a liberal share of puritanism and those two forces fought an unceasing battle in him. His father no doubt fighting his mother. For, for all I know, two beings may have looked out of Lawrence's eyes—a father-spirit who hoped you would put a little devil into him and a mother-spirit that dreaded that you would lead him outside the chapel-walks and persuade him not to wear flannel next his skin. It was no doubt something like that... But at that day, in my room, it was, I imagine, the mother-spirit that prevailed within him.

He wasn't at any rate going to take any material chances without weighing them very carefully. There he was in his teacher's job at Croydon, secure, making what he considered to be remarkably good money. Forty shillings a week. More than his father had ever earned and he was only twenty-one. And with sufficient hours of freedom during which he could write. He had to perform his mission: he had to write. So that there he was, to use a later phrase of his own, inside the cage. He would have to think twice before anyone persuaded him to get out.

For before that first interview had ended I had begun lightly to persuade him to get out. It was quite obvious to me that here was a young fellow who ought to write, who, indeed, would write, so the sooner he got to it the better. One would have to find some way for him. I was never one to be afraid of taking on responsibilities.

He shied a bit at that, plunging away, as if he had been a startled colt, from a too attractive novelty. It wasn't that the two thousand a year and establishment and titled company were not as real to him as his life in the cage. He felt himself as sure of the one as of the other. He was going to have them when the time came as certainly as he was going to have his next week's and all the ensuing weeks' salary from the Croydon School Board. He was quite tranquil about *that*.

And, before he had seen my office, he had made up his mind that I was the person who was to effect that translation. But the office had given him a bad shock. It hadn't seemed the proper frame for a person with influence, wealth, and the acquaintance of the titled. His own acquaintance with the world had been very limited and he imagined an Office, to be reassuring, must resemble the office of the colliery company for which his father worked—the handsomest, brick and shining granite building in the valley, with counters and swing-doors and brass and the clink of coins unceasing on the air.

So it had occurred to him that, even if he did take command of that ship of mine, there might not be behind it enough money to make the transition from his safe schoolmastership very advisable...

That was Lawrence—a continual fight between the jovial pirate father and the cautious, disapproving, Non-conformist, pale mother, going on all the while in the very current of his thought. And the struggle went on within him to the end of his life, though towards the end he was inclined to give his father altogether best. That alone should be sufficient to give the lie to those lugubrious, Freudian-psychoanalytic souls who try to explain the Lawrence riddle by asserting that he was obsessed by a mother-complex.[6] He wasn't. He was a little boy who had been sickly and who had had of necessity to depend on his mother for all the comfort and good things of his life whilst he was told that his father—who got drunk—by that deprived him of the new pair of shoes that he wanted for Sundays... If you have, in addition to that, complexes of an esoteric aspect, you had better explain him along the lines of Amen-Ra, the Egyptian All-Father–Mother, who united in himself the male and the female properties so that he was at once his own father and mother and his own wife...and husband. And his own children who were the other hawk, bull, and cat deities of Egypt. And it is better to regard Lawrence's own preoccupation with sex and its manifestations with the same composure. As a mother-suppressed child in a Nonconformist household he was shut off from the contemplation of all natural processes to such an extent that, when he grew to have control of himself, he was full of perfectly natural curiosities and, since he happened to be a writer, it was in the writing of speculations that he took his fling. If he had been a banker or a manufacturer he would have found other derivatives. As a child I was inhibited from ham and cream by a careful mother who considered them too expensive. So, when I came to man's estate, I indulged in orgies of ham and cream until for years I could not bear the sight of them. Now again I rather like cream but can do without ham unless it is the very best Virginian, such as one comes across only once every four years or so. Lawrence had the misfortune to become conscious of life in London and in a class in London that by a sort of inverted puritanism insisted that a sort of nebulous glooming about sex was a moral duty and a sort of heroism. That did not help him much. What he would have been if those influences had not bulked so largely on the horizon of his youth it is difficult to say. And it does not very much matter. He was good enough as he was. He had a white flame of passion for truth.

I cannot say that I liked Lawrence much. He remained too disturbing even when I got to know him well. He had so much need of moral support to take the place of his mother's influence that he kept one—everyone who at all came into contact with him—in a constant state of solicitude. He claimed moral support imperiously—and physical care too. I don't mean that he whined. He just ordered you to consider that there he was in Croydon subject to the drag of the minds of the school-children for hours of every day in a fetid atmosphere... And that is the great curse and plague of the schoolmaster's life...the continuous drag of the minds of the pupils pulling you down...and then with the tired mind to write masterpieces in the odd moments of silence.

And then came the scourge! He was pronounced tubercular. I don't know how we knew that he had been so pronounced. I don't think he ever mentioned it to me; perhaps he did not to anyone. It was a subject that he was always shy of mentioning. But Galsworthy and Masterman,[7] and even the solid, stolid Marwood—and of course several ladies—went about for some time with worried faces because Lawrence was writing masterpieces and teaching in a fetid atmosphere. He had to be got out of it. He ought to be allowed to resign his job and be given a pension so that he could go on writing his masterpieces. That was where Masterman, who was a Minister of the Crown and supposed to be scheduled as the next Liberal Prime Minister, came in. He was to use his influence on the educational authorities to see that Lawrence got a pension as having contracted tuberculosis in the service.

Alas, alas. Croydon was not within the Administrative County of London. The London County Council gave pensions to invalided schoolteachers. But the Kent[8] County Council did not. Not even the Crown could coerce a county into doing what it did not want to do... In the end, I think he was allotted a small lump sum. But one had had a good deal of anxiety.

There had been no difficulty in finding a publisher for him. The odd, accidental, as if *avant la lettre* notoriety that he had gained at the Trench dinner made several publishers be anxious to compete for his suffrages. They even paid him good little sums for his first books. He didn't have then, if ever, any very serious difficulties. And the London of those days was a kind place to people who were reputed to be writing masterpieces. There were kind, very rich people who asked nothing better than to be nice to young men of gifts. So that in a very short time Lawrence was writing home exultantly that he had dined with two Royal Academicians, several *Times* reviewers, Cabinet Ministers, and Ladies of Title, galore, galore. I don't mean that the exultation was snobbish delight at mingling with the Great. No, it was delight at seeing himself by so far on the road...towards the two thousand a year...

In the course of a good many Saturday afternoon or Sunday walks in the Gardens or Park, there came home to me a new side of Lawrence that was not father–mother derived—that was pure D. H. It was his passionate— as it were an almost super-sex-passionate—delight in the opening of flowers and leaves. He would see in the blackish grass of Kensington Gardens a disreputable, bedraggled specimen of a poor relation of the dandelion whose name I have forgotten...Oh, yes, the coltsfoot—the most undistinguished of yellow ornaments of waste places and coal dumps.... And immediately Lawrence, who had been an earnest *jeune homme pauvre* with a fox-coloured poll, drawing wisdom from a distinguished, rather portly Editor, would become a half-mad, woodland creature, darting on that poor thing come there by accident, kneeling before it, feeling with his delicate, too white and beautiful fingers, the poor texture of its petals. And describing how, the harbinger of spring, it covered with its sheets of gold the slag-heaps and dumps of his native countryside...With a really burning language!

And it was not the starved rapture of the Cockney poets to whom flowers were mysteries. He knew the name and the habits and the growths of every flower of the countrysides and of stoats and weasels and foxes and thrushes. Because of course Nottingham, for all its mining suburbs, was really in and of the country, and a great part of the time—the parts of his time when he had really lived—had been spent on the farms that surrounded his home... That, of course, you can gather from his books...

Above all from his books. The nature passages of the ordinary English novelist are intolerable—the Dartmoors and Exmoors and Woodlands and the bearded tits and comfreys and the rest. (I am not talking of naturalists.) But the nature passages of Lawrence run like fire through his books and are exciting—because of the life that comes into his writing even at moments when he is becoming rather tiresomely introspective. So that at times when you read him you have the sense that there really was to him a side that was supernatural...in tune with deep woodlands, which are queer places. I rather dislike writing just that because it sounds like the fashionable writing about Lawrence which gloomily identifies him with Pan—or Priapus or Pisces or phalluses—which you don't find in Nottinghamshire woodlands...

Well...He brought me his manuscripts—those of *The White Peacock* and *Sons and Lovers*. And he demanded, imperiously, immensely long sittings over them...insupportably long ones. And when I suggested breathing spaces for walks in the Park he would say that that wasn't what he had sacrificed his Croydon Saturday or Sunday for. And he held my nose down over this passage or that passage and ordered me to say *why* I suggested this emendation or that. And sometimes he would accept them and sometimes he wouldn't...but always with a good deal of natural sense and without *parti pris*. I mean that he did not stick obstinately to a form of words because it was his form of words, but he required to be convinced before he would make any alteration. He had learned a great deal from reading other writers—mostly French—but he had a natural sense of form that was very refreshing to come across—and that was perhaps his most singular characteristic. His father was obviously not a dancing teacher and minor craftsman for nothing.

And then one day he brought me half the MS of *The Trespasser*—and that was the end. It was a *Trespasser* much—oh, but much!—more phallic than is the book as it stands and much more moral in the inverted-puritanic sense. That last was inevitable in that day, and Lawrence had come under the subterranean-fashionable influences that made for Free Love as a social and moral arcanum. So that the whole effect was the rather dreary one of a schoolboy larking among placket holes, dialoguing with a Wesleyan minister who has been converted to Ibsen. It gave the effect that if Lawrence had not met that sort of religion he might have been another...oh, say, Congreve. As it was it had the making of a thoroughly bad hybrid book and I told him so.

I never saw him again...to talk to. But he did, in successive rewritings, change the book a good deal...at least I suppose there were successive rewritings...And I suppose I hurt his feelings a good deal. Anyhow I am glad I did not have to go through his manuscripts any more. I don't—and I didn't then—think that my influence was any good to him. His gift for form, in his sort of long book, was such that I could suggest very little to him and the rest of his gift was outside my reach. And, as I have said, he is quite good enough as he is—rich and coloured and startling like a medieval manuscript.

The last time I saw him was during the War when, of course, he was a pro-German and was supposed to be a good deal persecuted. That is to say, Authority—in the shape of the Minister of Information—was afraid that he was being persecuted and I was sent down to see what could be done for him, Mrs Wells—who was as worried as anyone else about him—kindly driving me the thirty or forty miles down into Sussex where Lawrence had been lent the house of Mrs Meynell, the poetess...But I was not talking without the book when I said that I never saw him again to talk to. The Gods saw otherwise. For the moment we arrived at that pleasant place, Mrs Wells, who was very small, and Mrs Lawrence, who resembled the Germania above the Rhine at Rüdesheim—fell into a discussion as to the merits of the Belgians. And, as Mrs Lawrence saw fit to address, on the side, unfavourable remarks to the uniform I was wearing, I thought it was better—because I *was* there to make a report to Authority—to retire to an outhouse and await the close of the discussion. So that the last image I have of Lawrence is his standing there, a little impotent, his hands hanging at his side, as if he were present at a dog fight in the beautiful, white-walled, shady, aesthetic room of Mrs Meynell.[9] He was smiling slightly, his head slightly bent. But his *panache*, his plume of hair with the sunlight always in it—and his red beard—were as disturbingly bright as ever.

NOTES

Ford Madox Ford (1873–1939), novelist and editor. Of Anglo-German parentage, he changed his surname from Hueffer to Ford during the Great War. He founded the *English Review* in 1908, met Lawrence in 1909, and published some of his earliest writings. A shorter version of his first encounter with Lawrence is given in his *Return to Yesterday* (New York: Liveright, 1932).

The latter account contains a few additional details of interest. When Ford invited him to dinner, Lawrence 'brought with him the young lady who had sent his manuscripts [Jessie Chambers]. But there was no confusion about them. The young lady asked the housemaid whether she was expected to take off her hat; Lawrence asked the servant who waited at table what knives he was expected to use with fish or asparagus. That being settled, he went on to talk and was completely at his ease' (p. 376). Visiting Lawrence in Nottingham (as he claims), Ford was

astonished at the atmosphere in which he lived though less astonished by then as to the great sense of culture in his work. Lawrence's father, of French extraction and great force of character, was a buttyman down the mine and one of his brothers also worked underground. His sister I think was, like Lawrence, a school teacher. Other young people from down the pit or from schools and offices drifted in and out of the Lawrences' house with the sort of freedom from restraint that I have only seen elsewhere in American small towns. I have never anywhere found so educated a society. Those young people *knew* the things that my generation in the great English schools hardly even chattered about. Lawrence, the father, came in from down the mine on a Saturday evening. He threw a great number of coins on the kitchen table and counted them out to his waiting mates. All the while the young people were talking about Nietzsche and Wagner and Leopardi and Flaubert and Karl Marx and Darwin and occasionally the father would interrupt his counting to contradict them. And they would discuss the French Impressionists and the primitive Italians and play Chopin or Debussy on the piano.

I went with them on the Sunday to a Non-conformist place of worship. It was the only time I was ever in one except that I once heard the Rev. Stopford Brooke, who was a Unitarian, preach a sermon on Tennyson. The Nottingham chapel—it was I think Wesleyan—made me of course feel uncomfortable at first. But the sermon renewed my astonishment. It was almost entirely about— Nietzsche, Wagner, Leopardi, Karl Marx, Darwin, the French Impressionists and the primitive Italians. I asked one of Lawrence's friends if that was not an unusual sort of sermon. He looked at me with a sort of grim incredulity.

'What do you suppose?' he said. 'Do you think we would sit under that fellow if he could not preach like that for fifty-two Sundays a year? He would lose his job.'

I asked him if the elder generation liked it. He said that of course they liked it. They wanted their sons to be educated people. And they liked it for itself. They could do their religious thinking without the help of preacher.

The fact is that that atmosphere was normal life to those young people. They could not imagine any other way of living. They lived like that 'of course'—and that ended it. By the Monday of that week-end I was pretty certain that the days of middle-class government in England were numbered. The time was passing when Mrs Sidney Webb would say that one person or another would not be able to be an official of the Fabian Society because he was not a gentleman.

(pp. 376–7)

Ford is a lively but sometimes unreliable witness, and it is not at all certain that he did in fact meet Lawrence's father.

1. Jessie Chambers.
2. English poet (1865–1923), resident in Italy from 1911.
3. See p. 14.
4. Published in 1923.
5. Actually in 1902.
6. Ford seems to have J. M. Murry's *Son of Woman* in mind (see p. 133 below).
7. See p. 147 below for Galsworthy's meeting with Lawrence. C. F. Masterman was a Liberal politician now remembered as the author of *The Condition of England* (1909).
8. Croydon was, of course, in Surrey, not Kent.
9. Viola Meynell, minor poetess and novelist, daughter of Wilfrid and Alice Meynell. She met Lawrence in 1914 and lent him her cottage at Greatham, Sussex, in 1915.

Lawrence Reads his Poems*

ERNEST RHYS

[At his London home Rhys held regular 'gatherings of young poets' who would read their work aloud to the assembled company.]

The most memorable of these nights was one when the late D. H. Lawrence, then a completely unknown poet, came with Ford Madox Ford (who was editing the *English Review*). He had written to say he had discovered a wonderful new poet in a young country schoolmaster somewhere in the Black Country, and wished to bring him along. When the two entered the room together, they made a curious contrast, for Ford always had the air of a man-about-town, well used to town occasions, while Lawrence looked shy and countrified, perhaps a little overwhelmed by the *fanfaron* of fellow poets heard in the room, with W. B. Yeats and Ezra Pound dominating the scene. . . .

The plan of entertainment on these occasions was a simple one. Every poet was supposed to bring an original poem and read or declaim it aloud. . . .

In his turn, Ford Madox Ford read us a witty burlesque, after which we persuaded D. H. Lawrence, who had been sitting silent in a corner, to read us some of his verse. He rose nervously but very deliberately, walked across to a writing desk whose lid was closed, opened it, produced a mysterious book out of his pocket, and sat down, his back to the company, and began to read in an expressive, not very audible voice. One could not hear every word or every line clearly, but what was heard left an impression of a set of love-poems, written with sincerity and not a little passion, interspersed with others written in dialect not easy to follow:

> Whativer brings thee out so far
>   In a' this depth o' snow?
> —I'm takin' 'ome a weddin'-dress,
>   If yer mun know. . . .
> '*Er* doesna want no weddin' -dress—
>   Why—? what dost mean?
> —Doesn't ter know what I mean, Timmy?
>   Why, tha must ha' bin 'ard ter wean.[1]

*From *Everyman Remembers* (New York: Cosmopolitan Book Corp., 1931) pp. 243–4, 246–7, 249.

Lawrence's reading went on and on, seemed as if it might go on the whole evening, and the other poets became restive, and chattered *sotto voce*. At the end of half an hour, these murmurings had increased, and one murmurer, with nod and gesture, seemed to ask his hostess to intervene. She appealed to me, and I whispered: 'What am I to do?'

'Tell him he must want a little rest.'

This I did, adding that if so inclined he might resume at midnight! He took it in good part, and getting up with an awkward little bow shut up book and desk, and retired to his corner. . . .

As the night grew late we tried to get Lawrence to give us one more lyric out of his black book, and impressed it on him that one only would satisfy our ritual needs; but Madox Ford took him under his arm and marched him off murmuring wickedly, '*Nunc, nunc dimittis.*'

NOTES

Ernest Rhys (1859–1946), author and editor. The occasion described seems to have taken place on 18 December 1909. See Arthur Mizener, *The Saddest Story: A Biography of Ford Madox Ford* (New York: World Publishing Co., 1971) p. 552.

1. Quoted (slightly inaccurately) from the sixth poem in the series 'Whether or Not', first published in *Love Poems and Others* (1913).

The Croydon Years*

HELEN CORKE

In the late autumn of this year, 1908, Agnes[1] tells me of a new assistant master recently appointed to the Davidson Road school. His name is David Lawrence—a young Midlander of college training but small practical experience. She says he avoids, or is avoided by, the other men on the staff (Arthur McLeod excepted) and looks lonely and unhappy. She talks to him in play-time, and reports that he has 'original ideas'. (Agnes, in her flair for the novel, is a veritable Athenian.)

Agnes invites David Lawrence to her home for a social evening with the family, and asks me to come and be introduced to him. A memory of Clarence and my nineteenth year inclines me to refuse, but Agnes is

* From *In our Infancy: an Autobiography*, Part One: *1883–1912* (Cambridge: Cambridge University Press, 1975) pp. 160–1, 166–7, 174–5, 177–8, 178–80, 184–6, 186–7, 187–8, 196–7, 200–1, 202–3, 213, 213–15.

insistent. I call, and am shown into the drawing-room; the newcomer is discovered in the centre of a family group, father, mother, two sons and three daughters. David Lawrence, seated on the floor, is telling fortunes with cards, chattering clever nonsense in three languages. When I am introduced he rises, and for a moment his interest is focused upon me with a peculiar awareness: it is as though he were isolating me from all present; then he returns to his fortune-telling patter...My call is short, but I carry away the impression of a tall, slim, lank figure, of thick, straight, ruffled hair, of keen, deep-set blue-grey eyes under a high forehead and heavy brows.

*   *   *

Agnes's interest in the young Midlander, David Lawrence, continues, and he spends more social evenings at her home. She tells me that he lodges in Colworth Road, Addiscombe, with an attendance officer and his wife, and that she thinks he is writing a book in his spare time. At weekends he takes long walks. On a fine Saturday in April she arranges that we shall meet after my lesson and introduce David Lawrence to Wimbledon Common and Putney Heath. He is polite and gay; he offers to carry my violin, but this is not permitted. When we reach the Common our talk turns upon Algernon Charles Swinburne, the poet, who died recently.[2] The house he shared with Theodore Watts-Dunton stands on the edge of the Common. . . . I have read Watts-Dunton's *Aylwin*, but scarcely anything of Swinburne's, with whom young Lawrence seems very familiar. While we sit under a clump of silver birches, on Putney Heath, he takes a small book from his pocket, and I hear, read with a restraint that intensified its exultation, the Chorus from 'Atalanta'. Within me there is an echoing exultance, an excitement that I hold tightly in check. This morning HBM[3] told me that he has secured a contract to play in the Covent Garden orchestra during its long season—April to the end of July—and that he may be able to afford a few days' holiday in August. Will I spend it with him, by the sea? He asks with a kind of desperation which makes me afraid for him—I feel that I cannot, and dare not at the moment, refuse. When I assent he tells me that he has not seen the sea since the days of his boyhood, when the whole family used to migrate each summer to Freshwater, in the Isle of Wight. He would like to visit the old place again. HBM, and an island—what a vision to warm the sunlight of a spring day! My horizon expands; the deeps of the blue sky become illimitable.

So Swinburne's poem is curiously apt. The spring sunshine glints on the bark of the silver birches as David Lawrence reads it.

> For winter's rains and ruins are over,
> And all the season of snows and sins,
> The days dividing lover and lover,
> The light that loses, the night that wins.

The talk following is gaily ironic, but Lawrence seems to sense the undertones in my mood, and meets it with a peculiar and penetrating sympathy. Something of wonder stirs in my perception of this young Midlander, whose intuition is so strangely acute.

*   *   *

Presently Agnes brings David Lawrence with her when she makes her evening call. He will sit down in a fireside chair, head thrown back, arms hanging over those of the chair, legs stretched across the hearth-rug, while Agnes and I play Mozart sonatas. The playing is very unsatisfying— Agnes's hard *fortes* and meaningless phrasing, my tonelessness. When the sonatas end we talk, desultorily, or Agnes and David talk, and I am silent. It is Agnes who will go to the kitchen to fetch coffee, or who makes it if my mother is out...and then the young man will suddenly bring a book from his pocket, with 'Listen! will you hear this?' Half a dozen lines from a poem...'What do you think of it? Shall we go on?' Or he will hand me, without speaking, a small thick note-book and point to a poem on the open page. There is always something arresting about these manuscript poems, something which lifts for a moment the weight of my inertia, jerks the sullen set of my brooding mind from its concentration upon memories. I am aroused to discussion—even, after the two have gone, to some reflection on what has been said.

David Lawrence is not without place in those absorbing memories. He had entered during the anticipatory spring time, that April day on the Heath, and I had spoken of him later to HBM, calling him *Wunderkind*. Now, in the autumn, he returns, with no less delicate a perception of the autumn in my heart. At first I am only aware of his unobtrusive sympathy, then of a tentative endeavour to reawaken my interest in literature and art, as related to personal experience. He will lure me from the isle of memory with the quiet voice of the sea itself.

> In Salamis, filled with the foaming of billows,
>   and murmur of bees,
> Old Telamon stayed from his roaming, long ago,
>   on a throne of the seas,
> Looking out on the hills, olive-laden, enchanted,
>   where first from the earth
> The grey-gleaming fruit of the maiden Athena
>   had birth.

Voice and rhythm enter into the pattern of my dream—that memory of an island where I saw romance and reality not as two eternals but as one eternal. On the mist-curtain enclosing that island I see the forms of the

Greeks, and hear, mingled with the pulsing of waves on its beaches, the tragic chorus of Euripides. Through Gilbert Murray, through Lawrence, the spirit of irony and pity inspiring Euripides brings the classic tragedy of the Troädes into touch with an individual tragedy, and they are woven together into the fabric of my life. Lawrence begins with the Chorus—then he ventures 'Will you hear the whole?'—and I lie hour-long in my chair on the opposite side of the hearth, conscious of the flicker and glow of the fire, which ever and again reddens David Lawrence's high forehead, the thick, straight, goldenish hair above, the bushy eyebrows over deepset eyes, the high cheekbones and slightly sunken cheeks.

*　　*　　*

David has a cough which he disregards, but which gives my mother concern when he appears on cold, wet nights. In February I hear from Agnes that influenza is keeping him from school. On a Saturday afternoon I call at his lodging in the Colworth Road, Addiscombe. His landlady says he is better, but still in bed, and shows me to his room. He is hoarse, but obviously glad to see me, and declares that he shall be out in a few days. There is a thick brown-paper parcel standing on the floor by the wall; he asks me to lift it on to the bed. Unpacked, it is the manuscript of a longish novel, with the title *Nethermere*.[4] He says it is his first novel, which has been accepted by the firm of Heinemann, but is returned to him for a final revision. Will I read the manuscript and give him my impressions? Especially marking passages that show prolixity.

Gaunt and pallid, but full of energy, he delivers the MS to me three days later. As I read the close, cursive, always legible script, my mind is lifted again from the personal, and sent on an excursion into a new country, the English Midlands, to see Lawrence as Cyril, the impersonal, almost bodiless intelligence, the observant wanderer, moving among a little community of Midland folk.

The raw February days mark a fresh stage in our relationship. Hitherto David Lawrence has been content to minister to the needs of my sick mind, and I to accept his ministrations. Now he makes his first demand on my activity. We enter a phase of co-operation which brings us together more frequently. I have a copy of the pianoforte score of *Walküre*, with its libretto printed in German; he suggests that we might improve our German by reading simple lyric verse, and he brings along a small collection bought for twopence on a second-hand bookstall. The German verse, long discussions relative to the revision of the novel, and other books he brings for my reading, may occupy three evenings a week. From *Nethermere* I get incidental impressions of his home life, but make no effort to co-ordinate them.

*　　*　　*

He returns to the subject of my Freshwater Diary later—comes with the request that he may take it and expand its theme—use the poems as basis for a more comprehensive rendering of the story. He will bring me the work as it grows; nothing shall stand with which I am not in agreement. It shall be a finished study in full accordance with my suggestions. He is very eager. I think of the music HBM should have lived to write. Indubitably David Lawrence is a poet. The power of grasping subtle analogies, of apprehending new rhythms, of capturing truth in symbols, is his in very great measure. There is an element of wonder in my contemplation of him, and in the coincidence of his appearance at just this juncture of my life. I consent.

One evening during this spring of 1910, DHL brings me the first chapters of a manuscript he has called *The Saga of Siegmund*,[5] saying that here is the beginning of a composition which must be a saga since it cannot be a symphony. He asks me to scrutinise it in detail, as I have done the manuscript of *Nethermere*. I cannot do this; my part in his work is that of guide: David must see and feel very clearly the personality of his subject. He must know Siegmund as I know him. It is the one thing I would do—realise for DHL the living image of HBM.

Life finds a purpose. The closing words of the Chorus in the *Alcestis*[6] become charged with a personal significance:

> There be many shapes of mystery,
> And many things God brings to be,
>   past hope or fear,
> And the end man looked for cometh not,
>   but a path is there where no man thought,
> So hath it fallen here.

At the spring weekends of 1910 David Lawrence and I ramble over the Surrey hills, pondering and probing the three major mysteries—life, love and death. The presence of HBM seems never very far away. Each Saturday morning we meet—at Purley, or Addiscombe, or Penge—all jumping-off points into open country. David knows the flora of the lanes better than I, and our talk is often mixed with incidental study of botany. I have a sense of peace, a detached kind of happiness; he is serious and whimsical by turns. One day we pass in a lane a fallen elm-tree, blown down by a gale but not utterly uprooted—a small thicket of bright green shoots is rising from its horizontal trunk. Perhaps my life is to be like that of the elm.

Sometimes, on our downland walks, David's mind reverts to his earlier experience, and I hear, casually, something of his Nottinghamshire home and its people. His talk is like an appendix to *The White Peacock*, but concerns chiefly the girl Emily, with whom Cyril, the narrator, has a detached kind of friendship. The original of Emily, I gather, is a farmer's daughter, Jessie Chambers, with whom David has shared his reading and study since their joint period at the Ilkeston Pupil-Teachers' Centre. She is now teaching in a Nottingham school, and keeping in close touch with David by correspondence. My very partial interest in her story is quickened when I hear that this friendship is being challenged by David's family, who voice local public opinion. 'They' declare that the time for a boy and girl friendship is over, and that David ought either to become engaged to Jessie, or put an end to the connection. It seems that he is miserably uncertain which course to follow. He seems to forget the personal problem only by absorbing his mind in the *Saga of Siegmund* tragedy.

One evening he brings me a recently written short story; its opening sentence runs: 'Muriel has sent me mauve primroses.' The 'Muriel' of the story is evidently Jessie Chambers. Thereafter JC is known to me as 'Muriel'; the change is the first instance of DHL's flair for relating name and personality. Between our three selves she is exclusively 'Muriel'; all her letters to me during the period are so signed.

David does most of his writing late at night. Self-absorbed, I scarcely notice how the *Saga* is taxing his nerves—imposing highly imaginative night work upon the strain of a wearing, noisy school-day. He tells me once that he writes half-drunk, but this I discount as a touch of the pose, which, evident a year ago, has almost disappeared. He brings the manuscript to me, chapter by chapter, as written. The intuition it shows, the rare symbolism, fill me with wonder. My regard for David Lawrence begins to be mingled with awe. Again romance and reality join hand. . . .

Early in July the writing of the *Saga* is finished. The MS has been shown, during the holiday week, to Muriel; her reaction to it seems to have disappointed David. He tells me now that he is sending it to Ford Madox Hueffer. I hear nothing more of it for many weeks. Our evenings of reading, English and German, continue; the good local library supplies us with current publications—poetry, philosophy and fiction; and David haunts Glaisure's bookshop in George Street, Croydon where pocket editions of the classics, well-bound, can be bought for a shilling. We exchange admired works—I lend David Olive Schreiner's *The Story of an African Farm*, he brings me H. G. Wells's *Tono-Bungay*, Arnold Bennett's *Old Wives' Tale*, E. M. Forster's *Howards End*, Walter de la Mare's *Henry Brocken*. Each, in its own way, is an illumination.

The long, June Saturday walks may begin at Purley, then a village; taking the track to the left of its tram terminus we climb Riddlesdown. Behind us, to the north, the Crystal Palace glitters in sunshine through a shawl of silver mist, ahead lies an illimitable prospect of sunshine and shadow—the uplands of Surrey flowing down to the Weald. David is a good walker, and swings along, developing an idea of following a line of thought as we go, but his thought never blinds him to the nature of the path or the variety of the plant life at our feet. Once, to his delight, he finds a wild orchid. Riddlesdown is left behind; we are on the downs above Warlingham, where the tracks are merely those made by the few wandering sheep and goats. We plunge north into a valley of tangled copses and rank undergrowth, to climb tediously again up into the sunshine warming gratefully the short turf of a hill summit. It is noon, and time to eat. David's landlady has given him sandwiches, I have biscuits and apples, and we share the food, sitting by the edge of a field of marguerite daisies, which, by our very feet, begins its descent to the Weald—the sunlit Weald of scattered red farmhouses linked by dusty white roads. Seen from our height it vanishes in a blue distance to the south. But we do not go down, we take a western track which slants, presently, into the Kenley valley, and so back to Purley . . . Or, if the day be wet, we may take a tram-ride to the Thames Embankment and visit the Tate Gallery. I have loved the Tate since childhood, when my father would take us there—my brothers and I—on a Bank Holiday, leading us first through the slum of Nine Elms, perhaps to quicken our sense of contrast.

David regards dubiously my preference for Luke Fildes, Landseer, Holman Hunt,[7] and in general for pictures which tell their own simple story. He leads me to the Botticelli Madonna, whose beauty enchants him. But my mind cannot yet bridge the centuries to meet with that of Botticelli. David loves the immortal trees of Corot—and so do I. A day or two later he hands me his pocket-book open at pages carrying two new poems—'Corot' and 'Michael-Angelo'.[8]

We propose to see an opera at Covent Garden Opera House, but the gallery slips are all sold and we cannot afford more expensive seats. How shall we spend the evening? (Six years later, when writing the novel *Neutral Ground*, my memory recalls in detail the pattern of that dismal night, and it is woven into the story.)

David is in an oddly irresponsible mood, and suggests that we go to a 'jolly old music-hall'. I refuse; the Puritan side of my unconscious strongly objects to music-halls. I release David to go if he wishes. He will not leave me, and we board a bus going to Hyde Park. A band is playing; we join the crowd of people strolling up and down the Broad Walk. David is fascinated; he stares, smiling, into the faces of the passers-by; his face has an expression I have never seen on it before. I hate my whole surroundings— the alien crowd, the painted faces of women, the stridency of the band, the hot glare of the coloured lights. I stop, release my arm from David's, and tell him I am going home. 'You don't like it?' he queries, still with that strange smile. We take a crowded bus to Victoria, and a train to Selhurst, without having spoken again, and I wish him goodnight at the garden gate without offering my hand. We have come, I feel, to a point where our paths divide, and on the day following write, telling him so.

* * *

In mid-July David announces that Muriel is coming to spend a week-end with him. Do I want to see her? Should I like to meet her? I am not incurious. We arrange that he shall bring Muriel to meet me on Hayes Common, for an afternoon walk, but I set out with misgiving, even prepared to dislike one whose claim on David is evidently so strong and subtle. She may resent my presence—and how detestable if I seem to intrude upon their older connection. Yet each of us has David's portrait of the other—I know her as 'Emily' of *Nethermere*—she has just read the manuscript of the *Saga*.

The afternoon marks a stage in my education. Indubitably, Muriel belongs to my world—she may enter it in her own right. I sense that she brings to it a new element. Light and colour, movement, joy and anguish that world knows; her presence will ensure it *warmth*. Not sun-heat, nor the unreliable blaze of a fire that scorches or sinks to ash, but a glow that relaxes, comforts, sustains...(In retrospect I always see her in a claret-red dress—perhaps it was the colour she wore on the afternoon of our introduction.) She is taller than I, but her shoulders are a little bent. Dark, silky hair waves over her tanned forehead and rests in little curls on neck and temples. She has a slight, gipsy tan, under which emotion may bring up a sudden flush. Her brown eyes, even when she smiles, are sorrowful— they have a grieved expression, as if, impersonally, she were always conscious of the pain of the world.

* * *

We return to David's lodging for tea. He, in cynical mood, lies on the hearth-rug and rends with slashing criticism a book of modern verse. It would seem that he is not pleased with the afternoon's development. I leave them immediately after tea. David sees Muriel to the railway station, and calls at my home later. He asks questions—what do I think of Muriel, what is he to do in relation to her—and what of ourselves?

I tell him that I think he will ultimately go back to her—how, I wonder, being conscious of her *quality* of life, can he do otherwise? He is cynical and impatient. It is almost as if he had hoped I would declare myself *against* his marriage to Muriel. As if he had expected me to produce evidence against her.

I feel that at the moment his desire is towards me—in such measure as I still represent the 'Helena' of his *Saga*. But there is no rest, no assurance in this love of David's, which will ultimately make an impossible demand upon me. A demand not only for passion given and reciprocated, but for the absorption of my being in his. 'He for God only, she for God in him'; I think he knows that he is asking the impossible, and refuses to admit it.

*   *   *

At the end of the half-term break David and I return from Nottingham by the midnight train. Muriel comes with me to the railway station; meeting David she is all too cognisant of the situation and his grief. We have a compartment to ourselves; David flings himself down in a window-seat; I take an opposite one. There is nothing to be said, and I cannot approach him for fear of imposing upon him the exhausting struggle with his sexual desire, so urgently towards me. He understands, and composes himself, as if to sleep. We arrive at King's Cross before dawn, and walk in silence to Victoria.

In 1964, when the *Complete Poems of D. H. Lawrence* were published, I read for the first time the one entitled 'Excursion Train'[9]—David's record of this journey.

*   *   *

David has reverted to his Eastwood self so fully that we meet almost as strangers at the beginning of the spring term 1911. He resumes calling at my home, perhaps from inertia, or because a later identity asserts itself when freed from the suppression of the Eastwood atmosphere. Gradually we build again a bridge of mutual comprehension. He brings me books, and we analyse and discuss them, sometimes crystallising a satisfactory definition or two from the argument. His preference is now for French and Russian authors. I read Maupassant, Baudelaire and Flaubert for the first time. Some of Baudelaire's poems convey a sort of rank beauty. I am too ignorant of the French language to appreciate the perfection of Maupassant. *Madame Bovary* makes no appeal to me—I dislike both subject and treatment. David insists upon the value of its masterly technique. Turgenev's characterisation in *Fathers and Sons* I can readily admire. Of modern English poetry David brings Ernest Dowson, who is lovable; and the Aubrey Beardsley drawings illustrating the volume[10] have a fascination which I admit without understanding.

The essential of great art, David now constantly affirms, is impersonality, objectivity, and an unassailable technique. My early conception of art defined it as the embodiment, in word, sound or material, of beauty. By 'beauty' I designate that quality towards which the flower of one's life instinctively turns. I assumed that the artist, with finer perception and greater sensitivity than the ordinary being, selects the more significant experiences of life, and presents them, clean of commonplace, in art-form, for the joy of such as have eyes to see or ears to hear. My own writing, slight as it is, has always been an attempt to sign and seal, in rhythmic form, the beauty I recognise, either in comedy or tragedy. David now challenges this conception. An art-form, he declares, is justified whether it excites loving or loathing. Moreover, the *subject* of a work of art takes a place of secondary importance in relation to its technique. He quotes Flaubert's dictum to the young Maupassant: 'When you can so describe this horse that no one may ever mistake it for another horse, believe that you can write.' He is obviously accepting French models.

Ford Madox Hueffer's criticism of the *Saga* has been taken very much to heart... The work is too molten, says the critic—by which I suppose he means too much the stuff of life itself. David has no defence ready.The arbiter of elegance has spoken, and David feels like one of his own school-boys sent back to his desk with a reprimand for indifferent work.

Early in the year he tells me that he has begun a new novel, with his home life as its background. Its title is *Paul Morel*.

* * *

With spring we resume Saturday rambles in the country. The Addington and Farley woods, the North Downs, Limpsfield Common. They are still remote from traffic and the crowd. We seek by-ways and walk silently, not disturbing the small wild creatures. In April we pick primroses in Farley Woods. I ask David—sitting on his haunches beside a tree-bole, what of *The White Peacock*? He turns up to me a white, expressionless face and shakes his head. 'I did think it would give me a start' is all he says.

The White Peacock has given David at least an entry into London literary circles. He makes the acquaintance of young Ezra Pound, red-headed eccentric, and brings me a corrected proof of Pound's book of verse, *A Lume Spento*.[11] The poems have a quaintly medieval flavour and much self-consciousness. David receives an invitation to call on a woman poet, Rachel Annand Taylor,[12] and lends me a collection of her poems, *Rose and Vine*—subtle and musical compositions. Especially appealing to me is one entitled 'Resurrection', beginning:

> There shall no blare of heavenly trumpets end
> The long, long lapses of oblivion.

David is also invited to hear Florence Farr[13] declaim the poems of W. B. Yeats. Something in the séance irritates him beyond bearing: on the following evening it amuses him to lampoon the company and the recital for my amusement. I resent his treatment of Yeats.

Tolstoy, Turgenev and Conrad come into our reading just now, also E. M. Forster's *Howards End*; and the American *White Whale* story,[14] the violence of which seems to attract David. Wells is represented by *The New Machiavelli*. I find the book a tonic; the freedom and energy of Wells' mind so charge his writing that realism is real without being drab, and the presentation of middle-class life escapes boredom. Wells is dynamic; he generates activity. But I am not ready for Shaw—*Man and Superman* repels me. David brings a public library copy of Schopenhauer's *The World as Will and Idea,* in which he is interested, but into this book I can dip casually—no more.

*   *   *

In the late summer of this year David is introduced to the critic and writer Edward Garnett,[15] and a friendship develops between them. Garnett is shown the *Saga of Siegmund* manuscript, which he approves and recommends to the firm of Duckworth. David, stung by Ford Madox Hueffer's ironic disapproval of the book's intensity, finds Garnett's attitude reassuring. . . .

On a wet evening in November David visits Garnett, walking the miles between Edenbridge station and the Cearne; he remains for hours in damp clothes. Pneumonia is the result. He is nursed in his Croydon lodging by his sister Ada.

Muriel is staying at my home during a part of the Christmas holidays; we visit him together. He is propped up in bed; his eyes burn blue from hollowed sockets, a tawny growth of beard adds to his age; his hands are wasted almost to transparency. Muriel speaks nervously, charged with love and pity she fears to show—I, in very reaction, am flippant. Ada Lawrence, a placid presence, like and yet so unlike her brother, sews in the background.

During January David writes asking my sanction for the publication of the *Saga.* The firm of Duckworth is prepared to take it. I cannot but consent. His new novel, *Paul Morel,*[16] is still unfinished. It is unlikely that after convalescence he will be able to resume teaching; he must have money. He says he is completely revising the manuscript. I stipulate that I shall see the revision before it goes into print. I wish he had not thought complete revision necessary; written at white heat it should keep the mould into which it ran—that is its truest form. Something of the kind I write to him—he replies from Bournemouth:

I am not altering the substance of the *Saga,* so that, in spite of my present tone, you will not find it perverted from what original truth it had. I recast the paragraphs and attend to the style. As soon as I can, I will send you the MS, that you may satisfy yourself. But, as you remember saying yourself, the *Saga* is a work of fiction on a frame of actual experience. It is my presentation, and therefore necessarily false sometimes to your view. The necessity is not that our two views should coincide, but that the work should be a work of art. I am not flippant with the *Saga.* But you shall see for yourself.

(David did not keep this promise.) The letter is dated 1 February 1912. A few days later, on his return from Bournemouth, I meet him at Waterloo station, we cross London to Victoria station for the Surrey train. He is going to stay with Edward Garnett at Edenbridge. I travel with him as far as Woldingham; it is a fine, calm evening and the Downs are a glowing, emerald green under the flush of winter sunset. In the train we are peaceful, for the instant gay and content, and our talk is like that of people who have just escaped a mutual danger. David tells me that after the visit to Garnett he will go home to Eastwood and concentrate for a couple of months upon the writing of *Paul Morel*. At Woldingham station I say good-bye with no more finality than usual, except for a wave of the hand, and take a train back to the suburb and the work that he is leaving for all time.

Two days later a letter comes from Edenbridge.

Should you like a walk with me one evening before I go? Should you like to meet me on Limpsfield Common, just outside the school, as early as you can one evening? Then you could walk down here and see The Cearne (Garnett's house). Perhaps you might even stay the night, if you would consent. You would not mind Garnett. He is most beautifully free of the world's conventions.

There is no sound but the fluttering of the logs on the open hearth... I am uneasy tonight.[17]

But no! it is too late. David's letter only makes more clear the division of our ways. I know the nature of his unease, and my incapacity to deal with it. I could enjoy a walk over the snow-covered common with David, but not a casual introduction by night to the house of the unconventional Garnett. Indeed, suddenly worldly-wise, it seems to me that David is politely observing certain conventions of a kind wholly unacceptable to me.

(Sixteen years later, in the 1928 edition of Lawrence's *Collected Poems*, I read for the first time the one entitled 'Passing Visit to Helen',[18] which was probably written at this point. A bitter clever poem, reflecting the mortification of that 'common man' of whom David's finer self was ruefully cognisant.)

David Herbert Lawrence and I never meet again...He returns to Eastwood, to work at the novel *Paul Morel*, ultimately published as *Sons and Lovers*. Early in May Muriel writes telling me briefly that he has gone abroad.

NOTES

Helen Corke (born 1883) was teaching in a Croydon school when she met Lawrence in 1908. They remained close friends until he left Croydon in 1912. Miss Corke later became a headmistress in Essex and wrote history textbooks. She also published *Lawrence and Apocalypse* (London: Heinemann, 1933), a commentary on Lawrence's *Apocalypse*, and a book on Jessie Chambers (see p. 31 above). In the latter she says that she was 'for three years in close association with [Lawrence] and his literary work' (p. 7). Lawrence's novel *The Trespasser* is partly based on Helen Corke's experiences. She herself used the same material as the basis of a work of fiction, *Neutral Ground* (largely written in 1918 but not published until 1933).

1. Agnes Mason, a colleague of Lawrence at Davidson Road School, Croydon, and a friend of Helen Corke.

2. Swinburne died on 10 April 1909.

3. H. B. MacCartney, a professional violinist, was a married man with four children and was fourteen years older than Helen Corke. After a shortlived affair with her he took his own life.

4. An earlier version of the novel that became *The White Peacock*.

5. An earlier version of *The Trespasser*.

6. In Gilbert Murray's translation, published 1915. Of Murray's translations of Greek tragedy, G. B. Shaw said that they 'came into our dramatic literature with all the impulsive power of an original work'.

7. English Victorian painters.

8. The editors of the *Complete Poems* have queried Helen Corke's account of the origin of the poem 'Michelangelo' (see pp. 983–4).

9. An earlier version of this poem was published in *The Egoist* on 1 April 1914 under the title 'Honeymoon'; the title 'Excursion Train' was adopted later.

10. The English artist Aubrey Beardsley executed illustrations for the *de luxe* edition of Ernest Dowson's play *The Pierrot of the Minute* published in 1897; he had earlier done the cover-design for Dowson's *Verses* (1896).

11. An early collection of poems by the American poet Ezra Pound, printed at his own expense in 1908.

12. Some of the poems of this Scots writer had been published in the *English Review*. Lawrence met her in 1910 and gave a lecture on her work to the Croydon branch of the English Association. The lecture was not printed until 1932; it was subsequently reprinted in *Phoenix II* as 'Rachel Annand Taylor'.

13. Maiden name and stage name of Mrs Edward Emery, actress and friend of Shaw and Yeats.

14. Melville's novel *Moby Dick*.

15. Edward Garnett (1868–1937), critic and man of letters, was introduced to Lawrence by Ford Madox Ford; from 1911 he acted as Lawrence's literary mentor. He was an editor for the publishing firm of Duckworth, and was the husband of Constance Garnett, the translator, and father of David Garnett (see p. 94).

16. The original title of *Sons and Lovers*.

17. There are numerous minor inaccuracies in Helen Corke's transcription of these letters: see *The Letters of D. H. Lawrence*, I, ed. James T. Boulton (Cambridge: Cambridge University Press, 1979) pp. 359, 362.

18. This poem was first published, under the title 'Intime', in *New Poems* (1918). A revised version appears in *Complete Poems*.

An Interview with Helen Corke*

MALCOLM MUGGERIDGE

HELEN CORKE: From 1908 to 1912 was my Lawrence period.

MALCOLM MUGGERIDGE: That was when you were teaching me, in fact. Can you remember, Helen, the exact circumstances in which you met D. H. Lawrence?

CORKE: My friend, Agnes Mason, was a mistress in the Davidson Road School where Lawrence taught. He was rather a lonely man at first. He didn't find friends among the staff. She invited him to her home and one evening she asked me to come and be introduced to this new member of the staff. She said he was rather unusual. She was always on the look-out for unusual people, and I was a bit sceptical, but I went along that evening and DHL was sitting on a hassock in the middle of the family circle telling fortunes with cards and chattering in two or three different languages. My first impression was: here's a poseur. But as soon as I was introduced, he stood up and looked at me for perhaps the space of a minute, and I began to feel there was something more than that in this new member of the staff.

MUGGERIDGE: Was he what you'd describe as an attractive man? Was he attractive to you?

CORKE: He must have been because I was not ordinarily attracted to young men at all. In fact I had somewhat of a contempt for them. My brothers were both younger than I, and for choice I would always talk to older people. So that Lawrence, being only 23, didn't interest me at first. Agnes Mason agreed, or rather tried to make me agree, that it was our duty to take him for walks, being a lonely young man with nothing to do on Saturdays. I remember once, on Wimbledon Common and Putney Heath, when he'd brought along a small volume of Swinburne and read the Chorus from 'Atalanta'.

MUGGERIDGE: Did he read his verses aloud to you?

CORKE: Very frequently he would come and show me a poem. He rarely read his own poems to me, but he would show me a new poem that he'd

* 'The Dreaming Woman—Helen Corke, in Conversation with Malcolm Muggeridge, Tells of her Relationship with D. H. Lawrence', *The Listener*, LXXX (25 July 1968) pp. 104–7.

written in his college notebook. But that was not until a year and a half later, when our association was something quite different from what it had been.

MUGGERIDGE: Your relationship with Lawrence then became quite different from this first superficial impression?

CORKE: At the time there was a good part of my life which I couldn't share with anyone. But I found that instinctively Lawrence would bring an understanding to it which no one else could.

MUGGERIDGE: I take it that what we're talking about is the theme of *The Trespasser* and of course of your novel *Neutral Ground*, and indeed the same theme described in your autobiography?

CORKE: Yes, the story's been told in *Neutral Ground*. And it was originally told in *The Trespasser*, but Lawrence became acquainted with that story in the autumn of 1909.

MUGGERIDGE: That was when this tragedy befell you.

CORKE: No, in the summer of 1909. But in the autumn of 1909 I was writing impressions of it myself and he asked if he might see some writings of mine. I gave him these—what he called prose poems—and he said: 'What are you going to do with these prose poems?' I said: 'Nothing. They're written, that's sufficient. I wanted the record.' And Lawrence said: 'But a book presupposes a reader.' And then he asked whether he might take it: it was a sort of diary and he asked whether he might take that and expand it, giving the full story and the leading up to the story. I wanted nothing better because the story had involved the death of someone very dear to me who should have lived to compose music. Lawrence said: it shall be a poem as it can't be a symphony, this story. And that was the beginning of the book that was called *The Saga of Siegmund* and became *The Trespasser*. I wrote in the copy of *The Trespasser* which Lawrence sent me eventually: 'I demand clothing for the soul of Siegmund, and voice for his silence.' That was the answer.

MUGGERIDGE: *The Trespasser*. And was it adequate clothing and a true voice?

CORKE: It was as true as it could be if you put David into the position of Siegmund. He did his very best psychologically to get into the same relation with me as Siegmund had done. But whether he did it instinctively and out of a sort of primal feeling for me, or whether he was actually much more interested in realising the character of Siegmund, I'm not quite sure. When the *Saga of Siegmund* was finished, Lawrence sent it to Ford Madox Ford, Ford Madox Hueffer as he was then, and Hueffer disapproved of it strongly because of its romanticism. He said, it's too *chargé*. Put it away and write something better, I think, was really what he meant, although he didn't use exactly those terms. And Lawrence put it away. But when he was ill in the winter of 1911–12 and knew that he wouldn't be able to return to teaching, there was this book which would bring him in some money. And he asked me then if I would sanction its publication. We had agreed that it wasn't to be published under five years. I gave my consent.

MUGGERIDGE: Reluctantly or readily?

CORKE: Readily, because I knew he must have some means; he had no means at all.

MUGGERIDGE: The fascinating thing is to know how far this version by Lawrence of a tragic incident in your life seemed true.

CORKE: Part of it was definitely pure fiction. The end of *The Trespasser* is Lawrence, complete Lawrence. But on the whole I couldn't quarrel with it.

MUGGERIDGE: And does Lawrence's account of the motives that led this man to take so terrible a step as to hang himself in his own home, with his wife and children there, explain the motives accurately? But perhaps we don't even know what those motives were.

CORKE: I think that the working out of the end part, the return home of the main character, is very vividly expressed.

MUGGERIDGE: Extremely.

CORKE: And there is sufficient in that, at any rate from Lawrence's point of view, to explain the act.

MUGGERIDGE: Now how did you work at it? You met a lot at this time.

CORKE: He used to come and give me German lessons, and we used to read German verse together twice a week. And we went for very long walks over the Surrey hills.

MUGGERIDGE: Helen, I want to go back to the time after the catastrophe which resulted from your visit to the Isle of Wight, when Lawrence became your comforter. He showed himself then, I take it, to be not only a highly perceptive man but also a very sympathetic person.

CORKE: That was so. My concentration then upon something which was past, something that could never be recovered, was a sort of cul-de-sac. He knew I could get no further in that direction, and he wanted to bring me back into some main road of life, really alongside himself. I was absorbed in my memories. It was only he who by his choice of reading, and by his sympathetic interest in the whole episode, came to show me that there was anything beyond those memories which was of value to me in life. I examined the fact of suicide and it led nowhere.

MUGGERIDGE: Otherwise you might have followed Siegmund.

CORKE: I had not the faintest hope that I should meet Siegmund in any other world. And when I realised that, presumably I was the more inclined to listen when David tried to show me that there was a way out. For instance, he read *The Trojan Women*,[1] and that tragedy in a sense came into line with the personal tragedy. Somehow he'd brought the personal tragedy in line with the universal tragedy.

MUGGERIDGE: That is how people are comforted.

CORKE: Then, you see, he used precisely the right method. It wasn't any exact effort to comfort. He tried to bring me into life again, so to speak, along these lines.

MUGGERIDGE: This, of course, as I imagine, developed between you two an extremely intimate relationship?

CORKE: It depends on what you call intimate. Lawrence, having put himself in the place of his character for the time being, felt personally in the same way as his character.

MUGGERIDGE: And in that capacity was in love with the heroine.

CORKE: Precisely. But I should imagine that after the writing of *The Saga* was finished, that connection gradually faded out.

MUGGERIDGE: If you'd been willing and prepared to co-operate, he could have enacted the part of Siegmund, couldn't he? In other words he could have been your lover?

CORKE: I think hardly so because, you see, he might have been my lover but I shouldn't have been his lover. I had a great affection for him. It wasn't a sisterly affection because he stood alone: he was someone quite different from all those in the ordinary run of life.

MUGGERIDGE: He would have liked you to look at it in a different way at that time?

CORKE: Oh, quite. But not, I think, while *The Saga* was being written. His affection for me moved more to the physical plane after it was done.

MUGGERIDGE: I have a strong suspicion that the Helen of Lawrence's poems and Helen Corke are one and the same person. No comment, you should say.

CORKE: I'm afraid I can't dispel your suspicion and we'll leave it at that.

MUGGERIDGE: Did you feel physically excited with him?

CORKE: No, not at all.

MUGGERIDGE: But he did with you.

CORKE: He did with me, yes, definitely.

MUGGERIDGE: And indicated it?

CORKE: Yes. I was sorry that we couldn't continue our intimacy along the same lines, but of course it was impossible. It certainly wouldn't have worked in the case of marriage. I was very much of a realist. And I'd seen what marriage between two people with practically no income shut into a suburban environment meant.

MUGGERIDGE: This is your father and mother?

CORKE: Yes, and others. All the surrounding people were the same. It was that environment. And I knew we should just kill one another; we should spoil the best in one another by any such intimacy. It was unthinkable. And then again there were other considerations, you see. Three was the consideration of Muriel—Jessie Chambers. That was a great complication.

MUGGERIDGE: We must come on to her.

CORKE: We can't get any further without her.

MUGGERIDGE: She really did love Lawrence?

CORKE: Yes, but it wasn't just a normal ordinary physical affection for a companion. She said to me once: 'David is one of the sons of God.' She looked upon him as a completely superior being. One has to admit that her experience had been very narrow: she hadn't known other men, and she may have formed an exaggerated opinion of him. But they had been for five years associated through the books they read. He had brought to her the books which he read at college and the books which he read in spite of college. And they had studied quite widely together. She was the only member of his environment who fed the literary appetite in him at all.

MUGGERIDGE: Did he try to make this a physical relationship also?

CORKE: I think yes. I think that she was not ready for any such physical relationship.

MUGGERIDGE: But he tried.

CORKE: That was really the crux of the matter between them. She, in normal fashion, looked to marriage. That was what she expected eventually. She thought they would have an ideal companionship in marriage. But his mother from the first was definitely antagonistic to their friendship because Muriel was living on another plane altogether.

MUGGERIDGE: Now we're going to get in a muddle over all these names. Why Muriel?

CORKE: Lawrence had brought me a short story in which the first sentence was: 'Muriel has sent me some mauve primroses.' And his mention of his friend as the original Muriel was the first reference that he gave me to his intimacy with Jessie Chambers.

MUGGERIDGE: First of all we've got Jessie Chambers—the girl's real name. Then we've got Emily in *The White Peacock*. Then we've got Miriam in *Sons and Lovers*. And now we've got Muriel because of this short story, which was the first time she was mentioned by him.

CORKE: And for the whole of our joint association she was invariably Muriel. We never used the word Jessie.

MUGGERIDGE: Now tell me something, Helen, was she an attractive girl?

CORKE: I think she was extremely attractive. She certainly was to me.

MUGGERIDGE: You really fell in love with her, didn't you?

CORKE: I did.

MUGGERIDGE: I always feel reading you that you were much more in love with her than with Lawrence.

CORKE: Yes, I suppose I could admit that.

MUGGERIDGE: You make her sound so marvellous, this girl. I almost fall in love with her just reading your accounts of her.

CORKE: We became very intimate friends.

MUGGERIDGE: What went wrong between Muriel and Lawrence?

CORKE: His mother's death had a good deal to do with it. It was discovered in the August of 1910 that the mother was a cancer patient and Lawrence knew that she would die within the next few months. He was already, as his poems show, full of pity for his mother on account of the life that she'd had with her husband. And the consideration that she would die from this terrible disease acted upon him to make pity the strongest feeling that he had at the time. Something must be done as far as he could do it to ameliorate his mother's pain and to give her what he could give her at that stage. I think it was from that feeling that he finally deferred to her decision and turned against Jessie. I should say Mrs Lawrence was extremely possessive. In fact, her attitude towards her son was rather that which in happier circumstances would have been the attitude to her husband.

MUGGERIDGE: The situation of a man with a passion for his mother, and the mother with a possessive attitude to her son, is the absolute casebook formula for producing homosexuality. Do you think there was anything of the homosexual in Lawrence?

CORKE: I have no evidence whatever.

MUGGERIDGE: You think he was a normally sexed man?

CORKE: Only in the sense that he was near what I would call the middle of the spectrum relating to sex, with the extreme masculine at one end, the extreme feminine at othe other end, and the intermediate position which has been, I believe, the position of some of our finest artists: of most of them.

MUGGERIDGE: In other words, to use the title of your novel, 'neutral ground': where you were yourself?

CORKE: Yes.

MUGGERIDGE: So that, in a sense, you and he, as it were, sexually corresponded.

CORKE: We were within the same range of the spectrum.

MUGGERIDGE: But not he and Muriel.

CORKE: She was much more a woman.

MUGGERIDGE: Than you.

CORKE: Yes.

MUGGERIDGE: And therefore her attitude to him would be different.

CORKE: Yes, it was very different. In fact, there's no comparison between the intimacy that he had with her and the intimacy he had with me.

MUGGERIDGE: Why was she so annoyed when he sent her the galley proofs of *Sons and Lovers*?

CORKE: She had known the manuscript from its beginning. She had shown her much more than he had shown me of the manuscript. And at one point she had actually advised him. But when he sent her the proofs the narrative had been so altered, presenting a completely different picture of herself, that she was not annoyed, she was devastated. That was the end of it. She sent back his letters.

MUGGERIDGE: And never saw him again or communicated with him again. When did you see her last?

CORKE: In 1940, when I was staying with a friend in Nottingham, and it occurred to me that we might arrange a meeting. I wrote and invited her, thinking that possibly she might invite me to her house. It was about 30 years after her marriage—she was married in 1915. We met in the noisy cafe in Nottingham which she had named as a rendezvous. I hardly recognised her. She was bent, terribly older than I had known her. Her eyes were the eyes of Muriel. But she was so deaf that conversation was almost impossible between us. I tried to get into touch with her but it was impossible, and eventually she rose and made her way to the door. She could see that it was impossible for us to have anything more to say to one another.

MUGGERIDGE: Lawrence obviously didn't like clever women, did he?
CORKE: He preferred the type of woman who was a mother or a mistress.
MUGGERIDGE: But not a wife who was his intellectual equal?
CORKE: I don't think he could conceive of such a person.
MUGGERIDGE: Such a woman didn't exist. Do you think you're a dreaming woman, Helen?
CORKE: I may have been, but I think most girls can be so described. There's a period for dreaming. And it was Lawrence's way of expressing what I was to him, you see. I had no reason for showing any practical ability as far as he was concerned. He always saw me when I was thinking. It was the more intellectual side of me which he saw and which he stimulated. I did occasionally make the coffee, but that was about all.
MUGGERIDGE: What was your last glimpse of him, of that tall fair-haired man?
CORKE: He had been down to Bournemouth for convalescence in the February of 1912, and coming back he was going down to Edward Garnett's to stay. But he wrote and suggested that we might meet at Victoria and chat on the way down, you see. We had tea in Victoria and travelled down as far as Croydon, where I intended to get out. But it was a lovely evening and we were quite gay, not discussing anything serious. So I went on as far as Woldingham and by that time the sun was set. It was February, and there was a lovely pink glow in the sky, and I got out at Woldingham. He was going on to Edenbridge. I just said goodbye and waved my hand at the window and that was that.
MUGGERIDGE: You never saw him or heard from him again?
CORKE: I did hear from him, from Edenbridge. But it was a letter that didn't please me.
MUGGERIDGE: What was in it?
CORKE: He suggested a meeting at Garnett's, which I thought was rather unjustifiable. 'Wouldn't you like to come and have a walk with me on the common some evening? Then we might go back to Garnett's. He is beautifully unconventional.' And so on. Everyone knew what that meant.

MUGGERIDGE: Did you just ignore the letter?

CORKE: I answered it.

MUGGERIDGE: Coldly?

CORKE: Yes: answered it in a manner which wouldn't have pleased him.

MUGGERIDGE: And that was the end of it?

CORKE: That was the end of it.

MUGGERIDGE: Do you think you could ever have made a wife for him?

CORKE: Not for him nor for anyone else.

MUGGERIDGE: But did you ever think that perhaps it might come to that?

CORKE: That I should marry him, do you mean? No. It was proposed by him, but even as he said the words he knew perfectly well that he was posing an impossiblily. Something that he himself couldn't face. I did sometimes blame myself for having committed him to the intimacy that aroused such feelings; I asked myself whether I was justified in bringing him into such a relation with the main character in *The Trespasser* as to temporarily, at any rate, upset the tenor of his own life.

MUGGERIDGE: Now you are enshrined in Lawrence's work; you're there, aren't you? For ever. A sort of everlasting memorial. What do you feel about it? Are you content with how you appear there?

CORKE: I am only there in those works in the sense that David's image of me is presented there. I don't think this distresses me because of necessity I must accept the image. And of necessity, in the case of anyone, an image only shows one facet of a character. It depends upon the individual who's forming the image rather than on the person whose image is being constructed. But I felt from the earliest association with Lawrence that here was an experience which in some way was out beyond the bounds of ordinary human experience. It's put very crudely, that. But the whole atmosphere of those three years when the three of us were associating is definitely marked out in different colours from anything else in my experience.

NOTES

On Helen Corke, see p. 77 above. Malcolm Muggeridge, author and critic, had been a pupil of hers in 1910. The interview was originally broadcast by the BBC; the title of the transcript published in *The Listener* is taken from Lawrence's novel *The Trespasser*, where he writes, of the character based on Helen Corke, that 'she belonged to that class of dreaming women'.

1.   Presumably in Gilbert Murray's popular translation, published in 1905.

First Meeting*

FRIEDA LAWRENCE

. . . And then Lawrence came. It was an April day in 1912. He came for lunch, to see my husband about a lectureship at a German University. Lawrence was also at a critical period of his life just then. The death of his mother had shaken the foundations of his health for a second time. He had given up his post as a schoolmaster at Croydon. He had done with his past life.

I see him before me as he entered the house. A long thin figure, quick straight legs, light, sure movements. He seemed so obviously simple. Yet he arrested my attention. There was something more than met the eye. What kind of a bird was this?

The half-hour before lunch the two of us talked in my room, French windows open, curtains fluttering in the spring wind, my children playing on the lawn.

He said he had finished with his attempts at knowing women. I was amazed at the way he fiercely denounced them. I had never before heard anything like it. I laughed, yet I could tell he had tried very hard, and had cared. We talked about Oedipus and understanding leaped through our words.

After leaving, that night, he walked all the way to his home. It was a walk of at least five hours. Soon afterwards he wrote to me: 'You are the most wonderful woman in all England.'

I wrote back: 'You don't know many women in England, how do you know?' He told me, the second time we met: 'You are quite unaware of your husband, you take no notice of him.' I disliked the directness of this criticism.

He came on Easter Sunday. It was a bright, sunny day. The children were in the garden hunting for Easter eggs.

The maids were out and I wanted to make some tea. I tried to turn on the gas but didn't know how. Lawrence became cross at such ignorance. Such a direct critic! It was something my High and Mightiness was very little accustomed to.

Yet Lawrence really understood me. From the first he saw through me like glass, saw how hard I was trying to keep up a cheerful front. I thought

* From *Not I, But the Wind* (New York: Viking Press, 1934) pp. 4–6.

it was so despicable and unproud and unclean to be miserable, but he saw through my hard bright shell.

What I cannot understand is how he could have loved me and wanted me at that time. I certainly did have what he called 'sex in the head', a theory of loving men. My real self was frightened and shrank from contact like a wild thing.

So our relationship developed.

One day we met at a station in Derbyshire. My two small girls were with us. We went for a long walk through the early-spring woods and fields. The children were running here and there as young creatures will.

We came to a small brook, a little stone bridge crossed it. Lawrence made the children some paper boats and put matches in them and let them float downstream under the bridge. Then he put daisies in the brook, and they floated down with their upturned faces. Crouched by the brook, playing there with the children, Lawrence forgot about me completely.

Suddenly I knew I loved him. He had touched a new tenderness in me. After that, things happened quickly.

He came to see me one Sunday. My husband was away and I said: 'Stay the night with me.' 'No, I will not stay in your husband's house while he is away, but you must tell him the truth and we will go away together, because I love you.'

I was frightened. I knew how terrible such a thing would be for my husband, he had always trusted me. But a force stronger than myself made me deal him the blow. I left the next day. I left my son with his father, my two little girls I took to their grandparents in London. I said good-bye to them on Hampstead Heath, blind and blank with pain, dimly feeling I should never again live with them as I had done.

Lawrence met me at Charing Cross Station, to go away with him, never to leave him again.

He seemed to have lifted me body and soul out of all my past life. This young man of twenty-six had taken all my fate, all my destiny, into his hands. And we had known each other barely for six weeks. There had been nothing else for me to do but submit.

NOTE

Frieda Lawrence (1879–1956) was born Emma Maria Frieda Johanna von Richthofen and was the daughter of Baron von Richthofen of Metz, Germany. In 1899 she married Ernest Weekley (1865–1954), who was at the time Lektor at the University of Freiburg; he later became Professor of French at the University of Nottingham, where Lawrence was in one of his classes, and author of some popular works on etymology. She had three children by this marriage. In April 1912 she met Lawrence; on 3 May she left her husband and children and accompanied him to Germany. Her marriage was dissolved on 28 May 1914, and she married Lawrence in London on 13 July of the same year. See also *Frieda Lawrence: the Memoirs and Correspondence*, ed. E. W. Tedlock (London: Heinemann, 1961), and the biography of Frieda by Robert Lucas, *Frieda Lawrence: the Story of Frieda van Richthofen and D. H. Lawrence* (London: Secker & Warburg, 1973).

First Meeting*

BARBARA WEEKLEY BARR

Much of what Lawrence said to me over twenty years ago is still quite clear in my memory, chiefly because he was so direct himself. He never hummed and hawed or offered the usual kind of cautionary advice which is supposed to benefit young people.

'The only thing worth living for is life itself,' he said. His strong influence on many people was due to the fact that he profoundly altered their sense of values. 'I shall change the world for the next thousand years,' he once said to Frieda, his wife. I believed him.

Although it was as a young woman that I really came to know Lawrence, I first met him when I was seven. My father was Professor of Modern Languages at Nottingham University, and Frieda was then his wife. There were three children: Monty, the eldest, Elsa, my sister, and I, the youngest.

In the early spring of 1912 Lawrence, who had at one time attended my father's evening classes, went to see him at the college to ask for a letter of recommendation for a post in Germany. He was invited to the house and so met Frieda. She had heard my father speak of him earlier, when he had said to her: 'I have got a genius in my evening class.'

One day, Frieda, Elsa, and I were walking along a country lane outside Nottingham when we met a tall, pale, cross-looking young man, who took us to Holbrook's Farm. My mother obviously knew him. It was Lawrence. A sister[1] of Jessie Chambers, the Miriam of *Sons and Lovers*, had married the farmer. Mr Holbrook showed Elsa and me over the farm, and gave us a ride on a horse. I remember that, as it reared up, I slipped off and was caught by Mr Holbrook.

When we went into the farmhouse, Elsa and I found that everyone else had gone out. There was a plate of rock cakes on which Lawrence had printed a notice, 'Take One'.

Later on we joined the others again in the parlour, where Frieda was

* From 'Memoir of D. H. Lawrence', in *D. H. Lawrence: Novelist, Poet, Prophet*, ed. Stephen Spender (London: Weidenfeld and Nicolson, 1973) pp. 8–9.

standing by a piano, singing. Lawrence, still pale and preoccupied, was sitting near her.

The story of their going away together has been told before. To Monty, Elsa, and me, it was a mystery for many years.

NOTES

Barbara Barr, née Weekley (born 1904), daughter of Ernest and Frieda Weekley. She met Lawrence briefly in 1912, again in 1923, and frequently from 1925; she was staying with him when he died (see below, pp. 283–9).

1. May Holbrook, née Chambers: see p. 7.

In Germany and Italy*

DAVID GARNETT

I was very pleased when my solitary existence in Munich was broken by the arrival of a letter from my father[1] suggesting that I should meet the author of *The White Peacock*, which I had read, and which had made a great impression on me.

On the heels of my father's letter came one from D. H. Lawrence, asking me to come out and see him, and adding as a postscript: 'I look fearfully English and so I guess do you, so there is no need for either of us to carry the Union Jack for recognition.' On the day appointed, I set out for Icking by the little light railway which winds along the valley, getting glimpses of the milky-green waters of the rushing Isar, of sloping fields of corn and white dusty roads, with wild Canterbury bells growing beside them.

At every station, the train stopped to set down summer visitors, day-trippers and holiday-makers in gay Bavarian peasant costumes; bevies of stout, laughing women with embroidered blouses, bare legs and sandals; or to take in real Bavarian peasant women in their best black stuff dresses, with occasionally a gayer male wearing a gnome's green cap, embroidered braces and be-ribboned leather shorts. Clusters of children, sometimes crowned or garlanded with flowers, crowded on the platform, waving handkerchiefs. I could hardly bear to wait in the train, for though we had all the windows open, the carriage was like an oven. I remember the clean beads of sweat on a healthy German woman's neck who was romping with her five children, while the rest of us sighed and wiped our faces.

* From *The Golden Echo* (London: Chatto & Windus, 1954) pp. 240–3, 244–7.

When I got to the right station, I did not need to linger, while the embracing Germans cleared away, to recognise Lawrence. He did look fearfully English. The bare-headed, slight figure moved towards me; I noticed a scrubby little moustache, and I was looking into the most beautiful lively, blue eyes. We set off to the house where he was living.

Lawrence was slight in build, with a weak, narrow chest and shoulders, but he was a fair height and very light in his movements. This lightness gave him a sort of grace. His hair was of a colour, and grew in a particular way, which I have never seen except in English working men. It was bright mud-colour, with a streak of red in it, a thick mat, parted on one side. Somehow, it was incredibly plebeian, mongrel and underbred. His forehead was broad, but not high, his nose too short and lumpy, his face colourless, like a red-haired man's, his chin (he had not then grown a beard) altogether too large, and round like a hairpin—rather a Philip IV sort of chin—and the lower lip, rather red and moist, under the scrubby toothbrush moustache. He looked like a mongrel terrier among a crowd of Pomeranians and Alsatians, English to the bone. He was the type of the plumber's mate who goes back to fetch the tools. He was the weedy runt you find in every gang of workmen: the one who keeps the other men laughing all the time; who makes trouble with the boss and is saucy to the foreman; who gets the sack; who is 'victimised', the cause of a strike; the man for whom trades unions exist; who lives on the dole; who hangs round the pubs; who bets on football and is always cheeky, cocky, and in trouble. He was the type who provokes the most violent class-hatred in this country: the impotent hatred of the upper classes for the lower. Certainly Lawrence had no need to carry the Union Jack.

He was all this, but once you looked into his eyes you were completely charmed, they were so beautiful and alive, dancing with gaiety. His smile lit up all his face as he looked at you, asking you silently: 'Come on ... let's have some fun', and the invitation of this look was irresistible, at least to me. I could no more hold out against it than a well-behaved spaniel can resist the mongrel terrier's invitation to slip off poaching. The mongrel gives one glance out of the tail of his eye, spreads his front legs, crouches on his elbows, yaps once—then they trot down the garden path and are away like the wind, scampering madly. Whistle and shout as you like, you'll never get your spaniel back now—not till he comes in yellow with sand from the bury, at the end of the day.

No doubt Lawrence made me talk about myself as we walked from Icking to Irschenhausen, and then into the woods where he said there were roe deer. In the afternoon we walked further down the valley through a wood by the river's edge. *Osmunda regalis* was growing in the shadow of the trees and the river tore past the rocks and the white sandbanks. I bathed amid clouds of horseflies and we went on to Wolfratshausen, where Lawrence led me into an orchard behind the house and introduced me to Frieda.

At first sight, she might have been a handsome sister of the sweating

German mother in the train: she had the same sturdy body, as strong as a horse, the same magnificent shoulders, but her head and the expression of her eyes were very different. Her head and the whole carriage of her body were noble. Her eyes were green, with a lot of tawny yellow in them, the nose straight. She looked one dead in the eyes, fearlessly judging one and, at that moment, she was extraordinarily like a lioness: eyes and colouring, and the swift power of her lazy leap up from the hammock where she had been lying.

I have always been particularly attracted by happy lovers and attached to them: Lawrence and Frieda were more than twice as attractive to me together than they would have been separately. I was completely charmed by each of them and at once worshipped them.

They on their part flattered me, buttered me up, laughed at me and became fond of me, accepting my worship and lecturing me for worshipping other people. After that first visit, they asked me again several times, introduced me to Frieda's sister and brother-in-law[2] and, in a week or two, I was at home in a new family circle.

*   *   *

[Later] I reached Mayrhofen, where I took a room in a house across the street from the Lawrences. I explained that Harold[3] was due in a day or two, and Lawrence and Frieda agreed to wait until he turned up.

There was an oleander in flower before the door and strings of mules, with swinging red tassels, loaded with huge Gruyère cheeses, came down the village street out of the forest and the mountains. Lawrence pointed everything out: he knew everyone in the village by name and all their peculiarities and love-affairs. Frieda and he had been there nearly a week.

He was just finishing *Sons and Lovers*, he was writing some stories and a lot of poems, but his work did not affect our daily life. It never occurred to me, or I think to Frieda, not to interrupt him, and we spent all the day together in one room, while he scribbled away at odd moments in the corner, jumping up continually to look after the cooking.

Scratch, scratch, scratch, went pen or pencil on the squared foreign paper; then, scratch, scratch, with the penholder at the back of his low-class head of hair. Scratch on the paper again—and then Lawrence would jump up and begin to make fun of himself, or else Frieda was bubbling over with some new thing she had seen out of the window, or else the soup was burning.

Lawrence was a natural copy-cat; indeed, he was the only great mimic I have ever known; he had a genius for 'taking people off' and could reproduce voice and manner exactly. He told you that he had once seen Yeats or Ezra Pound for half an hour in a drawing-room, and straightway Yeats or Pound appeared before you. The slightest affectation of manner or social pretence was seized on mercilessly. One realised the enormous aesthetic enjoyment which the poor are afforded by the spectacle of the imbecilities of the rich, of the endless 'copy' which they provide—but the person whom Lawrence most constantly made fun of was himself.

He mimicked himself ruthlessly and continually and, as he told a story, acted ridiculous versions of a shy and gawky Lawrence being patronised by literary lions, of a winsome Lawrence charming his landlady, a sentimental Lawrence being put in his place by his landlady's daughter, of a bad-tempered whining Lawrence picking a quarrel with Frieda over nothing. There was more than a little of Charlie Chaplin in his acting: but bitterer, less sentimental. Frieda and I laughed at him until laughing was an agony.

In the evenings we all three of us acted complicated nonsense charades, without an audience. The last time we met, Frieda asked me: 'Do you remember, David, the head of Holofernes?'⁴ and she collapsed helplessly with laughter and could only explain: 'Oh, you looked such a fool!' Alas, I have forgotten the Holofernes we acted at Mayrhofen.

There was one bad moment of the day for both of them, when the post came from England, but Lawrence's courage, his high spirits, his perpetual nagging mockery, kept us all gay. For his courage and his mockery of the slightest hint of self-pity rose with danger and difficulty and at that time both their difficulties were very great.

Lawrence and Frieda set off for Italy with twenty-three pounds between them and with no certainty of any more until *Paul Morel* was published, and *Paul Morel* had to be entirely rewritten and transformed into *Sons and Lovers*. About money Lawrence was almost painfully scrupulous, never getting a farthing in debt, extremely economical, and always ready to give money away. At Mayrhofen, I borrowed money from him and didn't pay it back, though my father did. Lawrence offered to lend me the money to accompany them into Italy, whence I should return to England by boat from Genoa. Though much tempted, I refused, and have regretted it ever since.

After I had been a few days at Mayrhofen, Harold joined us. He had not met Lawrence or Frieda before and very soon made great friends with them. Neither of them had the faintest trace of that hypocrisy which Harold hated more than anything else. They cared nothing about pretences or proprieties and Lawrence and Harold swopped bawdy stories and Frieda and I laughed at them. Harold, therefore, felt completely reassured, and Lawrence liked Harold because of his uncompromising honesty and natural force and Frieda was not untouched by his good looks and masculine charm.

A few days after Harold's arrival, Lawrence and Frieda sent off all their worldly possessions in two suitcases by train to Italy, and we set out to walk over the mountains rising up through the wet forests, with their yellow foxgloves and *noli-me-tangere* flowers, to the rocky pastures, where the trees stopped and the belt of *alpenrosen*, dwarf rhododendrons, began. Towards evening we found a Hay-hut Among the Mountains, which was not so bad as Lawrence makes out in his account in 'Love among the Haystacks'. . . .

Lawrence was interested in botany and loved flowers, which at that time played a large part in his symobolism and personal mythology. . . .

NOTES

David Garnett (born 1892), novelist and autobiographer, son of Edward and Constance Garnett (see p. 78), was a friend of Lawrence from 1912. Part of the above extract appeared earlier in a slightly different form as the introduction to Lawrence's *Love Among the Haystacks* (1930).

1. In July 1912.
2. Else and Edgar Jaffe. Else, who was a professor of social economics, subsequently translated many of Lawrence's books into German: *The Rainbow* is dedicated to her.
3. Harold Hobson, a friend of Garnett's.
4. In the Apocrypha, Judith cuts off the head of Holofernes.

Back in England*

CYNTHIA ASQUITH

My memory of the first time I ever saw [Lawrence] is very vivid. It was in the summer of 1913 that Eddie Marsh[1] brought him to visit Beb[2] and me at Kingsgate, near Broadstairs, where we had taken a small house for some months.

Except the mere facts that he wrote poetry, was the son of a coal-miner, and had a tendency to consumption, we at that time knew nothing whatever about Lawrence; but the moment a slender, lithe figure stepped lightly into the room, we both realised almost with the shock of a collision that something new and startling had come into our lives.

I don't believe anyone could have been in Lawrence's presence for two minutes without being struck by his difference from other people. It was not a difference of degree; it was a difference of kind. Some electric, elemental quality gave him a flickering radiance. Apart from this strange otherness, one could see at once that he was preternaturally alive.

With his broad, jutting brow, and clear, sensitive, extremely blue eyes— very wide apart—he looked half faun, half prophet, and very young. He

* From *Remember and Be Glad* (London: James Barrie, 1952) pp. 133–4.

had not yet grown the tawny beard with which most people remember him.

He wasted no time—he never did—on small talk, but dived with a clean plunge into some subject that interested him, and he could not fail to make it interest everyone else. Words welled out of him. He spoke in flashing phrases; at times colloquially, almost challengingly so, but often with a startling beauty of utterance. His voice was now harsh, now soft. One moment he was lyrically, contagiously joyous; the next sardonic, gibing.

Lawrence and Frieda stayed at Kingsgate for some weeks, during which they spent much of their time with us. He loved to stroll on the sands under the white chalk cliffs, watching the gulls swinging, as he said, 'like a half-born thought between the sky and the shore'.

You couldn't possibly be out of doors with Lawrence without becoming aware of the astonishing acuteness of his senses, and realising that he belonged to an intenser existence. Yet to some degree—and this was your great debt to him—he enabled you temporarily to share that intensified existence; for his faculty for communicating to others something of his own perceptiveness made a walk with him a wonderfully enhanced experience. In fact it made me feel that hitherto I had to all intents and purposes walked the earth with my eyes blindfolded and my ears plugged.

So receptive, so alert was he to every outdoor sight and sound, that I had the impression that he must know what it was like to be a bird or a wild animal—could feel himself inside the skin of anything living. I felt sure, too, that he would be able to see in the dark; would know the instant the wind changed; feel the turn of the tide and be affected by the moon.

NOTES

Lady Cynthia Asquith, Countess of Oxford and Asquith (1887–1960), married in 1910 the Hon. Herbert Asquith, son of H. H. Asquith (Prime Minister, 1908–16).

1. Sir Edward Marsh (1872–1953), senior civil servant and editor of *Georgian Poetry* (1912–22). See Christopher Hassall, *A Biography of Edward Marsh* (New York, 1959). Lawrence had published an enthusiastic review of *Georgian Poetry: 1911–1912* in *Rhythm*, a magazine edited by John Middleton Murry and Katherine Mansfield, in March 1913; it is reprinted in *Phoenix*. Lawrence's poem 'Snapdragon' had appeared in Marsh's anthology, and he contributed other poems to the 1913–15 and 1920–22 volumes. In a letter of 22 July 1913 he wrote, 'We are quite swells. Edward Marsh came on Sunday (he is the *Georgian Poetry* man and Secretary in the Admiralty to Winston Churchill) and he took us in to tea with the Herbert Asquiths—jolly nice folk—son of the Prime Minister. Today I am to meet there Sir Walter Raleigh [Professor of Poetry at Oxford]. But alas it is not he of the cloak' (Moore, p. 152).

2. Hon. Herbert Asquith, Lady Cynthia's husband.

First Meeting*

CATHERINE CARSWELL

I have read that to Richard Aldington in those days Lawrence looked like a soldier, and that to David Garnett he suggested a plumber's mate or the kind of workman that makes trouble with the boss. But to me, on that day in June 1914, when I first set eyes on him, the immediately distinguishing thing was his swift and flamelike quality, which was quite unlike anything suggested by even the most fascinating type of British soldier or workman. I was sensible of a fine, rare beauty in Lawrence, with his deepset jewel-like eyes, thick dust-coloured hair, pointed underlip of notable sweetness, fine hands, and rapid but never restless movements. The stiff, the slow or the unreal had as little part in that frame as had any mechanically imposed control, but he was beautifully disciplined. In any kind of paid manual or even mechanical labour, if he had undertaken it, I should have said that Lawrence would have risen quickly to a position of authority and would have been in favour because of his good workmanship. This is not the kind that 'makes trouble' in the accepted sense of the phrase, anyhow not so long as he is employed on a definite understanding. I have seen Lawrence under many circumstances but I never once saw him heavy or lounging, and he was never idle, just as a bird is never idle. At the same time I never saw a trace of strain or resentment in him when engaged in any of his manifold activities. In these two ways—never being idle, yet never seeming to labour—he was unlike anybody else I ever met. He was without human dreariness. . . .

Nothing memorable was said over tea. But afterwards, when we all walked down to the Finchley Road together to see the Lawrences into their bus, he and I walked in front; and as we passed the churchyard where my child was buried and I had paid for a grave for myself, I found that I was talking to him as if I had known him all my life. It was not that Lawrence encouraged confidences. He had none of the traits, still less the tricks of what is usually understood to be the 'sympathetic' man. There were no 'intimacies', either physical or mental. But he gave an immediate sense of freedom, and his responses were so perfectly fresh, while they were

* From *The Savage Pilgrimage: A Narrative of D. H. Lawrence*, rev. edn (London: Martin Secker, 1932) pp. 17–18, 18–19.

puzzling, that it seemed a waste of time to talk about anything with him except one's real concerns. . . .

NOTE

Catherine Carswell (1879–1946) was a novelist, biographer and reviewer. She contributed a series of articles titled 'Reminiscences of D. H. Lawrence' to *The New Adelphi* from November 1931 to March 1932, and these were expanded into her book *The Savage Pilgrimage*, published in 1932 by Chatto & Windus. After J. Middleton Murry threatened to bring an action for libel, the publishers withdrew the book and recalled stock. Before the end of the year Martin Secker issued a revised edition (repr. 1951).

Lawrence and the War*

CYNTHIA ASQUITH

About a year after my first meeting with Lawrence the war of 1914–1918 began. I had a letter from him in which he wrote, 'The outbreak of war finished me, it was the spear through the side of all sorrows and hopes.'

When I next saw him he really was visibly changed. At times he looked like one in acute physical pain. He spoke of the war as a 'colossal and deliberate horror'. Gusts of rage alternated with bitter grief. 'My soul is fizzling savagely,' he hissed, 'it is sending me MAD!' and, in truth, ever afterwards he did seem to me to have, though of course with radiant lucid intervals, a touch of delirium—to talk and write like one whose temperature is several degrees above normal.

A passionate subjectivist, now more than ever at odds with the nightmare facts of an objective world that impinged upon him on every side, he was reduced to gnashing, impotent misery. To him the war was not only the immediate horror it was to all of us; he had the despair of prevision as well. Convinced as he was that one war must always breed another, he saw it as a suicide-pact between the nations, as the beginning of the end—in his own words, 'the end of democracy, the end of the idea of liberty and freedom, the end of the brotherhood of man, the end of the belief in the reign of love, the end of the belief that man desires peace, harmony, tranquillity, love and loving kindness. The end of Christianity...the end, the end, the end.' Because to him 'the world on top was all torture and a flounder of stupidity', he conceived the idea of founding that small ideal

* From *Remember and Be Glad*, pp. 136–7, 139–40.

community on which from now on he set his heart and for which he was to search the world in vain. He repeatedly urged us to join this community, not a very practical suggestion as Beb[1] was in the Army.

Despite his loathing and denunciation of the war, Lawrence could not fail to recognise—and this fact obsessed him—that it did at least bring about what he called 'a slump in trifling', and trifling was what he detested. But that human beings should find in war an inspiration and fulfilment nothing else seemed able to give them, that this should be so, was to him a confession of failure; a blasphemy that filled him with despair. Some other moral equivalent must be found; new values proclaimed; a wholly different idea of life conceived.

The sense of separatedness to which Lawrence now felt himself condemned by his attitude to the war made him bitterly unhappy. He could not bear to feel that what he called the 'oneness of mankind' was broken in him. 'Believe me,' he wrote to me, 'I am infinitely hurt by being torn off from the body of my fellow creatures...but so it is ...and all heaven and hell lies in the chasm between.'

Rail too, as he might, against his country and her values; crave, as he genuinely supposed himself to crave, for an entirely new life in some distant land; yet his aching love for his own country was inextinguishable.

*   *   *

The following passages from my diary tell of an afternoon spent at that time with the Lawrences:

Littlehampton, 21 June 1915. The Lawrences came for the day. I wanted Beb and DH to have a talk, so to begin with I strolled with Frieda, leaving the two men together on the beach. She poured out to me about the difficulties of her life as the wife of a 'genius'. People, she complained, particularly women—particularly one woman—treat her as a mere appendage and will insist on 'explaining' her own husband to her, telling her that he is a 'being dropped straight from the sky'.

Later we all four sat on the sands. Lawrence talking, as he always does, with his entire body, railed against the war. He seems to have an obsession that to the minds of most soldiers destruction is an end, not the means to an end, a delusion which Beb—hard that by soldiering he of all people should be accused of indulging in an orgy!—in vain tried to dislodge.

In a discussion on the Germans, Frieda admitted that her countrymen had no sense of what the English mean by 'Fair Play'. Lawrence maintained that the German theory of war, though 'filthy', was perfectly logical, and that if all nations waged it in the same way, some conclusion might at least be arrived at, which with the present lunatic compromise between utter barbarism and half-hearted humanitarianism, could never be.

Then, with one of his sudden changes of gear, he became blithe and amusing, complaining how—small wonder—strangers always talked to him in the train, particularly colonels and curates, and imitating—he is a marvellous mimic—their faces, voices and vocabularies.

NOTE

For a note on Cynthia Asquith see p. 95.
1. Hon. Herbert Asquith, Lady Cynthia's husband.

Garsington and London*

LADY OTTOLINE MORRELL

These books[1] having excited and moved me, I felt how much I should like to know Lawrence himself, whose home had also been in Nottinghamshire, and to my surprise I found that Gilbert Cannan[2] knew him—indeed, Lawrence and his wife were at this time living at a cottage near them at Chesham.[3] Lawrence was pleased to hear that I admired his work, and one evening in February 1915[4] he and his wife came to see us. He was a slight man, lithe and delicately built, his pale face rather overshadowed by his beard and his red hair falling over his forehead, his eyes blue and his hands delicate and very competent. He gave one the impression of someone who had been under-nourished in youth, making his body fragile and his mind too active. Soon after coming to see us, they went to live at Greatham,[5] near Pulborough, in a cottage lent to them by Viola Meynell—one of a group of cottages built by old Mr. Meynell for his children. Here I went several times to see them, and except that one night I could not sleep on account of the cold, I was extraordinarily happy and at ease. When we met we at once went back to our memories of Nottinghamshire. We talked of the lovely wild commons, of Sherwood Forest, of the dark pit villages, of the lives of the colliers and their wives, and of all those scenes which he has described so vividly in his early books, scenes which were a part of his own life. He talked to me in the Nottinghamshire dialect which I loved to hear again. He also liked to talk of my family in Nottinghamshire, for he had a

* From *Ottoline: the Early Memoirs of Lady Ottoline Morrell*, ed. Robert Gathorne-Hardy (London: Faber & Faber, 1963) pp. 272–5, 279–80; *Ottoline at Garsington: Memoirs of Lady Ottoline Morrell, 1915–1918*, ed. Robert Gathorne-Hardy (London: Faber & Faber, 1974) pp. 35–40, 69–70, 77–9.

romantic feeling for them. He used to please me by saying that the 'Bentincks were always looked up to as being disinterested'.

The long bare room with its refectory table and luncheon cooked by Lawrence himself are all vivid in my memory. It was impossible not to feel expanded and stimulated by the companionship of anyone so alive, so intensely interested in everyone and everything as he was. Indeed, he seemed to possess a magnetic gift of quickening those he talked to and of making them blossom with new ideas, new enthusiasm, new hopes. His whole attention seemed concentrated on them. He who became so vehement in his writings was nearly always—certainly with me—gentle and tender in personal contact. Indeed, I felt when I was with him as if I had really at last found a friend, that I could express myself without reserve, and without fear of being thought silly. He felt the wind and the flowers with the same vividness that I did. He seemed to open up the way into a holy land by his gospel of instinctive development.

We used to go long walks through woods and over the downs. On one visit, when John Middleton Murry was staying with him, we climbed to the top of the Downs to look at the view towards Arundel and the sea—a view by which he said he tested the character of his friends. Murry lagged with a melancholy air behind us as we climbed. Another day in the early spring we went to the woods still bare of leaves, but he showed me the little flame-red buds of the trees not yet in leaf and said, 'See, here is the little red flame in Nature.' I looked at him as he was speaking and thought, 'In you, too, there certainly dwells that flame.' It was the central fire of his being, intermittent as nature is, and if he had been able to root himself in some soil this flame would have lit him through the seasons.

On one of my visits to Greatham I took Bertrand Russell with me and it appeared a great success. From the first these two passionate men took to each other and Bertie Russell, as we drove away, exclaimed, 'He is amazing; he sees through and through one.'

'Yes. But do you think he really sees correctly?' I asked.

'Absolutely. He is infallible,' was Bertie's reply. 'He is like Ezekiel or some other Old Testament prophet, prophesying. Of course, the blood of his nonconformist preaching ancestors is strong in him, but he sees everything and is always right.'

I reluctantly agreed. At the same time I had my doubts, which later on grew into a certainty, for he was much too impatient even then to see through all the layers and contradictions and subtleties of an English character. His insight was indeed very intense, but sometimes so bright that it distorted those it focused.

I find I wrote in my journal then:

'Lawrence is the spirit of flame. He has indeed a fire within him, a fire which flames into excitement and conviction when a subject or a controversy strikes a light. And what subjects do not strike a light? For that indeed is the rare quality that Lawrence has, he is interested in almost everything. Few subjects bore him. And by his wonderful capacity of being absolutely natural he stimulates those round him to be the same.'

Many people are interested in others in a superficial way, but his interest would penetrate and lay hands on his object, breaking down barriers. No wonder that there were those that resented it and resented what they thought was his interference in their private lives, that he would tell them that he knew better than they did what was good for them. He was not the child of an old cultivated family who inherits a natural restraint and respect for his neighbour's hidden and secluded lives; Lawrence's ancestors had never learnt the art of courtly bowing and curtseying. His old home was a small intense world where interests were passionate, direct and often violent. Poverty, hard work and an innate moral delicacy were the only restraints. Apart from that, it was a life untrammelled by middle-class conventions or decorum; kindness, curiosity, anger, were all freely and frankly expressed, and in this little world, Lawrence, young as he was, was supreme—for it was he who brought into it cultivation, excitement, intelligent talk and argument. The only one who remained outside was his father, who carried on his own hard-working, hard-drinking existence, and was often rough and abusive.

A miner's home in the Midlands is not the unlearned and untidy home of the south, and Lawrence's mother was obviously—from what he told me—a very remarkable woman, who had great delicacy of feeling and distinction of mind: clear, orderly, dominating towards the children. Anyone who has read *Sons and Lovers* and Lawrence's poems to her must have realised how important she was to him. But what an absorbing, troubling and agitating son Lawrence must have been to this delicately minded, orderly and capable mother who was the centre of the family, but above all was dominating and possessive of this son. And upon her he concentrated himself. She had so much in her character that satisfied him; she was sharp in retort and had a witty resistence—proud and erect—reserved—above all she had a complete admiration and devotion to him. No doubt as a result of her detachment from her husband she called forth his protective devotion and tenderness. The poems that he wrote to her show how lovely and tender was his feeling for her.

The early habits of his home life were never shaken off. He was quick and competent in cleaning a floor, washing up cups and saucers, cooking, nursing: violent in argument, free in expression and abuse. Burns and Lawrence are, I suppose, almost the only two important writers who have sprung from working-class homes. But Lawrence, unlike Burns, was never at one with his old companions. He could not have remained as Burns did, one of them. If he had been only a poet it might have been possible, but he was a seeker after life and a prophet preacher. He had to leave, to go out to wider fields, but he never really found a 'Home'.

*   *   *

The entries in my journal at this time seem very scanty, except jottings of despair about the war—'dull, grinding agony'. One was told at first that modern warfare was so terrible that it *could* not go on beyond a few weeks. I hardly believed this when it was said, people get accustomed to anything, however terrible. There is one entry as follows:

'I was sitting alone last night after dinner in the drawing-room, when in came, unexpectedly, Lawrence, bringing with him Katherine Mansfield, Koteliansky, Gordon and Beatrice Campbell,[6] and some other men. I was rather taken aback to see these great figures trooping in, and felt shy and lost, and I did not know how on earth I should entertain them as, except for Lawrence, they were complete strangers to me.

'Katherine Mansfield sat very silent and Buddha-like on the big sofa— she might almost have held in her hand a lotus-flower! The men looked immensely large and solid compared with Lawrence. The talk was, as far as I can remember it, mainly political. Campbell sat on a small chair near the fire; Lawrence knows him very well and they started a violent argument—or rather it was calm and irritatingly rational on Campbell's part; Lawrence stood over him shaking his arm above his head and every two or three minutes very quickly rubbing the tips of his fingers on his scalp in rapid friction, at the same time making a face, drawing back his mouth in a sort of grin which reached up to the top of his face, his voice mounting to a shriek—'You lie, you lie', or 'You know it is not true', and again and again more friction of the scalp.

'Somehow I could not take it seriously, nor did Campbell, or any of us. It all seemed rather comic and rather an access of exuberance. I don't think Lawrence was really angry. It was his method of controversy.

'But I should like to make this place into a harbour, a refuge in the storm, where those who haven't been swept away could come and renew themselves and go forth strengthened. But people are very difficult to manage. The young Cambridge men are so critical and superior and disdainful, and lift up their hands in horror at men like D. H. Lawrence who have fire and genius. They tolerate Bertie because he was at Cambridge and is of course intensely intellectual. I feel despondent about it all. People are so rigid, and only like to move in little circles on little toy railway lines surrounded by their admirers, they don't want to venture forth, and are afraid of possible persecution.

'But now I will bestir myself and ask some people here and have a party for my birthday. I will ask the Cannans and Lawrences and Bertie and Maria[7] will be here. Bertie and Lawrence can make friends and plan a 'revolution' and a 'New World', and write manifestos together. And as it is my birthday and lovely summer, they will have to be nice and kind to each other, and not rage and quarrel.

'I have had some nice letters from D. H. Lawrence lately.'

*   *   *

On June 15th [1915] I find the following entry in my Journal:
    'The birthday party arrived. The house, of course, was very unfinished, but I did my best to make them comfortable, and Lawrence was charming and sympathetic and interested in all that we are doing here. He helped us decorate with gold the panels in the red room. We were an odd looking company, tall and short, thin and thick, dressed in white overalls, egg-cups of gold paint in our hands, creeping slowly round the room, outlining each panel with a fine paint-brush. Someone had to climb up on to the steps to do the beams, and poor Bertie was sent up and nearly expired from the heat, but it was all fun and Lawrence of course did his far quicker and straighter than any of us. Frieda sat on the table in the middle of the room, swinging her legs and laughing and mocking at us, giving advice as to what curtains she would have. She has a terrible irritant quality, and enjoys tormenting, and she liked to taunt me because I was taking trouble to make the house nice. Of course to her, who hadn't a home, and who carries her belongings round the world in a few trunks, it seems absurd to spend time and trouble on making a house really nice, although when Philip offered to adapt the old 'monastic building' here into a house for them she required so much done that it would have cost far more than we could afford. It was an anxious visit for with Frieda one feels one is sitting with a tigress who will spring and rend either Lawrence or one of us at any moment. She was jealous that we all liked and admired Lawrence, or Lorenzo[8] as she calls him, and that we did not consider her as important a person as he is. She even said in a loud, challenging voice, "I am just as remarkable and important as Lorenzo". Indeed, in all our talks she was very aggressive and self-assertive. I began to fear she would make it difficult to be friends with him, she was already turning him against Bertie because Bertie didn't flatter her. She has educated herself on Nietzsche; she appears to be a woman that Strindberg might have married and hated, and is what is called a "clever fool". Naïvely, I did not realise that the Lawrences were not happy here, but apparently she became jealous and they had a miserable time together, fighting and quarrelling all night. He came down on the morning of their last day looking whipped, forlorn and crestfallen, and she went off in a high temper to London. I shall always see that unhappy, distraught, pathetic figure standing in the hall hesitating whether he should remain here or whether he should follow her to London. Philip strongly urged him to assert himself and leave her. Of course he didn't but meekly followed her to London. I retired from the controversy for I felt certain that he was too bound up with her ever to leave her. He is very weak with her, although he abuses her to us and indeed often to her face he shouts abusive things, yet she will always win if she wants to; for she had ten times the physical vitality and force that he has, and always really dominates him, however much he may rebel and complain. He is by tradition and instinct faithful to a wife, and far too timid and sensitive to face life alone, for although he has the flaming ideas of a propagandist he

has neither knowledge of the world nor the calm assurance that carries conviction. He soon becomes disappointed, angry, fierce and intolerant at not being attended to, and after a frenzy of angry barks he turns with a drooping tail and seeks refuge in Frieda, his 'dark abode'.

'How odd the effect two human beings can have on each other. Two ingredients separate may be good and balanced but mixed together beget havoc and discord. I always remember these lines of Browning:

> Once I saw a chemist take a pinch of powder,
> Simple dust 'it seemed—and half unstop a phial.
> Out dropped harmless dew. "Mixed nothings make," quoth he,
> "Something." So they did. A thunderclap but louder,
> Lightning flash, but fiercer, put spectators' nerves to trial.
> Sure enough we learnt what was, imagined what might be!

'Frieda and Lawrence mixed certainly put spectators' nerves to trial, and it is easy to imagine what might be! How well the soothsayer warned Antony beware of Caesar:

> Stay not by his side.
> Thy Demon—that's thy spirit which keeps thee—is
> Noble, courageous, high, unmatchable,
> Where Caesar's is not. But near him thy angel
> Becomes a fear, as being o'erpower'd—therefore
> Make space enough between you.

'Poor Lawrence, what a distraught creature he is underneath; the constant friction and fighting with Frieda will wear his nerves out in time. I fear he will have to kill all his gentle tender side, so as to have peace with her, and in time he will adapt himself more and more to her, although subconsciously he will resent it. But he will never part from her, he is too moral, and is bound to her by some need of his nature.'

After they had gone, Frieda in a rage with me and with everybody and Lawrence crushed and unhappy, but following her like a whipped dog, I thought I should never see them again. She accused me, I found out afterwards, of having ignored and slighted her and of having a "soul mush" with Lawrence. I thought he would never dare speak to us again, but I was to learn that such scenes did not have the permanent effect on them that they would have on most people. With the Lawrences they are like violent mountain storms that rage with thunder and lightning and then pass, and in a few hours the sky is calm, serene and sunny, for a brief spell at least. I wrote to him about *The Rainbow* when it came out, and told him that I thought the second half was very fine, and as he had had no praise for it my letter was welcome and made the sun to shine. He had the belief that he could, as with a wave of his hand bring a revolution to pass in

England, and that his friends were but poor, craven laggards who were too lazy and unbelieving to bestir themselves, but the failure of *The Rainbow* made him realise that at this time there were no ears open to him. *The Rainbow* was suppressed as immoral. Philip did all he could in the House of Commons to get the ban removed, but without success. We lent our copy to Sir John Simon[9] and other influential men, who read it with eyes that greedily swept the pages for indecent passages. The suppression of this book was a great blow to poor Lawrence. It had been a long piece of work into which he had put all his energies, and he was at the moment very hard up. The suppression was due to a hysterical newspaper review by James Douglas[10] in a Sunday paper. In my Journal I find:

'I went up to London for the day and went to see the Lawrences at Hampstead, in the little house which they have taken. Frieda was awkward and rather shyly aggressive and ashamed like a child, but I ignored it and was friendly to her. We had a long talk and went a walk on the Heath. Lawrence said he must leave England, and go to a country that has a future before it, a country that is in the spring of its life. Here in England the autumn had set in, life is dead, the land dead, the people are dead sapless sticks. He feels he must leave before he goes dead too. He is determined to go off to America and write for Americans. I think he may be right to go, although I think his judgement is all wrong about England. Of course while the War goes on everything is horrible. But he may be right to go for himself. Youth, genius, has an instinct perhaps to save itself, to protect itself from the depression and contagion of death; and it will be better for him to go to fresh fields than to stay here bemoaning and wailing the decay of England, especially as his health is very bad, and there is the complication of Frieda being aggressively German.

'Lawrence has a passion to preach, to dominate. His preaching, I fear, is too remote from what men need now. He is too isolated, too remote from the trend of thought of those that he would sway and influence. He really is not a practical leader although very inspiring and stimulating to individuals who understand him and who are anxious to learn from him. Just now he is very excited about two young men that he has met; he thinks they will do great things; to hear him talk of them, one would imagine the future of England is in their hands. One is a poet who has been at the War and is now in hospital and whose nerves are very bad, Bob Nichols,[11] and the other is a musician, Philip Heseltine.[12] He says that I *must* know them. He is determined that we should all go out and join him in Florida and make a community there, or perhaps on an island in the Pacific. It doesn't attract me at all! I certainly see no reason to leave England. And I feel one ought to remain and put all one's energies into helping on things here. Lawrence is too impatient, he has not got the political instinct, which means that one must have endless patience, tolerance and wisdom. He is far too reckless and rapid in denunciation, and Frieda urges him on in his intolerant denunciations, and so he rushes about with one idea after another like an excited dog, barking and barking at an imaginary enemy, but he cannot put forward any solid ideas, and mere denunciations do no good'.

*   *   *

In November of this year 1915, Lawrence came again to Garsington, indeed he came several times before the end of the year, sometimes alone, sometimes with Frieda. The visits when he was alone were far the happiest for him and for us all, as he was then quiet and natural. He helped me plant new hedges, and purple irises . . . .

He loved the touch and the smell of the dark clay, and the manual labour was natural and calming to his over-troubled soul. On an earlier visit he had made up his mind that a little arbour would be nice in one corner of the garden. Wood, nails appeared in a moment and in a few hours it was firmly erected. Climbing roses were planted to cover it, and Lawrence gave orders to the roses to flower with all their essential and primitive Rose-Force as rapidly and abundantly as possible, and to raise themselves up from the dark earth into sunshine. The little arbour was always preserved and propped up for the sake of the man who planned and built it, much to the annoyance of others who thought it absurd and suburban.

In the evenings he would read to us poems, generally poems from Swinburne, or he would tell some story from his own life, making the characters often so comic, and kindly and real, that one felt one was taking part in the scenes he described. We also went into Oxford and looked at the colleges, and museums; he felt it all 'dead and useless', but he enjoyed very much looking at the old illumined missals and books in the Bodleian, and we pored over them enjoying the fun and their grotesqueness. I got the librarian to take them out of the cases for him to see, as he wanted to copy some. It was enchanting being with anyone so sympathetic—he had that wonderful child quality of excitement over small things as well as over great ones. I had seldom met anyone that I felt so lovable.

One wet day, we (Mademoiselle Juliette Baillot and Maria Nys, Julian[13] and the Gilbert Cannans) were all whirled into acting a play— Lawrence's magnetism made us all forget ourselves and we became the characters that Lawrence apportioned to us. He himself was Othello, in a large straw hat and a real Arab coat. It was the only time I ever saw him look beautiful. I well remember, even at the time, realising how happy, fresh and gay I felt. We had all been liberated from our self-consciousness, and had had one afternoon's perfect freedom and gaiety.

Another day he was absorbed in copying most beautifully a Persian miniature, which I think he gave to Mrs Cannan. Lawrence's vitality and presence seemed to make every moment of the day throb with its own intense life, so that whatever one did with him was right and perfect to do. At this moment the memory I have of these days makes me see how rare that feeling is—how seldom one can look back and relive scenes without some regret.

But such happy good times do not last. The horror of war grew worse and worse and reverberated in Lawrence and nearly drove him mad.

*   *   *

On December 3rd, 1915, I find the following entry:

'Lawrence and Frieda have been here again, and they brought with them Philip Heseltine, a musician, and Kouzoumdjian ('Michael Arlen'),[14] also an Indian called Sarawadi, who is at Oxford, and who is a friend of Heseltine. What strange creatures Lawrence and Frieda attract to themselves. He is enthusiastic about both Heseltine and Kouzoumdjian, but I don't feel attracted to them, indeed quite the reverse. Heseltine is tall and blonde, soft and so degenerate that he seems somehow corrupt. Kouzoumdjian is a fat dark-blooded tight-skinned Armenian Jew, and though Lawrence believes that he will be a great writer, I find it hard to believe. Obviously he has a certain vulgar sexual force, but he is very coarse-grained and conceited. I cannot sit in the room with them for long. He and Heseltine seem to pollute the atmosphere, and stifle me, and I have to escape from their presence—also I get very tired of the continual boasting of what they are going to do. They flatter Frieda and pay her more attention than they do Lawrence, so naturally they are both great geniuses in her eyes, and she is enthusiastic about them—they are going down to Cornwall when the Lawrences go there. I do not understand the Indian Sarawadi. He is extremely anti-English, but like all Indians quite foreign and remote, though he seems more substantial and self-confident than most of his race.

'Frieda is devilish, and she really is a wild beast, quite uncontrolled, cruel to Lawrence, and madly jealous if she thinks anyone esteems Lawrence more than her.'

When I wrote this about Kouzoumdjian I little thought that he would develop into the successful novelist 'Michael Arlen'. I have never met him again since this time, but I constantly wear a little yellow shawl that he sent me, as he remarked that I was fond of yellow. And much as I felt repelled by him at that time I expect he is a kind man. I have always heard that when Lawrence was ill and poor he pressed financial help upon him— which Lawrence refused.

These visits to Garsington seemed like a lull before the most stormy time in Lawrence's life. Frieda had begun to growl and paw the ground. She was very much annoyed that he and I had so much in common—politics, love of England, poetry—and she became violently jealous of what she thought was my influence over him. In a letter to me she said:

'I would not mind if you and he had an ordinary love-affair—what I hate is this "soul-mush".'

She became more and more infuriated that I was detached from her, and she saw that she didn't impress me. I find an entry in my Journal: 'Frieda is turning Lawrence against Bertie Russell, because Bertie doesn't admire and flatter her, so she has made Lawrence mistrust him. She is certainly a sister to Potiphar's wife. She is turning him against me, for she tells him that I have been rude and contemptuous of her, and did not treat her with enough respect when she was here. So now he is angry with me, and writes to me about it. I am very unhappy about it, but she is so outrageous that I cannot bring myself to eat humble pie to her. I wrote her a nice letter but she even complains of that, and answered that my letter was impudent and an insult.'

It was, I believe, about this time that my mother-in-law told me that a young man at Balliol wanted very much to come and see us, and wanted me to invite him out. She said he was related to some of her old Oxford friends, and that he had the charming name of Aldous. I accordingly wrote a polite little note to the young man, Aldous Huxley, to ask him out to luncheon on Sunday.

A very thin, very tall, delicate young man, with a very beautiful serious face arrived, dressed in a corduroy coat and cut breeches and stockings. His eyesight was very bad, which made him stoop in order to view things closely. He was rather silent and aloof, and I felt as he sat on during the afternoon that he was rather bored, for we happened to be alone that Sunday. But, whether bored or not, he soon became a frequent visitor, and converted himself into being a son of the house. For years one of the bedrooms at Garsington was known as Mr Huxley's room. He came and met Lawrence when he was with us, and I suggested that he should go and see him at Hampstead when he was there. I think he was puzzled and rather overcome, and perhaps scared, at Lawrence's quick and immediate approach, brushing away all preliminaries—vetting him in fact, putting him under his X-ray. I was amused to hear that Lawrence claimed him immediately as a disciple and asked him to join 'the Colony' that he was planning in Florida. I felt how miserable Aldous, with his fastidious reserve, his delicate and perhaps over-intellectual temperament, would be if he went.

NOTES

Lady Ottoline Morrell (1873–1938) was the daughter of Lieutenant-General Arthur Cavendish-Bentinck of Welbeck Abbey, Nottinghamshire; her mother was a half-sister of the Duke of Portland. In 1902 she married Philip Morrell, MP, and subsequently became hostess to a brilliant circle of writers, artists and intellectuals at Garsington Manor, Oxfordshire, and in London.

1. *Sons and Lovers* and *The White Peacock*.
2. A popular novelist whose wife had previously been married to J. M. Barrie. Mark Gertler was staying with the Cannans, and the Middleton Murrys lived nearby.

3. The Lawrences lived in a cottage near Chesham in Buckinghamshire from August 1914 to January 1915; the Cannans lived at a neighbouring village.

4. Lady Ottoline's dating of her meeting with Lawrence must be inaccurate. On 3 January 1915 Lawrence wrote to her of visiting her 'again' (*Letters*, p. 213). By the end of January the Lawrences were living at Greatham (see note 5 below); Lawrence wrote to Lady Ottoline from there on 30 January (*Letters*, pp. 217–19), and she did in fact visit them there on 1 February (Moore, p. 180).

5. The village in Sussex where the Lawrences lived from January to July 1915.

6. Later Lord and Lady Glenavy. They met Lawrence in the summer of 1913 and were friends of the Murrys. Gordon Campbell was a witness at Lawrence's marriage ceremony.

7. Maria Nys, a Belgian refugee who later married Aldous Huxley.

8. Ottoline told me how, when they were quarrelling, she would sometimes draw herself up and say, 'Do not forget, Lorenzo, I am a baroness!' [Note by R. Gathorne-Hardy.]

9. The Home Secretary. Philip Morrell asked questions in the House of Commons on 18 November and 1 December 1915 concerning the banning of *The Rainbow*. In reply Simon explained that the action against the novel had been taken under the provisions of the Obscene Publications Act of 1857 (see Moore, p. 204).

10. A journalist who made a point of attacking what he believed to be dangerously immoral books. He was the prime cause of Radclyffe Hall's *The Well of Loneliness* being suppressed. He declared that he would rather give strychnine to a young person than this book. 'Strychnine,' he added, 'kills bodies. This book will kill souls.' [Note by Robert Gathorne-Hardy.]

11. Robert Nichols, poet and dramatist, met Lawrence in 1915 and again in 1929.

12. English composer, usually known by his pseudonym, 'Peter Warlock'. He met Lawrence in 1915 and lived near him in Cornwall in 1916–17. Lawrence wrote to J. Middleton Murry on 4 December 1915, 'I have found a nice man called Heseltine who will come to Florida' (*Letters*, p. 292). He portrayed him as Halliday in *Women in Love*.

13. Lady Ottoline's daughter.

14. 'Michael Arlen' was the pseudonym of Dikran Kouyoumdjian (usual spelling), a popular novelist born in Bulgaria. He settled in England and had a considerable success with *The Green Hat* (1924).

In Duncan Grant's Studio*

DAVID GARNETT

On my first visit to her house in Bedford Square Lady Ottoline[1] had asked

* From *The Flowers of the Forest* (London: Chatto & Windus, 1955) pp. 33, 34–7.

me about D. H. Lawrence whom she wanted to meet and I promised to introduce him to her next time he was in London. But before I was able to arrange it they had met and, when I went in to dinner the following Thursday, I found that Ottoline had placed me next to Frieda. On the opposite side of the table Lawrence was talking to E. M. Forster.[2] I had first met Morgan, as I afterwards learned to call him, when I was a boy of fifteen and he had come to tea with my parents in our workman's flat in Hampstead. . . .

After dinner we soon followed the ladies upstairs to the drawing-room and listened to a Mozart quintet, and after the music there was dancing. Duncan[3] was one of those who had joined the party after dinner and both he and I met with misfortunes that evening. I was dancing with a lively little Slade student with dark blue eyes, bright red cheeks and a small round head covered with short dark curls, called Barbara Hiles. She had arrived after dinner with Gertler[4] and Carrington.[5] It was Barbara's pretty little head that was my undoing, for after improvising a violent pirouette, she leapt into the air like Nijinsky and struck me full in the eye with the top of it and also made me bite my tongue severely. That was the end of my dancing for the evening. As she whirled happily away with her next partner, I watched, out of the other eye, Duncan dancing with Ottoline who was wearing a Spanish dress with a high comb and a lace mantilla. They were improvising free steps when Duncan caught his toe in her train, clutched her, and both of them lost their balance and crashed to the floor. Ottoline, fortunately, was unhurt, but Duncan was shaken and bruised.

*   *   *

Ottoline had talked to Lawrence about Duncan's pictures and, as Lawrence asked to see some of them, Duncan invited him and Frieda and E. M. Forster to tea in his studio the following afternoon. Morgan was the first to arrive. I came next, a woeful spectacle, as I had a very bad black eye. Then came the Lawrences. While we drank a cup of tea, Duncan brought out his pictures. On one very large canvas there was a green giant kneeling and overshadowing St Paul's Cathedral. The green giant was the spiritual form of Sir Christopher Wren. Then came an astonishingly good portrait of Ottoline—a three-quarter view of her head. Round the neck Duncan had pinned a string of Woolworth pearls. Lawrence had done a little painting himself and had his own ideas about the art. He was, indeed, to take up painting again and have his rather washy indefinite nudes seized by the police and destroyed by the order of a London magistrate.[6] But Mr Mead, on the bench in Marlborough Street, was not much stupider than Lawrence himself that afternoon. We all sat in silence as Duncan brought out one picture after another. Then Lawrence rose to his feet—a bad sign—and walking up and down the studio, began to explain to Duncan what was wrong with his painting. It was not simply that the pictures

themselves were bad—hopelessly bad—but they were worthless because
Duncan was full of the wrong ideas. He was barking up the wrong tree and
would have to learn to approach his subjects in a completely different
frame of mind if he wanted ever to become an artist.

Soon after Lawrence's first words, Morgan made some gentle remark
about catching the train to Weybridge and faded out of the studio.
Lawrence warmed to his subject and went on speaking with absolute
frankness, having decided that it was better to open Duncan's eyes and tell
him the truth. But as he talked he held his head on one side, as though in
pain, and looked more at the floor than at the pictures. Frieda,
unfortunately, was aware both of Duncan's feelings and of mine. Each time
that Duncan rose in silence and brought out another picture, she
exclaimed: 'Ah, Lorenzo! I like this one so much better! It is beautiful!' Her
interventions were ignored by both sides. Lawrence would give a wincing
glance at the new picture and discover in it new material for his argument.
Finally, in despair, Duncan brought out a long band of green cotton on two
rollers. I stood and held one roller vertically and unwound while, standing
a couple of yards away, Duncan wound up the other, and a series of
supposedly related, abstract shapes was displayed before our disgusted
visitors. That was the worst of all.

Before Lawrence had reached his peroration, there was a ring at the bell
and the lecture was held up while Duncan went down and returned with
an uninvited figure—a dark Russian Jew called Koteliansky[7]—who had
come to pick up Lawrence and Frieda with whom he had arranged to
spend the evening. He sat down and the lecture was resumed. Lawrence
paced uneasily up and down looking at the floor. Koteliansky sat black and
silent; Frieda occasionally burst out: 'But no, Lorenzo! We liked that
portrait so much!'

Duncan himself appeared to have developed toothache and sat with his
hands on his knees, rocking himself gently in his chair, not attempting a
word in defence of his works. Everything, however, has an end, and at last
Lawrence, feeling he had done his good deed for the day, said that they
must be going. Frieda and Koteliansky rose and followed and Duncan
showed them down the dimly lit stairs and ushered them politely out into
the foggy night. I stayed in the studio. The blast of Lawrence's attack had
been directed at Duncan, who no doubt felt that he had suffered an
unexpected assault, but he had lost nothing. I knew that the hope I had
nursed of happy hours with them both was vain. My two friends would
never understand each other.

When Duncan came back, I did not make any attempt to console him in
the style of Frieda. We stacked the canvases back against the walls and
washed up the cups and saucers in silence. Next day Lawrence who was
living in Sussex at a cottage lent him by Alice Meynell,[8] wrote [to Lady
Ottoline: see *Letters*, pp. 215–16].

From that spate of verbiage one might think that Lawrence was refuting ideas that Duncan had put forward. But I was a witness to the fact that Duncan had behaved like Tar-Baby while Lawrence had worked himself up into a passion like Brer Rabbit. In his letter, Lawrence was belabouring a figment of his imagination, as well as pouring out a lot of nonsense. What would an abstract statement of the instances of Rembrandt, Corot, Goya and Manet look like?

It seems certain that a memory of the visit to Duncan's studio inspired the passage at the end of Chapter xviii of *Lady Chatterley's Lover*. Mellors, the gamekeeper hero (Lawrence), is taken to the studio of Duncan Forbes, 'a dark-skinned taciturn Hamlet of a fellow with straight black hair and weird Celtic conceit of himself'. 'His art was all tubes and valves and spirals and strange colours, ultra-modern, yet with a certain power, even a certain purity of form and tone: only Mellors thought it cruel and repellent.'

NOTES

For a note on David Garnett see p. 94. The meetings described in the above extracts seem to have taken place on 25 and 26 January 1915.

1. See p. 108.
2. See p. 121.
3. Duncan Grant (born 1885), painter, met Lawrence in 1915.
4. Mark Gertler (1892–1939), painter, met Lawrence in 1914.
5. See p. 203.
6. In 1929.
7. Samuel Koteliansky (often known as 'Kot') (1882–1955). Of Russian birth, he settled in England and translated Russian authors into English. He met Lawrence in 1914.
8. Error for Viola Meynell (see p. 64); strictly speaking, however, the cottage belonged to Wilfrid Meynell, Viola's father.

A 'Brief and Hectic' Friendship*

BERTRAND RUSSELL

My acquaintance with Lawrence was brief and hectic, lasting altogether

* From *The Autobiography of Bertrand Russell*, vol. ii: *1914–1944* (London: Allen & Unwin, 1968) pp. 10–16, 59–61.

about a year. We were brought together by Ottoline, who admired us both and made us think that we ought to admire each other. Pacifism had produced in me a mood of bitter rebellion, and I found Lawrence equally full of rebellion. This made us think, at first, that there was a considerable measure of agreement between us, and it was only gradually that we discovered that we differed from each other more than either differed from the Kaiser.

There were in Lawrence at that time two attitudes to the war: on the one hand, he could not be whole-heartedly patriotic, because his wife was German; but on the other hand, he had such a hatred of mankind that he tended to think both sides must be right in so far as they hated each other. As I came to know these attitudes, I realised that neither was one with which I could sympathise. Awareness of our differences, however, was gradual on both sides, and at first all went merry as a marriage bell. I invited him to visit me at Cambridge and introduced him to Keynes[1] and a number of other people. He hated them all with a passionate hatred and said they were 'dead, dead, dead'. For a time I thought he might be right. I liked Lawrence's fire, I liked the energy and passion of his feelings, I liked his belief that something very fundamental was needed to put the world right. I agreed with him in thinking that politics could not be divorced from individual psychology. I felt him to be a man of a certain imaginative genius, and, at first, when I felt inclined to disagree with him, I thought that perhaps his insight into human nature was deeper than mine. It was only gradually that I came to feel him a positive force for evil and that he came to have the same feeling about me.

I was at this time preparing the course of lectures which was afterwards published as *Principles of Social Reconstruction*.[2] He, also, wanted to lecture, and for a time it seemed possible that there might be some sort of loose collaboration between us. We exchanged a number of letters, of which mine are lost but his have been published. In his letters the gradual awareness of the consciousness of our fundamental disagreements can be traced. I was a firm believer in democracy, whereas he had developed the whole philosophy of Fascism before the politicians had thought of it.

I don't believe [he wrote] in democratic control. I think the working man is fit to elect governors or overseers for his immediate circumstances, but for no more. You must utterly revise the electorate. The working man shall elect superiors for the things that concern him immediately, no more. From the other classes, as they rise, shall be elected the higher governors. The thing must culminate in one real head, as every organic thing must—no foolish republic with foolish presidents, but an elected King, something like Julius Caesar.[3]

He, of course, in his imagination, supposed that when a dictatorship was established he would be the Julius Caesar. This was part of the dream-like quality of all his thinking. He never let himself bump into reality. He would go into long tirades about how one must proclaim 'the Truth' to the multitude, and he seemed to have no doubt that the multitude would listen. I asked him what method he was going to adopt. Would he put his political philosophy into a book? No: in our corrupt society the written word is always a lie. Would he go into Hyde Park and proclaim 'the Truth' from a soap box? No: that would be far too dangerous (odd streaks of prudence emerged in him from time to time). Well, I said, what would you do? At this point he would change the subject.

Gradually I discovered that he had no real wish to make the world better, but only to indulge in eloquent soliloquy about how bad it was. If anybody overheard the soliloquies, so much the better, but they were designed at most to produce a little faithful band of disciples who could sit in the deserts of New Mexico and feel holy. All this was conveyed to me in the language of a Fascist dictator as what I *must* preach, the 'must' having thirteen underlinings.

His letters grew gradually more hostile. He wrote,

What's the good of living as you do anyway? I don't believe your lectures *are* good. They are nearly over, aren't they? What's the good of sticking in the damned ship and haranguing the merchant pilgrims in their own language? Why don't you drop overboard? Why don't you clear out of the whole show? One must be an outlaw these days, not a teacher or preacher.[4]

This seemed to me mere rhetoric. I was becoming more of an outlaw than he ever was and I could not quite see his ground of complaint against me. He phrased his complaint in different ways at different times. On another occasion he wrote:

Do stop working and writing altogether and become a creature instead of a mechanical instrument. Do clear out of the whole social ship. Do for your very pride's sake become a mere nothing, a mole, a creature that feels its way and doesn't think. Do for heavens sake be a baby, and not a savant any more. Don't *do* anything more—but for heavens sake begin to *be*—Start at the very beginning and be a perfect baby: in the name of courage.

Oh, and I want to ask you, when you make your will, do leave me enough to live on. I want you to live for ever. But I want you to make me in some part your heir.[5]

The only difficulty with this programme was that if I adopted it I should have nothing to leave.

He had a mystical philosophy of 'blood' which I disliked.

There is [he said] another seat of consciousness than the brain and nerves. There is a blood-consciousness which exists in us independently of the ordinary mental consciousness. One lives, knows and has one's being in the blood, without any reference to nerves and brain. This is one half of life belonging to the darkness. When I take a woman, then the blood-percept is supreme. My blood-knowing is overwhelming. We should realise that we have a blood-being, a blood-consciousness, a blood-soul complete and apart from a mental and nerve consciousness.

This seemed to me frankly rubbish, and I rejected it vehemently, though I did not then know that it led straight to Auschwitz.

He always got into a fury if one suggested that anybody could possibly have kindly feelings towards anybody else, and when I objected to war because of the suffering that it causes, he accused me of hypocrisy.

It isn't in the least true that you, your basic self, want ultimate peace. You are satisfying in an indirect, false way your lust to jab and strike. Either satisfy it in a direct and honourable way, saying 'I hate you all, liars and swine, and am out to set upon you,' or stick to mathematics, where you can be true—But to come as the angel of peace—no, I prefer Tirpitz[6] a thousand times in that role.

I find it difficult now to understand the devastating effect that this letter had upon me. I was inclined to believe that he had some insight denied to me, and when he said that my pacifism was rooted in blood-lust I supposed he must be right. For twenty-four hours I thought that I was not fit to live and contemplated suicide. But at the end of that time, a healthier reaction set in, and I decided to have done with such morbidness. When he said that I *must* preach his doctrines and not mine I rebelled, and told him to remember that he was no longer a schoolmaster and I was not his pupil. He had written, 'The enemy of all mankind you are, full of the lust of enmity. It is *not* a hatred of falsehood which inspires you, it is the hatred of people of flesh and blood, it is a perverted mental blood-lust. Why don't you own it? Let us become strangers again. I think it is better.' I thought so too. But he found a pleasure in denouncing me and continued for some months to write letters containing sufficient friendliness to keep the correspondence alive. In the end, it faded away without any dramatic termination.

Lawrence, though most people did not realise it, was his wife's mouthpiece. He had the eloquence, but she had the ideas. She used to spend part of every summer in a colony of Austrian Freudians at a time when psychoanalysis was little known in England. Somehow, she imbibed prematurely the ideas afterwards developed by Mussolini and Hitler, and these ideas she transmitted to Lawrence, shall we say, by blood-consciousness. Lawrence was an essentially timid man who tried to conceal his timidity by bluster. His wife was not timid, and her denunciations have the character of thunder, not of bluster. Under her wing he felt comparatively safe. Like Marx, he had a snobbish pride in having married a German aristocrat, and in *Lady Chatterley* he dressed her up marvellously. His thought was a mass of self-deception masquerading as stark realism. His descriptive powers were remarkable, but his ideas cannot be too soon forgotten.

What at first attracted me to Lawrence was a certain dynamic quality and a habit of challenging assumptions that one is apt to take for granted. I was already accustomed to being accused of undue slavery to reason, and I thought perhaps that he could give me a vivifying dose of unreason. I did in fact acquire a certain stimulus from him, and I think the book that I wrote in spite of his blasts of denunciation was better than it would have been if I had not known him.

But this is not to say that there was anything good in his ideas. I do not think in retrospect that they had any merit whatever. They were the ideas of a sensitive would-be despot who got angry with the world because it would not instantly obey. When he realised that other people existed, he hated them. But most of the time he lived in a solitary world of his own imaginings, peopled by phantoms as fierce as he wished them to be. His excessive emphasis on sex was due to the fact that in sex alone he was compelled to admit that he was not the only human being in the universe. But it was so painful that he conceived of sex relations as a perpetual fight in which each is attempting to destroy the other.

The world between the wars was attracted to madness. Of this attraction Nazism was the most emphatic expression. Lawrence was a suitable exponent of this cult of insanity. I am not sure whether the cold inhuman sanity of Stalin's Kremlin was any improvement.

*   *   *

[July 1915] Lawrence took up my time from morning till 10.30, so I couldn't write yesterday. We had a terrific argument but not a disastrous one. He attacks me for various things that I don't feel to blame about—chiefly, in effect, for having a scientific temper and a respect for fact. I will send you his written comments on my syllabus. I shall be glad to know what you think of them. He took me to see a Russian Jew, Koteliansky,[7] and [Middleton] Murry and Mrs Murry[8]—they were all sitting together in a bare office high up next door to the Holborn Restaurant, with the windows shut, smoking Russian cigarettes without a moment's intermission, idle and cynical. I thought Murry *beastly* and the whole atmosphere of the three dead and putrefying.

Then we went to the Zoo—the baboon gave me much cynical satisfaction: he looked long and deliberately at everybody, and then slowly showed his teeth and snarled, with inconceivable hatred and disgust. Swift would have loved him. Then we went up to Hampstead, to the Radfords, where Mrs Lawrence was staying. I was dead tired after the first hour, as we began arguing at once. I told Lawrence that I thought we ought to be independent of each other, at any rate at first, and not try to start a school. When he talks politics he seems to me so wild that I could not formally work with him. I hope he won't be hurt. He did not seem to be, as I put it very carefully. He is undisciplined in thought, and mistakes his wishes for facts. He is also muddleheaded. He says 'facts' are quite unimportant, only 'truths' matter. London is a 'fact' not a 'truth'. But he wants London pulled down. I tried to make him see that that would be absurd if London were unimportant, but he kept reiterating that London doesn't really exist, and that he could easily make people see it doesn't, and then they would pull it down. He was so confident of his powers of persuasion that I challenged him to come to Trafalgar Square at once and begin preaching. That brought him to earth and he began to shuffle. His attitude is a little mad and not quite honest, or at least very muddled. He has not learnt the lesson of individual impotence. And he regards all my attempts to make him acknowledge facts as mere timidity, lack of courage to think boldly, self-indulgence in pessimism. When one gets a glimmer of the facts into his head, as I did at last, he gets discouraged, and says he will go to the South Sea Islands, and bask in the sun with six native wives. He is tough work. The trouble with him is a tendency to mad exaggeration.

[July 1915, Tuesday] Yes, the day Lawrence was with me was horrid. I got filled with despair, and just counting the moments till it was ended. Partly that was due to liver, but not wholly. Lawrence is very like Shelley—just as fine, but with a similar impatience of fact. The revolution he hopes for is just like Shelley's prophecy of banded anarchs fleeing while the people celebrate a feast of love. His psychology of people is amazingly good up to a point, but at a certain point he gets misled by love of violent colouring.

NOTES

Bertrand Russell, later Earl Russell (1872–1970), was a mathematician and philosopher. He met Lawrence in 1915 through Lady Ottoline Morrell. In 1916 he lost his lectureship at Trinity College, Cambridge, on account of his opposition to the war.

   Lawrence visited Russell in Cambridge on 6 and 7 March 1915. Before the visit he had written to Russell, 'I feel frightfully important coming to Cambridge—quite momentous the occasion is to me. I don't want to be horribly impressed and intimidated, but am afraid I may be'—2 March 1915, in *The Collected Letters of D. H. Lawrence*, ed. Harry T. Moore (New York: Viking Press, 1962) I, pp. 327–8 (Lawrence's letters to Russell are not included in Huxley's edition of the *Letters*). Dining in hall, he sat next to the philosopher G. E. Moore, but conversation between them did not flourish; he seems to have got on rather better with the mathematician G. H. Hardy. The next morning J. M. Keynes was present at breakfast in Russell's rooms in Nevile's Court (see the next extract). On this occasion Lawrence was in a black mood and he wrote to Russell afterwards of his hatred for the Cambridge ethos: 'It is true Cambridge made me very black and down. I cannot bear its smell of rottenness, marsh-stagnancy. I get a melancholic malaria. How can so sick people rise up? They must die first'—(?) 19 March 1915, in *Collected Letters*, I, p. 330.

Russell's account in his autobiography, given above, is reprinted with minor revisions from *Harper's Magazine*, CCVI (Feb 1953) pp. 93–5. Part of the same material also appeared in Russell's *Portraits from Memory and Other Essays* (London: Allen & Unwin, 1956) and in *The Listener*, XLVIII (24 July 1952), pp. 135–6. His account provoked a reply from Mrs Frieda Ravagli (formerly Frieda Lawrence), who in a letter to *Harper's Magazine*, CCVI (Apr 1953) pp. 22–3 repudiates Russell's 'calling Lawrence an exponent of Nazism' and points out that Lawrence was 'a raw twenty-six' when he met Russell, who was already a well-known figure. (In 1915, however, Lawrence had attributed to Russell 'the inexperience of youth': see *Letters*, p. 235.)

1. See p. 120.
2. Published in 1915.
3. Letter from Lawrence to Russell, 26 July 1915, in Moore's *Collected Letters*, I, p. 355.
4. Letter of (?) 19 February 1916, ibid., I, pp. 432–3.
5. Ibid., p. 433.
6. Alfred von Tirpitz, German naval commander responsible for submarine warfare in the First World War.
7. See p. 112.
8. See p. 133.

Lawrence in Cambridge*

J. M. KEYNES

I can visualise very clearly the scene of my meeting with D. H. Lawrence. . . . But unfortunately I cannot remember any fragments of what was said, though I retain some faint remains of what was felt.

It was a breakfast party given by Bertie Russell in his rooms in Nevile's Court.[1] There were only the three of us there. I fancy that Lawrence had been staying with Bertie and that there had been some meeting or party the night before, at which Lawrence had been facing Cambridge. Probably he

* From 'My Early Beliefs', *Two Memoirs* (London: Hart-Davis, 1949) pp. 78–80, 103.

had not enjoyed it. My memory is that he was morose from the outset and said very little, apart from indefinite expressions of irritable dissent, all the morning. Most of the talk was between Bertie and me, and I haven't the faintest recollection of what it was about. But it was not the sort of conversation we should have had if we had been alone. It was *at* Lawrence and with the intention, largely unsuccessful, of getting him to participate. We sat round the fireplace with the sofa drawn across. Lawrence sat on the right-hand side in rather a crouching position with his head down. Bertie stood up by the fireplace, as I think I did, too, from time to time. I came away feeling that the party had been a failure and that we had failed to establish contact, but with no other particular impression. You know the sort of situation when two familiar friends talk *at* a visitor. I had never seen him before, and I never saw him again. Many years later he recorded in a letter, which is printed in his published correspondence, that I was the only member of Bloomsbury who had supported him by subscribing for *Lady Chatterley's Lover*.[2]

That is all I *remember*. But Bunny's[3] story suggests some inferences to me. In the passage of his life which Bunny has described I think that Lawrence was influenced by two causes of emotional disturbance. One of them centred round Ottoline.[4] As always, Ottoline was keeping more than one world. Except for Bertie, the Cambridge and Bloomsbury world was only just beginning to hold her. Lawrence, Gertler,[5] Carrington[6] were a different strand in her furbelows. Lawrence was jealous of the other lot; and Cambridge rationalism and cynicism, then at their height, were, of course, repulsive to him. Bertie gave him what must have been, I think, his first glimpse of Cambridge. It overwhelmed, attracted and repulsed him— which was the other emotional disturbance. It was obviously a civilisation, and not less obviously uncomfortable and unattainable for him—very repulsive and very attractive. Now Bunny had come into his life quite independently, neither through Ottoline nor from Cambridge and Bloomsbury; he was evidently very fond of Bunny; and when he saw *him* being seduced by Cambridge, he was yet more jealous, just as he was jealous of Ottoline's new leanings that way. And jealousy apart, it is impossible to imagine moods more antagonistic than those of Lawrence and of pre-war Cambridge.

But when all that has been said, was there something true and right in what Lawrence felt? There generally was. His reactions were incomplete and unfair, but they were not usually baseless. I have said that I have forgotten what the conversation was about. But I expect it was pretty brittle stuff—not so brittle as Frankie Birrell's[7]—but pretty brittle all the same. And although it was silly to take it, or to estimate it, at its face value, did the way of responding to life which lay behind it lack something important? Lawrence was oblivious of anything valuable it may have offered—it was a *lack* that he was violently apprehending. . . .

If, therefore, I altogether ignore our merits—our charm, our intelligence, our unworldliness, our affection—I can see us as water-spiders, gracefully skimming, as light and reasonable as air, the surface of the stream without any contact at all with the eddies and currents underneath. And if I imagine us as coming under the observation of Lawrence's ignorant, jealous, irritable, hostile eyes, what a combination of qualities we offered to arouse his passionate distaste; this thin rationalism skipping on the crust of the lava, ignoring both the reality and the value of the vulgar passions, joined to libertinism and comprehensive irreverence, too clever by half for such an earthy character as Bunny, seducing with its intellectual *chic* such a portent as Ottoline, a regular skin-poison. All this was very unfair to poor, silly, well-meaning us. But that is why I say that there may have *been* just a grain of truth when Lawrence said in 1914 that we were 'done for'.[8]

NOTES

John Maynard Keynes, later Lord Keynes (1883–1946), economist. He was Fellow of King's College, Cambridge; served in the Treasury, 1915–19; author of *Economic Consequences of the Peace* (1919). The memoir from which the above extract is taken was written in 1938. David Garnett states that 'Keynes was one of my friends whom Lawrence most disliked' (*Two Memoirs*, p. 75). Soon after the meeting described here, Lawrence wrote to Garnett: 'when I saw Keynes that morning in Cambridge it was one of the crises of my life. It sent me mad with misery and hostility and rage . . . ' (letter of 19 April 1915, quoted in *Two Memoirs*, p. 77; not included in either of the standard collections of Lawrence's letters). See also F. R. Leavis, 'Keynes, Lawrence and Cambridge', *The Common Pursuit* (London: Chatto & Windus, 1952) pp. 255–60.

1. In Trinity College.
2. *Letters*, p. 728. The accuracy of Lawrence's statement was disputed by Clive Bell (Nehls, I, pp. 574–5).
3. Nickname of David Garnett (see p. 94).
4. Lady Ottoline Morrell (see p. 105).
5. See p. 112, n.4.
6. See p. 203.
7. Francis Birrell (1889–1935), son of Augustine Birrell and friend of David Garnett. For a further impression of Birrell a few weeks later, see *Letters*, pp. 223–4.
8. In a letter to David Garnett dated 19 April 1915 Lawrence wrote, 'You must leave these friends, these beetles. Birrell and Duncan Grant are done for forever. Keynes I am not sure...' (quoted in *Flowers of the Forest*, p. 54; the letter is not included in either of the major collections of Lawrence's letters). Birrell and Grant had spent the previous weekend with Lawrence.

'A Vivid Impression' *

E. M. FORSTER

. . . it was then or about then—that is to say, in the spring of 1915—that I met him three or four times. I did not know him well, or meet him again subsequently, but he leaves a vivid impression—so quick with his fingers and alive in his spirit, so radiant and sensitive, so sure that if we all set out at once for one of the South Sea Islands we should found a perfect community there which would regenerate the world. Shelley[1] must have been a little like that, but Lawrence was a rougher, tougher proposition than Shelley; there is a vein of cruelty in him, and though he did beat his wings against society in vain, he was ineffectual as a bird of prey rather than as an angel.

NOTES

E. M. Forster (1879–1970), novelist, met Lawrence in January 1915 at a dinner-party given for the latter by Lady Ottoline Morrell, and described him in a letter to Forrest Reid a few days later as 'a sandy haired passionate Nibelung'—quoted in P. N. Furbank, *E. M. Forster: A Life*, II (London: Secker & Warburg, 1978) p. 5. (See also pp. 4–13 of the same volume for a detailed account of Forster's short-lived relationship with Lawrence.) They exchanged letters and books, and Forster visited the Lawrences at Greatham, but the two writers soon quarrelled. Forster referred to Lawrence's work in his *Aspects of the Novel* (1927), and he came magnificently to Lawrence's defence after the publication of some of the obituary notices (see his letters to the *Nation and Athenaeum*, 29 Mar 12 and 26 Apr 1930). Thirty years later Forster appeared as a witness for the defence in the celebrated *Lady Chatterley* trial at the Old Bailey, when Penguin Books were prosecuted for publishing the unexpurgated version of Lawrence's novel.

1. For a similar comparison, see p. 117 above.

* From 'D. H. Lawrence', *The Listener*, III (30 Apr 1930) p. 745; originally broadcast as a talk by the BBC on 16 April 1930.

'The Florida Scheme' *

ALDOUS HUXLEY

To those who knew Lawrence, not *why*, but *that* he was what he happened to be, is the important fact. I remember very clearly my first meeting with him. The place was London, the time 1915. But Lawrence's passionate talk was of the geographically remote and of the personally very near. Of the horrors in the middle distance—war, winter, the town—he would not speak. For he was on the point, so he imagined, of setting off to Florida[1]—to Florida, where he was going to plant that colony of escape, of which up to the last he never ceased to dream. Sometimes the name and site of this seed of a happier and different world were purely fanciful. It was called Rananim,[2] for example, and was an island like Prospero's. Sometimes it had its place on the map and its name was Florida, Cornwall, Sicily, Mexico and again, for a time, the English countryside. That wintry afternoon in 1915 it was Florida. Before tea was over he asked me if I would join the colony, and though I was an intellectually cautious young man, not at all inclined to enthusiasms, though Lawrence had startled and embarrassed me with sincerities of a kind to which my upbringing had not accustomed me, I answered yes.

Fortunately, no doubt, the Florida scheme fell through. Cities of God have always crumbled; and Lawrence's city—his village, rather, for he hated cities—his Village of the Dark God would doubtless have disintegrated like all the rest. It was better that it should have remained, as it was always to remain, a project and a hope. And I knew this even as I said I would join the colony. But there was something about Lawrence which made such knowledge, when one was in his presence, curiously irrelevant. He might propose impracticable schemes, he might say or write things that were demonstrably incorrect or even, on occasion (as when he talked about science), absurd. But to a very considerable extent it didn't matter. What mattered was always Lawrence himself, was the fire that burned within him, that glowed with so strange and marvellous a radiance in almost all he wrote.

---

* From the Introduction to *Letters*, pp. xviii–xix.

NOTES

Aldous Huxley (1894–1963), the son of Leonard Huxley and brother of Julian Huxley, was a prolific and versatile writer, best known as novelist and essayist. He met Lawrence in December 1915; a few days later Lawrence wrote to Lady Ottoline Morrell, 'I liked Huxley *very* much. He will come to Florida' (*Letters*, p. 298). At about the same time Huxley wrote to his brother, who was in America:

> What if I came next year, D[eo] V[olente] and W[eather] P[ermitting] of course, to visit your transatlantic Home . . . . Furthermore, there is a good man going to Florida, one D. H. Lawrence, a novelist and poet and genius...whose recent work *The Rainbow* was regrettably burnt by the common hangman for obscenity, supposed by the magistrate who had not read it to be subversive to England, Home and Duty...well, well, this good man, who impresses me as a good man more than most proposes, how unwisely soever it may appear, to go to the deserts of Florida there, with one Armenian ['Michael Arlen'], one German wife and, problematically, one young woman called Dorothy Warren, to found a sort of unanimist colony. The purposes of which are to await a sort of Pentecostal inspiration of new life, which, whether it will come is another question. But Lawrence is a great man, and as he finds the world too destructive for his taste, he must, I suppose be allowed to get out of it to some place where he can construct freely and where, by a unanimous process, the rest of his young colony, might do the same. The gist of all of which is that when, and if, I go and see you, I shall very likely go and see him also, to spend, perhaps, a little while in his eremitic colony...which, I am sure, would be quite particularly medicinal to my soul. (*Letters of Aldous Huxley*, ed. Grover Smith [London: Chatto & Windus, 1969] p. 88)

Their real friendship, however, began late in 1926. In Florence, Huxley 'passed some very delightful hours with D. H. Lawrence, whom I like so much' (*Letters of Aldous Huxley*, p. 275). He saw a good deal of Lawrence in 1926–30, and was with him when he died (see below, pp. 289–91).

The character of Rampion in Huxley's novel *Point Counter Point* (1928) is based on Lawrence. In a letter Huxley wrote that 'Rampion is just some of Lawrence's notions on legs' (*Letters of Aldous Huxley*, p. 340). Lawrence himself said that 'your Rampion is the most boring character in the book—a gas-bag' (*Letters*, p. 758).

1. According to Murry (*Reminiscences*, p. 73), Lawrence planned to sail in December 1915 but was unable to obtain a passport.

2. The word was taken from a Hebrew chant which Lawrence learned from his friend Koteliansky (see p. 112) and was used to signify a colony of chosen spirits which he hoped to found in some part of the world (see *Letters*, pp. 221, 291). David Daiches has suggested that in coining the word Lawrence was incorrectly recalling Koteliansky's chanting of the Hebrew words which open Psalm 23; this suggestion was confirmed by Murry (*Times Literary Supplement*, 6 Jan 1956, p.7; 3 Feb 1956, p. 69).

'A Judge of Character' *

JOHN COURNOS

I met D. H. Lawrence for the first time at the Aldingtons'[1] flat in Hampstead. Lawrence also lived in Hampstead, in the so-called Vale of Health. He was in a perverse mood, for when I was introduced, HD[2] or Richard—I forget which—asked Lawrence for politeness's sake if he had read my translations of Sologub.[3] Yes, he had, and he did not think much of Sologub. Nothing wrong in that. But he said it rather truculently, as though it were intended as a reflection on me. He left after issuing an invitation to visit him the following Sunday. I stayed away. The 'joke' of it was that he immediately asked the Aldingtons why I didn't come. They gave some excuse about my being busy, but he waved it aside with the words: 'I knew he wouldn't come! I knew it!' That interested me and amused me. It proved to me that he was aware of his own truculence, which was perhaps even deliberate. Again, it proved what a judge of character he was thus quickly to gauge the measure of my pride. Lawrence had almost a sixth sense about people. In the Aldington apartment he saw a woman I know well cross the room, and though he never met her before he remarked after she left that here was a woman who was unhappy with her husband. She was, in fact; how did he know? Yet she was a suave woman who knew how to conceal her emotions.

I met Lawrence again, however, a little later, and he was quite friendly. I liked the way he poised his head to the side, like a bird, when he laughed as he gave utterance to a satirical remark. Still later in the war I saw him once more, a strangely morose, brooding figure, silent and sulky, shut in within himself, and emanating waves of blackest despair. He was happier, and friendlier too, when I met him again long after the war in a train between Assisi and Perugia, when we agreed to meet in Florence. There he acted his most charming self toward me and my wife; and he went to an infinite amount of trouble to procure one of his books which he wished my wife to have.

* From *Autobiography* (New York: Putnam, 1935) pp. 283–4.

NOTES

John Cournos was an American author and journalist who first met Lawrence late in 1915.
1. On Richard Aldington, see p. 225.
2. Hilda Doolittle, the American Imagist poet who wrote under the initials 'HD', had married Aldington in 1913.
3. Russian Poet.

Sussex and Cornwall*

JOHN MIDDLETON MURRY

On 16th February 1915, I went to stay with the Lawrences at Greatham in Sussex, in the cottage lent them by Viola Meynell. Katherine Mansfield had gone to Paris, and after a few days I had found myself rather lonely in Buckinghamshire and followed the Lawrences. The floods were out. I had hard walking from Pulborough to Greatham in the dark, and I stumbled into a good deal of water. Since I had the remains of an influenza upon me, I was pretty wretched when I arrived. 'The Lawrences were very good to me to-day,' I wrote in my notebook. 'May I requite them!'

In fact, I was distinctly ill, though in those days I had great difficulty in recognising that I was ill. It was not due to any kind of courage, but to a sort of physical stupidity—a trait in my composition which Lawrence found particularly irritating, for he himself possessed an instinctive sapience about the condition of his own body, without which his life would have been much shorter than it was. On this occasion, Lawrence assured me, vehemently, that I *was* ill. He made me go straight to bed, and did not let me get up until he was satisfied that I was better. Lawrence was in his element looking after someone, especially someone rather stupid about his body. He liked 'bossing' one for one's good. There is no more perfect likeness of the man I knew than the picture of Lilly looking after Aaron Sisson in the little flat near Covent Garden, in *Aaron's Rod*.

In this matter of the body, Lawrence knew more about me than I did myself, and I was glad to obey his orders. In this submissive condition, I was half inclined to take it for granted that he knew more about me than I did in other matters too. At this moment it happened that Lawrence was brimful of one such matter. I was, or had been, on terms of intimate

* From *Reminiscences of D. H. Lawrence* (London: Jonathan Cape, 1933) pp. 52–6, 59–64, 73–81.

friendship with a man whom Lawrence also knew well. For this man I had a deep affection, and certainly I had been attached to him more closely than I knew. I had made the discovery, rather painfully, a little while before, when the friend (whom I will call D) without warning or excuse failed to come down to stay the week-end with me in Buckinghamshire as he had promised. I was very sore at the dereliction, and the pain I felt was a revelation to me of what I had really felt for D. It took a long while for the wound to heal.

Of this friendship of mine Lawrence disapproved. He knew of the crash, which had taken place only a fortnight before; and, as I think now, he discerned in my soreness and disillusion an opportunity to eradicate the friendship. As I lay in bed, he told me that he had been talking to D a day or two before, and that D had said to him: 'What there was between Murry and me was the most regrettable part of each of us.' I was completely bewildered. Something in me simply would not admit that there was anything at all regrettable in the depth of my feeling for D, and now, fifteen years afterwards, I am much farther from admitting it than I was then. There was perhaps an almost childish intensity in my affection for him; but I shall never believe that intensity of affection is wrong. What I have learned is something different, namely, that intense affection lays one open to a corresponding intensity of pain which, if it were possible to avoid it, would be better avoided. If it were possible . . . but it is not possible without blunting the fine point of one's soul in the process.

So I felt some tinge of resentment against Lawrence. Rather dully I was aware that he was trying to force me to an admission which I could not and ought not make. I wanted him to leave the matter alone; I was not going to recant. I had loved D and there had been a smash; but to say that my love for him was wrong—that I could not. Let us leave it alone. But Lawrence would not. He shifted his ground, and declared that D was 'nothing but a callous materialist underneath'. I did not find that any better. Again, I simply could not admit then, and do not admit now, that D was essentially different from what I believed him to be. And I find that, after fifteen years, my instinctive faith in this matter is not greatly changed. I believe, more firmly than I did then, that to see the truth of anything, or any man, or any woman, you must love it, or him, or her. As Lawrence 'stuck to the solar plexus', I stick to that, though I acknowledge that what one means by love is a matter of long and painful discovery.

So we compromised—Lawrence and I. I did not admit that my affection was either wrong or blind; on those points I was not to be moved; but I did admit, quite candidly, that it was all over between D and me. What there was between us was gone, and could never return. As indeed we both of us recognised, and as it proved. With that admission Lawrence was content. And, it seems to me now as I look back, that from that time onwards whatever capacity I possessed for affection towards a man was turned towards Lawrence himself. That, I suppose, was what he wanted.

In a day or two I was fairly fit again, and we began laying green linoleum together. Lawrence did the cutting, as he would have done, and I did the tacking; and he cut, and I banged, for hours together. A trivial recollection perhaps, but it so happens that some of my most precious memories of the man are of precisely these trivial odd jobs done together, and I am sure that many others of his friends feel the same. Then 'the flow', as Lawrence called it, was really between himself and another. We did not have to, we did not want to, talk; and it was good between us, better than I have ever known with a living man.

Still, in the evenings during those days we did talk. Lawrence was serious and sad; to be fully conscious, in those days and perhaps always, made him sad. For the first time, there at Greatham, I felt distinctly that the sense of a personal 'doom' was upon him.

*   *   *

[21 February 1915] In the evening we talked about the 'revolution'. Lawrence said it was no more use writing now; we had first to change the conditions, for without that change people either would not hear, or our words be only a tale. At first, though I agreed, I felt an uneasiness— whether I was playing the hypocrite in agreeing; I wondered whether I was merely trying to cling on to his skirts because I knew he was a proven writer with a tried audience. But then I felt sure that I was independently on the same track...I said that in writing a novel (I was getting towards the end of my first, which was actually finished as Greatham) I began with an assumption, even in matters of sex and morality, which was beyond obtaining conditions. He agreed, and said: 'What novels we could write, if we wrote of the whole good we knew, instead of the good that may be in this world.' We loosely planned a scheme for publishing weekly pamphlets in which the revolution should be expounded by us individually. After expounding *The Rainbow*, Lawrence said he felt he would write one more novel and no more. He was sad, he said, because he was a fore-runner, like John the Baptist before the Christ, whose destiny it was to surrender and make way. He asked me at what moment, in normal life, I thought that a man came to wait for the coming generation. I said, When he reached the outer edge of the inmost circle within which he knew that his true achievement began and ended.

'So I suppose,' he said, 'that my achievement begins and ends with preaching the revolution of the conditions of life—why not?' He said that he felt he was clumsier than I. 'My lack of clumsiness,' I said, 'was largely nervelessness.' 'Yes,' he replied, 'there is a lot of inertia in you, but that is valuable. Your effort somehow seems to be purer than mine. I am more temporal, you are more permanent.'

'You have more strength,' I said.

'Yes, of a certain kind; but less again than you, of another kind.'

Lawrence seemed sad, and in the incomprehensible mood of believing that I was somehow to succeed him.

* * *

Three distinct Lawrences live vividly in my memory: first, the man of immediate contact and overflowing humanity, who gave out 'virtue'; whose approach to another human being was never social, but always personal; who had no barriers and saw none; with whom one was incomparably at ease; whose naturalness was so pervasive that it made one natural. Then, there was an impersonal Lawrence who would as it were dispossess the personal man; this impersonal Lawrence is to me the most memorable of all. There would come a moment of strange intensity, and I would suddenly feel that I was in the presence of a man of destiny, a prophet, a Messiah. It is easy for the sceptic to dismiss such feelings as hallucinations. To me they are perfectly real. I know Lawrence far better now than I ever did while he was alive, and all the deeper knowledge of him that I have gained since his death has only served to confirm the immediate and indelible impression which the living man made upon me at such unforgettable moments, of one of which the foregoing note is the bald and inadequate record. At such a moment I passed completely under his spell. If he said these incomprehensible things about me, well it was *he* who said them, and no matter how strange or seemingly inordinate they sounded, I accepted them. At such a moment, I could not even dream of not accepting them. Though, of course, this acceptance had nothing to do with understanding them. I might try to bring myself to my sober senses afterwards, but no matter what I did, the central impression was ineradicable. Lawrence was a significant and symbolic man, in a special and particular sense of the instrument of destiny.

How it comes that there are such men, how it came that I should have known one, and known him at such moments, I do not pretend to know. That there should be such men is to me not mysterious at all; it is what I expect to happen sometimes. In another age, Lawrence would have been more easily recognised for what he essentially was. But in the twentieth century, and in England, we have no place for a prophet in the scheme of things. In the prophetic order, the utmost our scheme of things allows for is a Mr Shaw, or a Mr Wells, or a Dean Inge.[1] And from them Lawrence was totally different.

By calling Lawrence a prophet, I do not mean that he prophesied truly. I am convinced that much of his actual prophecy was false—and some of it even pernicious. What I mean is hard to convey, except in peculiar terms. But I might say that in Lawrence life itself was making an experiment towards a new kind of man, and that the experiment was crucial. Everything that he did and was, was therefore significant; it had a meaning transcending Lawrence's own personality.

He was a dedicated man. And sometimes, in his presence, I was immediately conscious of this. No other man I have known has ever produced this overwhelming impression upon me, or one remotely resembling it. Moreover, Lawrence made this impression upon me not only when I was a young man of twenty-five, but also when I was ten years older, and any facile impressionability I may formerly have possessed was thoroughly worn away. The impression was not vague and fleeting, but distinct and permanent; the vagueness arises only from the difficulty of defining or communicating it.

The third Lawrence was terrifying. In this condition he also was not any more a person, but a man possessed. A sort of paroxysm of rage or hatred engulfed him wholly. He appeared to me then demented, or as one possessed by the Furies. Though I was often the witness, I was only once the actual victim of one of these outbursts of rage, and then it passed into a kind of delirium during which he would call out my name in the night with all manner of strange and to me unintelligible denunciations. But this was more than a year after the period of which I am writing now. And then again the impression made upon me was ineradicable. It was a turning point in our relation. Never again did I feel really *safe* with him, as I had always felt before. The simple trust I had in him was gone; nor did it ever return.

* * *

. . . in November [1915], Lawrence was planning to depart for Florida, where an American friend of his possessed an estate. If he could find a place there to settle, we were to follow, and all of us 'live on no money at all'.

'If only it will all end up happily,' he said, 'like a song or a poem, and we live blithely by a big river, where there are fish, and in the forest behind wild turkeys and quails: there we make songs and poems and stories and dramas, in a vale of Avalon, in the Hesperides, among the Loves!'[2]

Lawrence let his little flat and sold his furniture, though not the beautiful rug. On 4 December he was in hopes of sailing from Glasgow to Key West on 20 December. But a week later, when I returned to London, I was told that he could not get a passport, and that he was going to spend the Christmas with his sister Ada at Ripley. Anyhow, he had determined to leave London for good. Within a day or two more he had made up his mind to go to Cornwall.

At the New Year I went back to Katherine to Bandol, charged with this message from Lawrence to her:

I want it now that we live together. When you come back, I want you and Murry to live with us, or near us, in unanimity: not these separations. Let us all live together and create a new world. If it is too difficult in England, because here all is destruction and dying and corruption, let us go away to Florida. But let us go *together*, several of us, as being of one spirit. Only let there be no *personal* obligation, no personal idea.

The Lawrences went first to the Beresfords'[3] house at Porthcothan. There Lawrence fell seriously ill, and reached a nadir of depression. He wrote that he had lost all faith whatever in humanity and in the future. The only hope was in the superhuman, the miracle; and failing the miracle, he was finished. He ended, ominously, by saying that he did not intend to accept this human life. It was foul muck. What had he to do with it?

I say 'ominously' now; but I was not then in a position to interpret the omen. It did not occur to me as a possibility that Lawrence, or any other man, should make a deliberate attempt to *escape* from accepting human life. To me the impasse seemed absolute. There was the horror and madness of the war which in one's soul one must repudiate; but there it was. Nor God nor demon could undo the done. It was real, not a nightmare from which we should awaken. The fearful reality on the one side; on the other the individual soul which must repudiate it. What was to be done? There was nothing to be done, except to submit, to suffer and to go on suffering until something died within oneself—the something which suffered, and wept and could not be comforted. Ultimately, the only thing to be done was to take the attitude which is expressed in the great prayer of Christ: 'Nevertheless, not as I will, but as Thou wilt.' And that was not an attitude that could be *taken*; it had to happen. It was a surrender, but it could not be a deliberate surrender; it had to be wrung out of one by the sheer compulsion of the things that were.

I am writing now out of whatever wisdom has come to me in the fifteen years which have followed since that winter of 1915–16. In those days I knew nothing of it. What I was then is pretty faithfully revealed in the curious essay 'There was a Little Man...' which was my contribution to the *Signature*; I was engaged, positively distraught, by a feverish struggle to keep my personal consciousness alive against the horror of the war; I was fighting against the death that threatened my 'ego'. And Lawrence, as I now see the situation, was engaged in the same kind of struggle, though the form it took was very different. Lawrence had conceived the idea of escaping from the intolerable suffering which the war inflicted upon his sensitive spirit, by divesting himself of the spiritual consciousness altogether. He would sink back into a 'mindless' existence, and put off altogether the condition of those

to whom the miseries of the world
Are misery, and will not let them rest.

It was, I think, at the beginning of this year, 1916, only an idea, a dim possibility, in Lawrence's mind; and I believe he shrank from it. The alternative way of making existence endurable, as it presented itself to him then, was to have Katherine Mansfield and myself living together with him and Frieda; and that we should by a united effort create a little world in which we could maintain ourselves free from the contagion. It may appear a selfish plan; but the alternative was some sort of madness, or so it seemed. Lawrence's appeal to us was of a kind that we could not resist. It was made with all his amazing tenderness and deep affection. We two were the only people remaining in his life, he said; he looked at the rest across a grave. Would we come? The nervous strain had made him badly ill; he felt that if he went on caring, he would die. The earth seemed to be slipping under his feet. If we would promise to come, he would find a place for us all to live, somewhere in Cornwall. He liked Cornwall, and did not want to leave it; it had a kind of pre-human magic. We could be happy together somehow there.

The personal appeal was not to be resisted. Without it, I suppose, Katherine Mansfield and I would have stayed where we were, at Bandol. There, for a few short months, we actually were happy; it was the only period of real happiness vouchsafed in our life together. It would have ended soon; it was bound to end. We had no right to it. It was stolen in the teeth of circumstance. And Lawrence's unhappiness, more than anything else, awoke us to the fact that it was stolen. He wrote joyfully to tell us that he had found a cottage near Zennor, with one for us beside it. We must return. We said good-bye to the tiny Villa Pauline with a pang, and returned.

It was a cold, slatey-grey day in early April when we arrived at St Ives. Lawrence was on the platform. The white gulls wheeled about, crying desolately; and our hearts sank. We tried to be gay, not to disappoint Lawrence, as we drove out to the Tinners' Arms at Zennor; but we felt like weeping. Our fairy-tale was over.

We pulled ourselves together and set about furnishing the cottage at Higher Tregerthen. Lawrence helped, as he always did. He and I would march off together to Benny's sale-room at St Ives, where things were incredibly cheap. They needed to be, for we were all incredibly poor. I remember that I bought a wooden bedstead for one shilling, and a half-dozen chairs for eighteen-pence apiece. These last, for some reason, I painted a dull funeral black. Lawrence and Frieda, and even Katherine, were rather astonished at this outburst, and stood watching with a sort of mild dismay while I stolidly blackened the chairs on the grass between our cottages. It did not seem at all funny to me. A dead and lustreless black seemed to me an eminently appropriate colour just then.

From the beginning the experiment was a failure. There were wonderful moments of happiness; but they were seldom. We fell back into a depression from which it seemed impossible to escape. Katherine was very unhappy, and conceived a hatred of Cornwall that lasted for the rest of her life. And Lawrence, at times, was positively terrifying: a paroxysm of black rage would sweep down upon him, and leave us trembling and aghast. Sometimes he hated me to the point of frenzy. One night it became a kind of delirium, and I heard him crying out from his bedroom next door: 'Jack is killing me.' I was bewildered, and terrified; more bewildered, and really more terrified, when the next day Lawrence would be kinder and more affectionate than ever towards me. Life began to be an awful phantasmagoria. We tried to blot out these black visitations from our memory, and to behave as though nothing had happened. But people living in the intimate relation in which we were living could not go on pretending. Katherine and I would talk things over, and wonder what was the matter. Was Lawrence really going mad? It belonged to the hopelessness of the situation that neither of us dared to ask him point-blank what *was* the matter?

A very great deal was the matter, of which we were totally ignorant. And it was as well that we were ignorant, for we could have done nothing to help. His desperate struggle was completely outside the range of our experience; and his idea of escape from it completely beyond our imagination. Some partial record of what was actually happening in him will be found in the chapter of *Kangaroo* called 'The Nightmare'; but it is very partial. The lapse into the mindless world which he there describes was upon him now like a temptation. Half he wanted to resist it, half he desired to succumb. The real function of Katherine and myself was to help him resist it, but at other moments he wanted me to go with him. And all this was never formulated, never openly expressed between us. He wanted me to swear to be his 'blood-brother', and there was to be some sort of sacrament between us. I said, perhaps rather childishly but with perfect sincerity, that I thought I was his 'blood-brother', and I did not see the need of any kind of sacrament. 'If I love you, and you know I love you, isn't that enough?' No, it was not enough: there ought to be some mingling of our blood, so that neither of us *could* go back on it. For some cause or other, I was half-frightened, half-repelled, and I suppose my shrinking away was manifest. He suddenly turned on me with fury: 'I hate your love, I *hate it*. You're an obscene bug, sucking my life away.' The vindictiveness with which he said it made me almost physically sick. But the words were burnt into my brain.

Now, I was scared and utterly out of my depth. The only thing to do was to go away. Katherine had long been anxious to go; she had been miserable ever since she returned from France. We told Lawrence that it was too cold and bleak for us, and that we wanted to live on the south side of Cornwall. He was rather glum, and so were we. I went across and found a cottage at Mylor, near Falmouth, while Katherine went for a little while to London. Lawrence helped me to pack our bits of furniture on the cart. We were very silent, and very sad. Before I rode off on my bicycle, he said he would come to see us very soon. In a fortnight or so he did. There is a little picture of him in one of Katherine's letters of June 1916.

Lawrence has gone home again. We walked with him as far as the ferry and away he sailed in a little open boat pulled by an old, old man. Lawrence wore a broad white linen hat and he carried a rucksack on his back. He looked rather as though the people of Falmouth had cried to him as the Macedonians did to Paul and he was on his way over to help them.

That was a good time, and the bad time at Higher Tregerthen seemed then like a bad dream. A little while afterwards he came again with Frieda, and once more we were happy, although we nearly drowned ourselves in a small boat. But from this time forward we were conscious of a certain hostility. It was not a personal hostility: as persons we were very fond of each other still. But I was now vaguely aware that we represented different principles and were bound to go different paths, and I think Lawrence was acutely aware of it.

NOTES

John Middleton Murry (1889–1957) was an editor, critic and prolific writer on a wide variety of subjects. He met Lawrence in 1913 and was a witness at Lawrence's wedding on 13 July 1914. He saw a good deal of Lawrence during the war and again in 1923–5. Murry was married to the New Zealand writer Katherine Mansfield (pseudonym of Kathleen Mansfield Beauchamp; 1888–1923). He edited the *Athenaeum* (1919–21) and the *Adelphi* (1923–30). In 1931 he published *Son of Woman*, a biography of Lawrence which Aldous Huxley described as an example of 'destructive hagiology'; it represents the then fashionable psychoanalytical approach to literary biography and did no service to its subject's reputation in the period immediately following his death. Catherine Carswell's *The Savage Pilgrimage* (1932) included an attack on Murry: see above, p. 97. Earlier Murry had published in the *Adelphi* two articles on Lawrence: 'The Poems of D. H. Lawrence' and 'The Doctrine of D. H. Lawrence' (the latter a review of *Lady Chatterley's Lover*); these were reissued in 1930 as *D. H. Lawrence: Two Essays* (Minority Press, Cambridge; repr. 1970 by University Microfilms, Ann Arbor).

The *Reminiscences*, from which the above passages are taken, were originally published in the *Adelphi* (June–Aug 1930). Some of the same material is used in Murry's autobiography *Between Two Worlds* (New York: Messner, 1936).

1. W. R. Inge, Dean of St Paul's (1911–34) and author of many popular works on theology and ethics.

2. *Letters*, p. 287.

3. J. D. Beresford (1873–1946), novelist and friend of Murry, had a house at Porthcothan, near Padstow, Cornwall.

Lawrence as a Neighbour*

THE HOCKING FAMILY

STANLEY. It was in March 1916 that I first saw D. H. Lawrence. Only a few days previous he had arrived at the Tinner's Arms at Zennor, and his ambition seemed to be to find a cottage to live in here in Cornwall. He and Frieda walked across the fields from Zennor to our farm, and I remember him asking about the cottages which were quite near to us. We told him the name of the owner, Captain Short, and he soon found him. Soon after that he and Mrs Lawrence moved in. I was only a lad then, I know, and I had not long left school. But he struck me as being a rather queer-looking individual with his red beard and his tall, thin figure. We soon got to know him and to like him.

WILLIAM HENRY. Lawrence often came into the fields with us when we were at work, whether it was hay-making or harvesting, and would work along with us the same as if one of us. Of course hay-time and harvest, as you know, are fairly hot times of the year. Often we would be waiting for what we called *croust* to come—which would be perhaps 'elevenses' today, or a meal at four or half-past four in an afternoon. While having one of those meals I passed the remark to him, 'You are getting more like one of us every day, Mr Lawrence'. He made a smile at that. Of course he looked sweated—you know, with his shirt open with the warm weather, and we were the same at those times of the year.

STANLEY. If he got tired of working, he would come out in the fields for a couple of hours and slog away, carrying or binding sheaves with us, just like one of ourselves. But he couldn't cut corn with a scythe—he admitted that. We used to cut a lot of corn with a scythe in those days, but he could not use a scythe. He could tie sheaves in his particular method, but they weren't tied really firm enough to hold handling. He had a Midland method which he tried to show us, but the knot was different to the Cornish method. For several handlings like sheaves of oats have from the field to the threshing machine, they need to be tied very firmly. But his, I must admit, were not tied firmly—they would come adrift on the second handling. We showed him our Cornish method, but he never seemed able to do it. We had a

*First published in Nehls, I, pp. 365–7, 425–6. The interview was originally broadcast by the BBC on 14 and 22 November 1953.

method of tying it and twisting it and shoving it in with a bang which, if it's done properly, you could never undo.

INTERVIEWER. Will you tell us about Lawrence as a gardener?

WILLIAM HENRY. He had a little corner of a field of mine and planted almost every kind of vegetable that I knew of at that time—and some that I didn't know. He kept them clean, and apparently had a good crop.

INTERVIEWER. Extraordinary that in spite of his ill health he was able to do so much manual work.

WILLIAM HENRY. Yes, it was rather surprising. He could work very hard indeed, but not for a whole day like we would. We often used to put in twelve or fourteen hours a day.

STANLEY. If he chose to break off in the middle of the afternoon, well, he would do so. I often used to think then that he'd got some material to write a novel or an article with, and that he would go in and jot it down while he remembered it, you see.

WILLIAM HENRY. Yes, and perhaps our talk—he would go right back then while he remembered it.

STANLEY. All the time he seemed to be busy writing, and some famous people visited him while he was here at Tregerthen, including Thomas Hardy and Aldous Huxley.[1]

WILLIAM HENRY. He often came to our house in the evenings when we were perhaps having supper, and would often stay for a bit of a chat. I also had some of my friends coming in the evenings, and we made kind of a merry group at times. He was never short of a story or an answer for us, and, well, I think we amused him and he also amused us.

MABEL. He used to like to come down to talk to my mother. If he went out, you know, he would come down sometimes and talk to her because she was here quite often.

STANLEY. His favourite seat was a little corner seat by the old-fashioned Cornish range.

MARY. That was his seat.

MABEL. He liked 'the bench', as he called it.

STANLEY. When my mother would be getting something for supper, he would very nicely and cautiously take, for instance, a fried potato out of the frying pan and eat it with great delight. He was very amused at this. He used to come so often.

INTERVIEWER. Did he write here?

MABEL. Oh, no, he never wrote anything here. He wrote at the cottage. He didn't do any writing at all down here, not that I'm aware of anyhow.

INTERVIEWER. When he came up in the evenings, he taught you French, didn't he?

STANLEY. Call it 'coming down', actually, because the cottages are above the farm lanes.

INTERVIEWER. What did he teach you?

STANLEY. French.

INTERVIEWER. Did you learn much?

STANLEY. Oh, yes.

INTERVIEWER. You were able to speak it?

STANLEY. Oh, yes. I could hold a little conversation with him in those days. But I'm afraid I've forgotten it all now. In a letter he remarked to me: 'I suppose you've forgotten all your French, but never mind.' The war was on then, you see. He said, 'Better than going to France to learn it.' Oh, yes, he was educated. He was a university man. He had no accent at all. You couldn't detect what part of England he came from.

INTERVIEWER. Some people say he had a high-pitched voice. Is that right?

STANLEY. Yes, rather effeminate. His was a feminine disposition on the whole...he was so tall and thin and delicate.

INTERVIEWER. Was he particular, or did he just go around wearing any old thing?

MABEL. He used to wear the corduroys, of course. Green, I think, mostly, and a green corduroy coat.

INTERVIEWER. It must have been unusual down here in those days, I should think.

MABEL. Well, I don't know. He had different colours. He had a brown he used to wear. Frieda used to wear red stockings.

INTERVIEWER. Why did the Lawrences leave Cornwall in the end?

MABEL. Well, they had to leave, as far as I know, because the war was on. They couldn't remain here because they were too near the coast.

INTERVIEWER. And there was a lot of nonsense about submarines and things?

MABEL. Well, it was said that lights were seen, but I don't think so.

STANLEY. The First World War was on while the Lawrences were here; and, being strange to the locality, they were naturally looked on with suspicion. At the same time German submarines were active off our Cornish coast, and I distinctly remember one little incident in August 1917. A German submarine had been spotted and was being hunted by our destroyers and seaplanes and an airship. The noise of exploding depth charges was terrific, and Mrs Lawrence remarked to me: 'What an awful thing war is. In that submarine may be some of the boys I went to school with.' As you know, she was a German. Anyway, the submarine was destroyed, and huge patches of oil remained on the sea for several days.

INTERVIEWER. Do you think those wrecks had anything to do with the suspicion that grew around the Lawrences?

STANLEY. Oh, not in the least.

INTERVIEWER. You don't?

STANLEY. No, I don't think that.

INTERVIEWER. What do you think started that suspicion?

STANLEY. Well, the fact of them being strangers and probably Mrs Lawrence being a German. That's all.

INTERVIEWER. How did they go in the end? In a great hurry or not?

STANLEY. Well, I remember Frieda Lawrence coming down to the farm one evening in a very distressed state. Apparently somebody had been to the cottage, she said, and searched the place and turned everything upside down. She couldn't just understand it. My mother and sister remembered seeing two men, one of whom they thought was a policeman, up there in the afternoon. Apparently it was the police and a military officer who had searched their cottage. Soon after that they had notice to leave Cornwall.

INTERVIEWER. Did you drive them to the station?

STANLEY. Yes.

INTERVIEWER. Will you tell us what you remember about that? Did you pick them up at the cottage?

WILLIAM HENRY. Yes. The day they left I drove to the cottage and took them into St Ives station, and there the police were again. That's about all I know.

NOTES

The Hockings were friends and neighbours of the Lawrences in Cornwall in 1916–17.

1. Almost certainly an error; there seems to be no record of Hardy visiting Lawrence, though the idea is intriguing, and, curiously enough, Hardy and his wife *were* in Cornwall in September 1916—see F. E. Hardy, *The Life of Thomas Hardy* (London: Macmillan, 1962) p. 373. Nor is it certain that Huxley visited him there: according to Sybille Bedford, Huxley's biographer, the two men met only once during the war, and that was in Hampstead—see *Aldous Huxley: A Biography*, I (London: Chatto & Windus, 1973) p. 178.

A Visit to Cornwall*

CATHERINE CARSWELL

My visit to Cornwall was all happiness—one of the quietest kind. It was my first stay with the Lawrences. I was their only visitor, sleeping in the other cottage, which I 'made' myself each day. Nothing particular happened. Chiefly we talked—though even that not so very much. We also walked, but not so very much either, as the weather was not of the best. One of the reasons I got on with Lawrence was that I enjoyed 'doing' ordinary things.

I seem to recall that Lawrence spoke a good deal of Dostoievsky. Murry

* From *The Savage Pilgrimage*, pp. 65, 67–9, 76–7, 79–81, 82.

had writtern a book about him and had sent a copy to Lawrence. Lawrence perfectly disagreed with Murry's findings, and was incisive as well as eloquent on the subject. . . .

We carried on the daily work of the cottages without help from outside. With Lawrence one seemed, in such a case, to have enough time over for anything else one wanted. But the necessary daily jobs seemed so much a part of life that one did not fret to be done with them. Certain literary critics have found that in estimating Lawrence as a writer it is beside the point to note that even while washing up dishes he radiated life. But those who washed dishes with Lawrence know that it is not beside the point.

More than by his unceasing interest in my novel, which he had made me bring with me, I was pleased when he said that I 'fitted in' with their cottage life better than the Londoners did. Perhaps from his North Midland upbringing and origin, Lawrence had a warm feeling for Scotch people. 'I don't care if every English person is my enemy,' he wrote to me once later; 'if they wish it, so be it. I keep a reserve for the Scotch.' He had not a good word to say for the Irish character. He detested anything like professional 'charm'. There was prejudice here, of course, but it could be tracked down to a racial feeling.[1] The inexpressiveness of the Northern temper, implying, as it does, a distrust of easy verbal expression, was congenial to him just as the so different Latin mentality with its subtle realism was congenial. In the facile intellectualising of emotion he found evidence of a certain poverty of nature. He saw this at its worst in the Irish and the Americans. Here, however, he was perhaps not more characteristic of the North than of the English working-class generally, whose experience it is to associate true warmth with verbal inexpressiveness. 'I think one understands best without explanations,' he said often. Or of those who talked and talked—'they don't *want* to understand'.

Another strongly 'working-class' trait in Lawrence was his extreme distaste of anything that could be regarded as indecent. It would indeed be easy to call him prudish. One night in Cornwall, after having just begun to undress for bed, I found I had left my book in the sitting-room, where Lawrence and Frieda still were, and I returned to fetch it. I had brought no dressing-gown with me, but there seemed to me no impropriety in my costume—an ankle-length petticoat topped by a long-sleeved woollen vest! Lawrence, however, rebuked me. He disapproved, he said, of people appearing in their underclothes. No doubt, if I had not privately believed my *négligé* to be attractive as well as decent, I might neither have ventured to appear in it nor have felt so much abashed as I did by Lawrence's remark. So, essentially, Lawrence was right after all! How more than horrified he was—furious—when from his flat in Florence, looking across the Arno, he was compelled to overlook also a stretch of mud and shingle which the Florentine *gamins* found a convenient spot for the relief of nature. He hated the domestic dog on account of its too public habits. In such respects Lawrence was no advocate of what is often, but wrongly, called 'the natural'. Still less was he an apostle of the nude. I am sure that he put down all our civilised indecencies—our coquetries as well as our callousnesses, our sophisticated desire to shock as well as our prurience—to a departure from natural reticence. On first thoughts this may seem strange to those who have not considered the matter closely. On second thoughts it will be seen that such a man, and only such, could have become the author of *Lady Chatterley's Lover*.

* * *

I have said I was present at many rows between these two extraordinary people, the one so richly endowed with physical life, the other subtly and magnificently endowed with mind, responding with natural delight to the minds of others, yet bending all the force of his own to break the dominance of mind in our modern ways, and to destroy 'ideal' reactions in favour of true reactions out of which life would come trembling and renewed.

When I first arrived in Cornwall they told me in concert of a quarrel that had taken place shortly before. I don't remember what it was about— probably Frieda's children—but it had been fought out to what Lawrence took to be a finish, and he had gone into the scullery at the back to wash up. While he was thus engaged, with his back to the living-room door, singing quietly to himself (Lawrence was slightly deaf) and working with a bit of a clatter at the enamel wash bowl, Frieda came in from the living-room carrying one of the stone dinner plates. His unconcerned roundelay after what had just passed (I only wish I knew which song, sacred or profane, Lawrence chose on this occasion) so wrought upon her that her wrath boiled up afresh. Down on the singer's head she brought the dinner plate.

It hurt him very much and might, of course, have injured him seriously. But he was as far from bearing Frieda a grudge as from turning the other cheek. 'That was like a woman!' said he, turning on her viciously, but on this occasion too much astonished to strike back. 'No man could have done such a thing when the quarrel was over, and from behind too! But as you *are* a woman,' he added ruefully, 'you were right to do as you felt. It was only lucky you didn't kill me. You might have. These plates are hard and heavy'.

* * *

I hope I have made it clear that a miserable account of Lawrence at this time, or any other, would be a false and misleading account. He had far too magnificent a talent for enjoyment, far too fine a capacity for work, to be miserable in the true sense of misery, which is dreariness, regret, sterility and doubt. He had an aim worth struggling for to the utmost, and he felt himself growing strong in and for the struggle. One day you might hear him say he felt like never writing another line. And this he said, not so much in despair, as in the furious determination that life held better things than books. But within a week or so he would be sending you a volume of new poems in MS, or one of a series of essays that nobody would publish, or telling you that he was triumphantly typing the last chapter of a novel. At intervals he burned piles of MSS. Once he almost set the chimney on fire and revelled in its roaring. He enjoyed warming his hands at such fires of outgrown life. All along, when no entirely new thing was clamouring to be written, there would be something lying by, which waited upon his mood for its last revision. I came to take it as a sign, when Lawrence wrote to say he was writing nothing, that even as I read his letter he would be deep in some new undertaking.

When not engaged on a book or a story, Lawrence would be working at something else with precisely the same ardour and economy and dislike of outgrown accumulations. Once he bought a gauze shawl of Paisley pattern for Frieda—cheaply, because it had the moth in it—and set himself to make it whole without delay by mending it himself. It took him two entire days, working well into the night, and allowing only the shortest intervals for his meals. When I say I never saw Lawrence idle, I do not mean that he was that wretched thing, a time-haunted man. He was that as little as he was the Shavian 'writing machine'. He did not seem to be 'driven', either by clocks or by conscience. He worked more as a bird works, eagerly and unceasingly till the job on hand was finished. But he certainly valued time as any good worker must, and he was shocked in a light passing way when he noticed other people dilly-dallying or spending their hours on trivialities or lying unduly long in bed of a morning. I have heard him say that he needed nine hours' sleep out of the twenty-four, and he observed this as a rule, being neither a late sitter-up nor an unduly early riser. But throughout his fifteen-hour day he was 'doing things' all the time.

Besides, Lawrence was happy in that he had no struggle to create. The 'frail, precious buds of the unknown life', which for him were the only possessions worth fighting for came into being without his groaning or travailing. He had to struggle only for the condition—the 'small, subtle air of life'—in which alone these 'unborn children of one's hope and living happiness' could appear, and he had to shelter them in their growth from meddling or destructive hands. The happy demon of creation was his. All that was demanded of him was the courage to see that the demon's mouth was stopped neither by the world's disapproval nor by his personal fears.

So there was always happiness for Lawrence. He was always engaged upon something supremely worth while, with no less in constant view than a new heaven and a new earth. . . .

One day I bewailed to Lawrence how unproductive my life appeared by the side of his. 'Ah, but you will have so much longer than I to do things in!' he answered quickly and lightly. Though we saw he was delicate, this certainty of his was so shocking that we did our best, with remarkable success, to believe him wrong. There was no mistaking his own certainty that time for him might not be lost.

NOTES

For a note on Catherine Carswell see p. 97.
    1. Personal sympathies apart, Lawrence regarded 'Celtic' influences—whether Welsh, Irish or Scottish—as essentially destructive of the English genius and culture: this especially in politics. [Catherine Carswell's note.]

'A Subtle and Deadly Poison' *

CECIL GRAY

The truth is that Lawrence was always inclined to treat his friends and acquaintances as if they were characters in one of his novels, and sought accordingly to mould their characters and direct their actions as he desired. When he failed in this—and he invariably did fail—he took his revenge by putting the said friends and acquaintances, recognisably, into his books, and there worked his will upon them. In this respect Lawrence's life and his art were curiously intermingled. But whereas he was wont to claim that his art was a kind of overflow from his life, it was, in fact, the precise contrary, a substitute for life: to such an extent, indeed, that it is exceedingly probable that he would never have felt the urge to write his novels—the later ones at least—if he had been able to have his way with living personalities. Practically all his novels are essentially a form of wish-fulfilment, an imaginary gratification of his desires. Throughout all the later ones he himself stalks, thinly disguised as the hero, surrounded by malevolent caricatures of those who, for some reason or other, had failed to respond completely or to submit themselves entirely to his will in actual life. This is what happened in the present instance; as we shall see later, a particularly offensive caricature of Philip[1] is to be found in one of his novels, *Women in Love*, for no other reason than that Philip declined to allow himself to become a mere puppet or marionette in Lawrence's hands.
    The fact is that Lawrence demanded more from a friend than anyone

* From *Peter Warlock: A Memoir of Philip Heseltine* (London: Jonathan Cape, 1938) pp. 119–20, 121–2.

has the right to demand or anyone the power to give—a complete surrender of one's personality, which no one with any personality at all could make. . . .

Such was the power of his genius and the magnetism of his personality, however, that so long as one was with him one was hypnotised into accepting him unreservedly. In the curious glamour that he cast around him, his dark gods, mystic underworlds, and all the rest, became actual living realities; it was only when one got away from him that one suddenly awoke, dazed, as if out of a dream which, however inconsequent and absurd it might seem on waking had, while it was in progress, a reality and a significance, which no one who had not the experience of coming into close intimacy with Lawrence could possibly understand or appreciate.

What ultimately brought Philip to break with Lawrence, then, was not, I think, so much his refusal to subordinate his personality, nor even his acute perception of Lawrence's absurdities and inconsistencies, though these certainly played their part; it is rather to be found in the phrase of the letter to Delius quoted [before this extract]—'he acts like a subtle and deadly poison'. This is absolutely true, at least of the Lawrence of these days, although it is difficult to believe that he could ever have changed greatly in this respect. The Lawrence that Philip knew, that Mr Nichols[2] knew, that I knew, was a very different one from the characteristically feminine idealisation which is presented in the pages of Mrs Carswell's *The Savage Pilgrimage*—the wise, kind, lovable, sympathetic friend and man of genius. That side certainly existed, and I too can gladly testify to its existence. Many were the wonderful and unforgettable moments I spent in his company, but there was another side to the picture, which was very much in the ascendant during that period of his life: dark, sinister, baleful, wholly corrupt and evil. I believe myself that this aspect of Lawrence was the real and fundamental one, and that those who were unaware of it or to whom he did not choose to reveal it simply did not know him.

NOTES

Cecil Gray (1895–1951) was a music critic who knew Lawrence in Cornwall and London in 1917.

1. On Philip Heseltine ('Peter Warlock'), the subject of Gray's biography, see p. 109, n. 12.

2. On Robert Nichols, see p. 109, n. 11.

'Searching Not Flattering' *

BRIGIT PATMORE

[After leaving Cornwall towards the end of 1917, the Lawrences lived for a short time in a London flat belonging to Richard Aldington. During this time Brigit Patmore visited London and invited them to have lunch with her.]

When I arrived Frieda had a bad cold and was in bed, but was anxious not to spoil the luncheon. She insisted on Lorenzo (the name she always used for him) and me setting off together. A theory of mine is that most people like contrasts and I asked him should we go to a newish place under the Rialto Cinema. It was rather pretentious but served fairly good food, considering war conditions.

'Yes, let's go and see your world.'

'It isn't my world.' I protested, rising always to the bait that I was the parasite of a rich useless class. Lorenzo's teasing was his way of touching you with a kind of affection. If he wanted to attack he was quite direct and forthright.

He had been through much suffering and humiliation in Cornwall, but I knew nothing about it, I only saw that he was thinner and seemed taller. He had straightened up the way proud people do under the lash; he had the indifference in look and manner which goes with agony endured, especially cruelty inflicted by one's fellow-men. He had grown a beard and wore a brown velvet coat and fawn corduroy trousers, which made harmony with the deep russet of his uncovered head. His pale skin and the expression of his face showed great sensitivity, but strength was in the slight ruggedness of his features.

We arrived at the restaurant. The waiters were shocked in their vulgar consciousness of Lorenzo's unconventional clothes and they did not disguise it. I refused table after table with the nonchalant impertinence they take for good manners. Lorenzo did not seem to notice their rudeness, but I felt like a watch-dog.

When at last we were settled, he enjoyed advising me about food and wines—very elder-brotherly.

* From 'Conversations with Lawrence', *London Magazine*, IV (June 1957) pp. 31–4.

Back in Mecklenburgh Square we found Frieda sitting up in bed by the side of the fire.

'Well, Frieda, are you all right? Do you feel better?'

'Yes. *So* much better, Lorenzo. So lovely and *warm* here. But *such* a stupid book. No *reality*, no *feeling*. How stupid people are! I can't *bear* it.'

'Of course we're never stupid, are we? The woman thinks she's perfect, does she? Well, well.' Putting a fresh glass of lemonade on the table by Frieda's pillow. 'Brigit took me to the Elysian fields. Think of that. And the waiters didn't approve of Brigit's guest so she turned very haughty and great lady. She wanted to drink claret and I wouldn't let her.'

'How *like* you, Lorenzo. Such a *bully*. Poor Brigit, he would go against you just to exercise his power. You *must* not give way.'

The stress Frieda laid on certain syllables was not for intensity. It was a musical call for attention and gave life to whatever she said.

I laughed and Lorenzo brimmed with the inward smile Frieda's mocking love always evoked. Why have people written so much about quarrels between this couple? Could they not see that most of the time he was lashing out at the world, at them? Frieda was the whipping-lass for all society, and she offered herself to his wrath with her gay gibes and wilfulness in the way a tigress draws the play-fight of her cubs. Later, in his pain and weakness he grew bitter, but who would not allow a man rage under torture rather than tears?

We sat in front of the fire. For some reason, Lorenzo never lolled: he sat with knees crossed and body hunched over them and looked like a contemplative bird brooding over a fish about to be caught. He would look at you out of eyes a little closed and ask question after question, which you would answer more in surprise than gratification, for they were searching not flattering.

'So you're married and have two children. Do you like them?'

'Very much.'

'Hm, what does your husband say to that?'

'Oh—why—women…the home…discipline…children are company for women…'

'Well, they're quite young yet, aren't they?'

'The elder is about seven.'

'A little too young for jealousy . Your husband's rather vain, I suppose? Both boys. Poor Brigit.'

'Why? I'd be much more miserable about girls.'

'Did you want to have children?'

'Well…it's a pretty horrid world, isn't it? Especially for women.'

'Didn't you like your father?'

'At first, then afterwards…'

'He treated your mother badly?'

'Yes.'

'Is she alive?'

'No.' Longish pause.

'What did he do?'

'He drank...and then...'

The thought of a son's agony over his mother in *Sons and Lovers* made it easier to allow these probings. After we had absorbed comfort from the flames for a while, I said:

'It's strange, although it was years before I could even mention my mother, and I ran away from my stepmother, I managed to forgive—or rather—to understand my father a little...yet somehow I can't get over it.'

'No,' Lawrence said at once. 'One can't. One is cut down to the quick. You know? The quick. There's no more sensitive part of one's life than that. One can't forget that. One is never the same after that.'

NOTE

Brigit Patmore, writer and translator; she met Lawrence 'a few years before the war of 1914' and saw him intermittently until their last meeting in 1928.

In Augustus John's Studio*

CYNTHIA ASQUITH

D. H. Lawrence's irruption into John's studio is one of the incidents most deeply etched on my memory. I had been lunching with him at Queen's Restaurant in Sloane Square. Hearing I was about to sit nearby, he took it into his head to come and see my portrait.

The collision between the two Red Beards was enthralling. D. H. was in a queer, challenging mood. Why the atmosphere of a studio and the impact of a brother artist should thus have affected him, I have no idea, but whatever spiritual revolt he felt made him—strange symptom—speak in Latin, a quite uncharacteristic vagary.

With his wide-brimmed black hat in his hand, he walked into the studio like some nervous, lightfooted woodland animal on the look-out for something to shy at.

There was some minutes silence during which he prowled about the studio, gloomily, mutely surveying the finished and unfinished works of

* From *Haply I May Remember* (London: James Barrie, 1950) p. 106.

art. Then, like a clock rustily clearing its throat to strike, he muttered, 'Mortuus est. Mortuus est,' several times. Gathering volume, his voice became a tolling bell. Suddenly, raising his head, he summed up the situation with the sepulchral utterance, 'Let the DEAD PAINT THE DEAD!' Pacing up and down, he knelled this lugubrious refrain several times.

John showed wonderful tolerance of this curious behaviour. That he had been pronounced to be dead did not seem to distress him. To one so plentifully endowed with vitality, the cap, I suppose, was too obvious a misfit to matter.

Whatever his unspoken feelings, the artist expressed great admiration for the writer's 'head', and asked him to sit for a drawing. Lawrence consented, but unfortunately this plan never came off.

NOTE

For a note on Lady Cynthia Asquith see p. 95. Augustus John (1878–1961) is widely known for his portraits of celebrities. His biographer, Michael Holroyd, dates the episode described above 1 November 1917 and quotes from Lady Cynthia's diary: 'I thought it just possible John *might* add another to the half dozen or so people whose company Lawrence can tolerate for two hours. It was quite a success. John asked Lawrence to sit for him . . .'—*Augustus John: A Biography*, vol. II: *The Years of Experience* (London: Faber & Faber, 1975) p. 67. In his autobiographical volume *Chiaroscuro* (London: Jonathan Cape, 1952), John offers his own account of the occasion (p. 85):

I met D. H. Lawrence in the flesh once only. Lady Cynthia Asquith whose portrait I was painting brought him round one day to my studio. Lady Cynthia would have liked me to paint Lawrence and I would have been interested to do so. But Lawrence protested that he was too ugly. I didn't agree. I never did insist on an Adonis for a model, and I thought Lawrence's features would have done very well for my purpose; even if they didn't conform to any known canon of beauty, they didn't lack character. Besides, did I not recognise in them the mask of genius? On this occasion the poet made a point of compensating himself for his physical drawbacks by a dazzling display of cerebral fireworks. Originality or Death seemed to be his motto. Lady Cynthia treated us to a box at the Opera that evening. A resplendent guardsman was of the party: Frieda Lawrence who also was present assured us all that her German husband's uniform was much grander than that of this officer. On leaving what Sir Edwin Lutyens used to call the 'uproar', DHL announced that he would like to howl like a dog . . . .

The visit to the opera is depicted in *Aaron's Rod*.

'That Provincial Genius'*

JOHN GALSWORTHY

[13 November 1917] Lunched with Pinker¹ to meet D. H. Lawrence, that provincial genius. Interesting, but a type I could not get on with. Obsessed with self. Dead eyes, and a red beard, long narrow pale face. A strange bird.

*From H. V. Marrot, *Life and Letters of John Galsworthy* (London: Heinemann, 1935) p. 433.

NOTES

John Galsworthy (1867–1933), novelist and dramatist. Lawerence wrote an essay on Galsworthy (first published in *Scrutinies* in 1928; reprinted in *Phoenix*) in which the novelist's later work is condemned as 'purely commercial'. Galsworthy's reactions to *Sons and Lovers* are contained in a letter written on 13 April 1914— Edward Garnett, *Letters from John Galsworthy, 1900–1932* (London: Jonathan Cape, 1934) p. 218.

1. J. B. Pinker, well-known literary agent.

The Lawrences at Home†

DOUGLAS GOLDRING

It was probably at Koteliansky's house in Acacia Road, St John's Wood, that my first meeting with Lawrence took place. I had recently moved from Yeats's maisonette in Woburn Buildings to a house in St. James's Terrace, Regent's Park, a few minutes' walk from Acacia Road. Lawrence used to come to lunch with us sometimes, when he was staying with Kot.

† From *Life Interests* (London: Macdonald, 1948) pp. 84–6.

He was a delightful guest for a poor and servantless household, because he always made a point of helping to set the table and of washing up. He really enjoyed these simple domestic tasks and used to insist that the washing up should be done immediately after the meal and that the dirty plates should not be left to accumulate. Betty, the Dublin girl to whom I was at that time married, interested him. He admired her large brown eyes, her 'big nose' and what he called her 'silent quality', and was anxious that she should play the part of 'Mrs Holroyd' in the play he had recently written and was eager to have produced.[1] If Lawrence was a perfect guest in an unpretentious home, he was an equally good host in his own. Betty and I once spent a week-end with the Lawrences at Hermitage in Berkshire, where he had rented a small cottage from Margaret Radford.[2] The details of this visit will always remain clearly in my memory. The way he kept his Prussian wife, Frieda, 'in her place' was slightly embarrassing at first. There was a painful moment just before the midday meal on Sunday. The potatoes were cooking in an open pot on the fire and Lawrence was watching them. Suddenly Frieda made some remark which he found particularly exasperating. His blue eyes crackled with rage, his red beard bristled, his hand shot out to the potatoes. Only our presence, I am certain, restrained him from 'saying it with missiles'. But in a few moments, the storm was over. His aunt Ada[3] and his rich and respectable uncle, who owned a stocking factory somewhere in East Anglia, were coming to lunch and Lawrence and I went off to the pub to buy them some beer. Lawrence was now in the highest spirits. He was determined to tap the uncle for enough money to enable him and Frieda to bolt for Italy—the English climate made him ill and depressed —and throughout the meal he was at his chirpiest. During the afternoon, when the relatives had returned to the inn, after inviting him to dinner, we went for a walk and hatched plans for extracting the necessary cheque. (I may mention, in parenthesis, that to go for a walk with Lawrence through the English countryside was an unforgettable experience. It is one of the characteristics of genius to be able to see things which normal people miss. Lawrence made me feel that I had never really 'seen' a wood before.) Later in the evening we sent him off to his dinner, and wished him luck. He returned triumphant, in a few hours' time, waving a cheque for £10 and we had an evening of rejoicing. When I came downstairs the next morning I found Lawrence and Frieda singing South German folk songs at the tops of their voices while they laid the breakfast table. Life with Lawrence could never be *dull*, but I doubt if he would have found any Englishwoman with the nervous solidity to stay the course. Voluble, full-bosomed, Prussian Frieda was built to weather storms. Like a sound ship, broad in the beam, slow but seaworthy, she could stand any amount of buffeting. And I have no doubt that she found the Von Richthofen card a useful one. Lawrence, I should say, was less of a snob than most people, much less of a snob, for example, than the 'inverted snobs' who are to-day so prevalent. But the fact that his wife was sprung from a 'baronial' family was not lost on him. Indeed, he never seems to have discovered how little it really meant.

As soon as I displayed my eagerness to be of use to Lawrence, Koteliansky uttered a salutary warning. 'If you don't want to lose Lawrence's friendship,' he said, 'you must be very careful never to let him guess that you are doing anything for him.' I had no difficulty in taking the hint because, much as Lawrence the man attracted me, it was Lawrence *the writer* to whom, out of a love for good literature, as disinterested as Ford's or Ezra Pound's, I wanted to be of service.

NOTES

Douglas Goldring, novelist and critic. As Hueffer's (Ford Madox Ford's) sub-editor on the *English Review*, he first saw Lawrence in 1908; however, he only met him in 1919.

1. *The Widowing of Mrs Holroyd*. There was an amateur production of this play at Altrincham in 1920, but the first professional production (at the Kingsway Theatre) was not until 1926. It had been published in 1914.

2. Daughter of Ernest and Dollie Radford (see p. 117).

3. Ada Beardsall, the sister of Lawrence's mother, married Professor Fritz Krenkow, an Arabic scholar.

Hermitage*

CECILY MINCHIN

One could never be dull in Lawrence's company, or Frieda's, for the matter of that. They were so full of fun and life, and I regret that we were so busy and had so little time to spend with them. They occupied two bedrooms at Grimsbury Farm, and when I suggested to Frieda that it would ease things if they shared one, her reply was that she did not wish to be too much married. What that implied I have no idea. Maybe it was DHL's illness. I remember Frieda saying how much she missed her children who were at school in London, and how welcome a child of DHL would be. But she was, I believe, several years older than DH, and the advent of a child would have been a remote possibility. In any case I doubt if one would have had much of a welcome. They were very poor, and DH hated staying in one place for any length of time and at any moment had the urge to travel to any part of the world. He hated possessions and roots,

* From a short memoir first published in Nehls, 1, pp. 503–5.

and Frieda craved for a home and solidity. Frieda, I remember, started her visit to us by succumbing to bed for the first few days and expected to be waited on. Most of this fell to DH. We were far too busy and overworked to do any nursing, except in an emergency, which certainly this was not. To this day I can see DH in a raging temper, carrying a brimming chamber down to the front garden and emptying it over our flower beds which rather horrified us, to say the least of it, although there was little else he could do. The sanitation was of the most primitive—an earth closet far down the garden. Our bathroom was a tin bath in the scullery with rain water drawn up by a hooked pole from a well outside the house in the front garden. Drinking water had to be fetched in pails from a spring some distance away. The going and return must have measured a quarter of a mile. It seemed like five to us.

The bohemian life of the Lawrences appealed to me, and DH's desire to avoid being cluttered with possessions, free as air and untrammelled, excited my sympathies. Frieda I thought did not realise her luck in being able to go all over the world with all plans made for her. I remember her worrying DH for money for red curtains for a flat somewhere. He raged and told me he had less than fifty pounds in the bank and 'Frieda wants red curtains! Imagine it! Red curtains!' How they found money for travelling expenses puzzled me. Somebody had great faith in his literary powers: this must have been his compensation and inspiration. And it always seemed he felt time was likely to beat him. So much must be accomplished before the dreaded bronchials gave up the fight. This probably was the reason he rushed from place to place getting copy for his books. I could in a way sympathise with Frieda. She was more phlegmatic and easy going, and every woman really needs roots. It seemed on the face of it very selfish on DH's part, but I think he felt he would not last the full span, and besides he could write in any environment and knock off a short story to pay expenses anywhere.

He had a diabolical temper in keeping with his red beard. At times when he was irritated (and this was fairly often and for some trifling reason, almost nothing), his rage would burst out enveloping all and sundry who were unlucky enough to be in his vicinity. The intensity of it was completely shattering. On one occasion when staying at the Farm Frieda borrowed Miss Monk's sewing machine and had inadvertently had some small mishap with it. I forget what it was really—not very serious—but anything happening to Miss Monk's possessions was a major calamity in her eyes. It was mentioned in front of DH, and the result was a tornado so shocking that even we were terrified, fearing the outcome. He slated Frieda unmercifully, saying she was lazy and useless and sat around while we did all the work. He then ordered her to clean our kitchen floor which was large with the old-fashioned, well-worn bricks, none too easy to get scoured, in fact real hard labour. To our amazement she burst into tears and proceeded to work on it, fetching a pail of water and sloshing around with a floor cloth in a bending position (although he had told her to kneel), bitterly resentful at having to do such a menial task quite beneath the daughter of a baron, at the same time hurling every insult she could conjure up at DH, calling him an uncouth lout, etc. He appeared to love an opportunity to humiliate her—whether from jealousy or extreme exasperation one could never tell. I was only surprised that she listened to his abuse or obeyed his orders. The quarrel simmered down, but if I remember rightly she went back alone to Chapel Cottage, and he stayed on at Grimsbury Farm to finish his book which he spent most of the day writing in one room—*The Lost Girl*, I believe it was. Anyway the manuscript was sent on for us to type, or rather Miss Monk typed and I read it to her, some weeks later.

We were nearing the end of our farm experience, and the Lawrences were planning to move. Frieda was hankering to get back to Germany to contact her family again; DH was off somewhere else. They would meet later. I well remember the morning he was leaving. My playing job took me out in the mornings some days, and this was one. We hired a pony trap (a little tubby thing) which the banker's daughter used to drive, and on this particular morning she had another woman to take, and it meant four of us in this little vehicle. DH was highly amused. He came out to give us a send-off and remarked that it looked like a flower pot. I expect we all had different colour clothes and hats and that we must have looked a funny sight.

For the first time since we had met, DH was dressed in a lounge suit of a dark material. The change was startling. He looked the well-dressed and smart man-about-town and exceedingly handsome, striking in fact with his red beard (groomed) and his intense blue eyes. His lean figure lent itself to well-cut clothes, but I remember him saying that he hated orthodox clothes and dressed in the blue coat and odd things because he liked to create attention. 'I like people to look at me', he said once. Frieda was, I believe, at the cottage gathering their few possessions, and DH was seeing her off to Germany and going to London himself.

NOTE

Cecily Minchin, née Lambert, knew Lawrence in 1918–19 when he was staying at Hermitage, Berkshire. Her recollections were written in 1955.